O'Mandingo!

O'Mandingo!

The Only Black at a Dinner Party

Eric Miyeni

Published by Jacana Media (Pty) Ltd.
10 Orange Street
Sunnyside, 2092
Johannesburg
South Africa

1st Edition February 2006
Reprinted May 2006
Reprinted July 2006
Reprinted October 2006

ISBN 1-77009-187-4
    978-1-77009-187-0

Set in Ehrhardt 12/15
Printed by CTP Book Printers

See a complete list of Jacana titles at www.jacana.co.za

Contents

Why O'Mandingo!?

O'Mandingo! is a collection of opinion pieces that covers subjects as varied as politics and movie reviews, but at the centre of this seemingly disparate collection of thoughts is one theme: black pride, strength, unity and prosperity. If this theme is not overtly invoked, it is subtly promoted by the quality of the insights in each article.

Some call this foregrounding of black pride racist. To them I say think of a family you know working hard to raise youngsters who will become upstanding citizens. Would you call that family hateful of the other families on the block? I suspect you wouldn't. Black people have been brutalised for centuries. To heal, we need moments of pride. We need to focus our attention inward on joy and the will to be better and successful. The time to look outward only to be rewarded with even more brutality is behind us. *O'Mandingo!* is an attempt to galvanise this shift from an outward to an inward search for validation.

O'Mandingo! began as a response to a negative take on black people by a black person. This man's badly written piece, published in a "black" South African newspaper that has since improved greatly in both content and design, was seemingly designed to denigrate black people. In it I was called a "has been" amongst other insulting and libelous epithets.

My choices then included responding with an article of my own in that same newspaper, suing or responding outside the newspaper in a dignified manner that was uplifting. I chose the latter option – it was beneath me to be published alongside what I considered the drivel in that newspaper. As it turned out (perhaps fearing a lawsuit), that newspaper lifted my piece from the Internet and published it almost verbatim – despite

9

my protests otherwise. A simple response to bad journalism, writing and manners – a piece I wrote and circulated via the internet called "Yeoville" (page 153) – soon grew into an Internet newsletter with a cult following around the world. Over time subscribers sent it on to more and more people worldwide to share the views expressed and to debate them.

Why O'Mandingo? Simply put the name means "the people who are called Mandingos". "O" is Zulu and means "the people who are called..." Mandingos are Mandinkas, the warrior people of West Africa who gave us the kora, one of the oldest string instruments in the world. *Griots* (storytellers) amongst the Mandinkas told stories that passed down centuries-old traditions, norms and customs from generation to generation. The name is a visual if not physical embodiment of unity across Africa – north to south, east to west and back. Zulu and Mandinka joined at the hip in one word: *O'Mandingo!*

Four years have passed since that first article and it seemed fitting to publish a compilation of some of the articles written between 2001 and 2004. If you have been a supporter of *O'Mandingo!*, I hope this book will take you on a beautiful journey down memory lane. If you are new to *O'Mandingo!*, then give the book a chance. email us at editor@omandingo.co.za and share your own thoughts. The pieces selected for this edition are almost exactly as they were when *O'Mandingo!* subscribers first received them in their e-mail boxes. That is to say we have kept their immediacy and the sense of urgency with which they first appeared. This intention was to preserve a certain emotional history, as well as the integrity of the original thought and what sparked it off in the first place.

Every endeavour succeeds because of a team of people. No human being is an island. You know the drill. My mother, Mavis Thenjiwe Miyeni, taught me from an early age to stand up for what I believe. She taught me not to be too quick to judge but to be decisive in my actions. Her teachings are embodied in the articles in this book, and I am eternally grateful to this miracle woman of God. Mother, I promise to put less and less emphasis on race in my future analysis of events.

Lara Gochin is godmother to *O'Mandingo!* I write this thank-you note without having seen this dear friend for well over fifteen years! But almost from the day I started publishing *O'Mandingo!*, Lara proofread every piece from as far away as Italy and as close as Cape Town. She has never complained or made me feel ashamed of my dependence on her. For all this, Lara, I am deeply thankful.

Without Mike Pnematicatus, South African Greek godfather to *O'Mandingo!*, the *O'Mandingo!* website would not exist. This wonderful man made it possible for *O'Mandingo!* to be on the Internet for all and sundry to read at no cost. In the process his organisation endured impatient demands and criticism but stayed focussed on being useful to us with a monk-like steadfastness. As though that was not enough, he became the inspiration for "Black legacy" (page 42). Mike, thank you for your generous spirit.

To all *O'Mandingo!* readers and supporters, first amongst whom I put my brothers Theri, Errol and Rhulani, my son Dumisani, and my dear friends Al Zoya and Petra Fischer, I say thank you for reading my unsolicited advice, and for often responding to it with such passion. I am lucky to have you in my corner.

Eric Miyeni
Johannesburg 2005

Questions

ARE YOU REALLY A BANK ROBBER?

A friend of mine always says, "Bank robber" whenever anyone asks what he does for a living. I asked him once why he did that and he said that he does not want to be liked, let alone loved, for the wrong reason.

In response to further probing, he said if he gave you a card with his name on it and his title was, say, "Dr", and then you phoned him all nice and sweet, well, he wouldn't know if you were phoning because you liked him or because the title on his card was "Dr". He does not want anyone to love him for what he does or for his achievements, thank you very much. He wants to be loved for who he is. That's it.

When I asked around, I discovered that this thinking is quite prevalent. And when you think about it, it makes total sense. EVERYBODY WANTS TO BE LOVED FOR WHO THEY ARE, DON'T THEY? Not for their achievements. Not for their possessions. Not for their qualifications. But for WHO THEY ARE.

Now here's what I find strange. Once (back in the day when I used to act full time and appeared in newspapers frequently for my acting work) I had a girlfriend who had the amazing habit of seeing my picture on the front page of a newspaper in my presence and paging straight past it like it was not there to a page with some word game of sorts without ever commenting on the story about me or my picture. After the word game came a cover-to-cover perusal of the newspaper and still no comment! This hurt a lot at the time.

You might be saying, oh Eric, puhleeeeeze get a grip on your ego already! And I would be the first to reluctantly admit that,

13

yeah, my ego had a bit to do with the pain I felt at being snubbed in this way by someone I cared about so much. But in hindsight I think I was also hurt by how dismissive she was of what I did, my career and achievements.

If we all want to be loved for who we are, then the question to ask is who are we? Unless you are ashamed of your profession (what you do for most of the day), and your possessions (the result of your profession) are a source of some pain or disgrace, unless your qualification (what you spend a massive chunk of your life studying and practising to be) is an embarrassment of some kind to you, then all these things are a major part of who you are. When someone actively plays them down or belittles them in some way, you'll discover just how big a part of you they are.

If you meet a person who loves you for the way you look, the way you dress, the car you drive, the house you own, the job you have and the money in your bank account, that's really okay. These define in great measure who you are. The question is does s/he love the way you think, make love, eat, walk, tilt your head when you doze off, construct an argument, your passions, friends, the kind of family you'd like to build?

Does h/she love you for the softer issues too? The sounds you make when the words don't come. The way you smell. How you behave in restaurants. What would happen if you got fired, lost your car and your glamorous friends deserted you? Would this person stay? That's the biggest fear, is it not? Can you guide the future?

While you had this person's attention – because of all the superficial things they loved about you like your smile, the "Dr" on your business card, the firm handshake – you should have earned that person's desire to stay, whatever your circumstances. Or you weren't worth it. We are all attracted by the superficial, but we stay for the deeper qualities. Or we are repelled by them. Love is earned minute by minute. You can't sit on your laurels and hope to keep it forever.

So ask yourself this: once the Porsche is removed and you can't afford the oysters any more, are you worth it?

CAN YOU SIT WITH YOUR BACK TO THE WORLD AND FEEL SAFE?

Since 9/11 I have observed western countries, those northern to us, spend more and more time and effort on security. It amazes me that some humans believe that they can create a security system that other humans can't breach. I am amazed but I shouldn't be as we all know that these nations overflow with arrogance. They think: "I am cleverer than they will ever be. I will invent a security system they could never decipher because I'm top of the heap, king of the concrete jungle. Come on, I'm the man. What Iraqi could possibly beat me at the security game?"

To those of us who respect others it is obvious that interfering with other people's lives means you can never be safe. Logic dictates to us that whatever security measures you create in terms of fingerprinting procedures at airports, X-ray equipment all over the show, big brother cameras at every corner of the length and breadth of this vast universe, whatever "ingenious" safety measures you conjure up, you can never escape the wrath of a man or woman done wrong.

The emphasis on security in the absence of real respect for the other reminds me of the gangster who never sits with his back to a room. I ask you this question, Mandingo: can you sit safely with your back to the world?

We know that America can't, despite being called the world's only superpower. Too many people in the world feel bad just thinking about that country, the Henry Kissingers it produced and their hatred-driven slaughter of innocents on foreign shores in the name of the American people. We know that Britain can't because of its legacy of colonial conquest. We know that the Belgians can't because of what King Leopold did to the people of the Congo centuries ago. We know that France can't until she begs her former colonies for forgiveness. Spain can't because the lost civilisations of South America demand its repentance. Deeds haunt in differing guises until a goat is killed and its blood is shed – or the equivalent thereof in your

15

culture – and forgiveness is sought from the ancestors of those who have been wronged.

And so we do not applaud but are appalled by what the Chechen rebels did to those poor children in Russia. The number of innocent people who died because of the bombings in Spain upsets us. We are still shaken by the vision of the Twin Towers falling, of innocent people flinging themselves out of windows to avoid burning to death instead. Yet we have to ask the question: why do these countries have such ruthless enemies? If those who came before me visited horrors upon others in my name, am I without blame if, when my turn to rule comes, I do not return to the wronged to seek forgiveness and offer to atone in some way (as the Germans are doing to the Jews who Hitler wantonly attacked, tortured and killed for what appears to be no reason but pure hatred)?

How many people in your life walk around feeling that you should just disappear, Mandingo? How many people would stand up in your defence if for some reason you came under attack? How much goodwill does your life produce to help you sit safely with your back to the world, Mandingo?

When you create bad things for people around you, it's a matter of time before worse things befall you. Remember that the world's memory is long. In a twist of irony, a Mayan King who had slain his own brother by slitting his throat from ear to ear so that he himself could be king was locked in a room and told by the Spanish to fill it up with all the gold in his kingdom to attain his freedom. He did as he was told and was killed anyway. That does not mean the Spaniards will not pay for their deeds; it shows how decisively the wheel of fortune turns.

Hate the Germans if you will, but amazingly they are the only Western country, that has truly looked at its past, apologised and sought forgiveness. Countries like England, America and Australia still gang up to produce more enemies for future generations. Who amongst these has a chance at real peace? Which amongst these would you emulate? That's an interesting question but the answer is even more interesting: none of the above. Why? The answer is simple and maybe less interesting: apologising for horrible deeds is never as good as not committing those deeds at all.

Is South Africa a good example of how you should shape your life? Almost. We should never have attacked Lesotho. That was a mistake. I'm glad we are talking to everyone now and saying we want a better world, worldwide. I'm glad that we stand on principles in terms of world governance. I hope and pray that we are not likely to repeat Lesotho soon. Peaceful negotiation, Mandingo. Goodwill wherever you tread. Wanting the best for yourself and all those around you. Knowing that there's enough for everyone in the world and that sharing is wonderful. That's the way of angels. Emulate them, Mandingo, and feel the heavens protect you as you sit with your eyes closed, your back to the world.

SHOULD I SAY SOMETHING?

I was having a chat with someone very dear to me the other day. I said, you know, there's this guy in my group of friends who is constantly making abusive overtures towards women. I told her that I hate it and that finally I had told the guy. I said I am personally sick of hearing you spew abuse at women every time I am around you. I told him it makes me sick and I don't need it in my life. I told him don't do it and if you must, do it in your own time when you are alone.

Later this dear person in my life asked if she could join me to watch the last half of the Greece vs Portugal Euro 2004 soccer game. I agreed, but knowing her I added, let me warn you that two of my friends who I know to have wives or steady girlfriends are here with women I don't know. I know you will feel uncomfortable, so I'm warning you in case you arrive and are shocked. That's when she accused me of hypocrisy because how, she asked, could I be intolerant of a man who abused strange women and yet sit with men who abuse women I know,

17

their girlfriends and/or wives, by being with other women?

Because I hadn't condoned this behavior, I was taken aback. In fact I had indicated my discomfort with it. Knowing that she would be even more uncomfortable with it, I had sounded an advance warning, but I wasn't about to get off easy. How, she wanted to know, could I sit with my friends doing what they were doing and not object? Considering that this is someone I love very much, someone with whom I am trying to build trust, I couldn't take this lightly and just let it roll, you know what I mean?

So why did I sit with my friends, watch them be what seemed, superficially at least, unfaithful to women they love?

The first thing I said in my defence was that there was no abuse going on. Not on the surface. Here were two men I know with two women I did not know, who seemed to be having a great time without coercion, all very voluntary. In fact, the last time I looked one woman seemed to be giving one guy a voluntary genital massage although, of course, she thought no one could see, but I did. The problem was not the women who, for all we know, could have been lied to and told that these friends of mine were single and available. The problem was the men and my involvement in their seeming deceit.

My second defence was probably better. I told my beloved this true story: Some years ago, when apartheid Yeoville was still the ultimate example of what South Africa could become post-apartheid, I left Tandoori Chicken (before it was as many youngsters know it to be today – no Tandoori Chicken for sale!) and walked to The Coffee Society (now non-existent) three doors up the road. Before leaving Tandoori Chicken, I invited James (not his real name) to come with me. He said no, he couldn't come as he was waiting for Jane (not her real name), his girlfriend at the time. I said fine and walked to The Coffee Society.

When I reached The Coffee Society, Jane, who was busy kissing Tom (not his real name), blocked my entry. I stood in shock watching. When the two were done kissing, Jane looked at me and gave me a smile that said there was nothing wrong going on and said hullo before she sauntered down to Tandoori Chicken to meet James. Then I bumped into Sipho (not his real name) who was James' best friend in high school or earlier. I asked him what I should do as I believed that Jane's behaviour was not cool. He, to my surprise, said he was not about to get involved in issues that were none of his business. I told him I would, as Jane was behaving repulsively and disrespectfully to say the least. Sipho said go ahead and I did.

To this day I regret it. James, who I thought I was helping, stopped talking to me for a millennium after that. He did not believe what I told him and thought I was just out to ruin the beauty in his life. More than eight years later, he has still not mentioned the incident to me ever. Later I discovered that Sipho roomed with Tom, and when Tom wasn't around, Sipho slept with Jane! And there I was in the middle of this heap of trash and James wasn't even a close friend!

What did I learn from this?

There is always more than what meets the eye. Tread carefully. As if to prove me right, the next day one of the friends I was accused of hanging out with without calling him to order for "cheating" on the mother of his child, his live-in lover, came to me.

"Eric," he said, "I just want you to know that it is over between Nontando (not her real name) and me. It ended some time back. We were totally incompatible from a financial perspective. There are no hard feelings. We just know and agree that we can't be together in that way. As for the woman you saw me with, she knows where I stand. I can't jump straight into another serious relationship at this stage. She asked me if we could and I told her no, we couldn't. We both know where we stand."

Now imagine if I had come in all moralistic-holier-than-thou-judgmental only to discover this after the fact! I might have lost a friend!

My take is simple: if you abuse people in my presence, I will stand up and say something against that and you. But if you behave in a totally normal and loving way towards someone I don't know when I know you to be with someone else I know, I will wait for the facts before I open my mouth. How am I to know, without being told, that you and your girl/boyfriend or spouse have an open relationship, for instance, and are allowed to see other people even while you are in a relationship with each other?

I believe that people should be honest with each other. You can't want an open relationship and convince someone you love that you only want monogamy and then act like s/he agreed to an open relationship. That can only hurt them deeply later and you'll lose them forever. It's harder, but try your best to be honest, Mandingo. As for other people's affairs, well, I suggest you keep an open mind until you know all the facts. Different folks do prefer different strokes after all. Take your time before you judge, Mandingo.

IS FREEDOM ALL THAT IT'S CUT OUT TO BE?

I have had suicidal thoughts periodically throughout my adult life. Now don't get me wrong. I love life. I do. And trust me when I say I am not weak. I have never spent a day in hospital for physical reasons. Those who know me will attest that I do not have any overt psychological deficiencies either. I am mentally and physically strong and I enjoy life to the fullest. Yet, despite these qualities, I have considered suicide. Why is that?

Growing up I was baffled and somewhat irritated by reports of men who killed themselves for whatever reason (oddly enough I remember very few incidents of women killing themselves back then). Suicide was a man thing and it seemed so weak. Not only because men were meant to withstand it all in this patriarchal society but because it seemed like such a cop-out. You can't handle your problems and so you kill yourself. Come on, get a life! That's how it seemed to me as a young buck, that's how I interpreted it.

Most male suicides I heard about in my youth involved women the men had loved. Nowadays, as the appallingly high instances of femicide show, this anger has been externalised. South African men today simply kill the women who leave them. If they are going to kill themselves, then the woman must die too. Back in my childhood, men simply went into the bush and hanged themselves, leaving a note declaring their love for the woman who left them or wouldn't have them. I don't remember any suicides from my childhood that did not involve love stories gone sour.

Never once did it occur to me to kill myself over anything all the way up to freedom day. And then suddenly it seemed that this could be a wonderful way to rest, you know. I would be in an aeroplane and the thought of it crashing would bring a smile to my face. Suddenly it all seemed too much - I just felt tired, spent, literally ready to die. In those moments it would not seem dark and miserable as I had always thought it must feel to those on the brink of suicide. On the contrary, it would seem as if angels were calling. Imagine being exhausted and invited into a beautiful room with a big bed, wonderful linen and fluffy pillows everywhere. Now imagine the addition to this fantasy of an individual of your utmost liking ready to massage you as you fell asleep for good to rest. That's how it felt to me when it hit me; all my problems would melt away softly, tenderly, beautifully, and I would be totally free. I even settled on the best way to commit suicide. What is puzzling is that I really haven't had monumental problems to surmount. I have had a pretty easy life compared to many people and yet here I was, ready to let my surmountable problems melt away through my own death.

In those moments, my son, whom I love with the deepest part of my soul's heart, did not even feature. Neither did my mother or any member of my wonderful family or the friends I cherish. It was just me, and my angels calling, softly, softly, and what I imagined was a Godly smile on my face and no one would guess what was in my mind at the time. It was just me and the blissful moment of possible death.

I'm not alone in this because friends have confessed to having this very same feeling. I do not know how it hits them and how

21

they feel when it does because I haven't asked. Maybe they cry because at that very moment they desperately want to live but the call of the angel of death that they recognise as such is too strong. Maybe they grow angry because they feel that they do not deserve to have to wrestle with these demons in the prime of their life. Maybe they too smile like I do. Maybe they are indifferent as they wait for the moment to pass. Maybe they grit their teeth in desperation as they wait for the moment to pass. I honestly do not know what they feel when those moments come. What I know is that they too are going through this tunnel over and over in this time of freedom. And so I've had to ask myself, why? Why now when there's seemingly so much to look forward to?

Why is it that now, when all seems destined for our success in a world supposedly free of institutionalised prejudice, do we feel this pull towards suicide? The only answer I have is what most mountain climbers who have done it will tell you about reaching the top of Mount Everest. The summit, you see, is the halfway point. You still have to come down, and many die on the way down because they never planned for that final stretch. The answer, I suspect, also lies in what Mandela said in his book; when you reach the top of a mountain, all you see are more mountains to scale. That is the quest for freedom in a nutshell. It's never over when you think it's over. That can be a killer.

When we have done what we have done to be free and suffered through all that we suffered through to get here, to have such a short moment of rest to appreciate our accomplishment before we have to go down again, only to begin yet another climb up yet another peak on the journey to final and total liberation, can be completely debilitating and painful. I don't think most of us understood how hard it would be just to survive after liberation. I don't think most of us knew how much fighting still had to be done after the main battle had ended and suddenly, we had to find hidden reserves to continue or die.

22

The thing about oppression is that it forces the oppressed to walk a thousand miles in order to gain a millimetre. Now that we are free, we run the same thousand miles in order to gain a metre. Our oppressor on the other hand used to gain a thousand miles for every millimetre s/he ran but now gains eight thousand miles for the same effort. We have made progress but it's small and our former oppressor still benefits more from our sweat and what is rightly ours than we do. The struggle is not over yet. There is much to do. But we are exhausted. This is the source of my suicide call.

I look at the effort I have put into everything I have done after the fall of apartheid and often I wonder why am I getting so little reward? And this darkens my days. At least during apartheid, I knew that my efforts were not to be rewarded. Today my expectations are high, my work ethic is sharper and when nothing or little comes of this effort, I suffer more. What is most disturbing is that I often suffer this feeling of empty gain at the hands of black people who should know better than to make me feel worthless at the end of a hard slog. Not that suffering this same fate at the hands of white people makes it easier. My gains should be visibly bigger because apartheid has fallen. That they are not cuts deeply, with sharpness beyond description.

I am not a psychologist and I haven't tested my theory with any qualified psychologist but I am sure that this lies at the heart of every black South African suicide emotion: after having reached the summit of the highest peak in the world under the toughest circumstances, the need to be carried down and forward is immense. Am I not allowed to rest a while for God's sake? Should I not be rewarded while others continue the struggle if there is a struggle to move forward?

But we all know that's not how it will roll, don't we? And that's why I haven't committed suicide despite the beautiful calls I have had. If you reach the summit, you must come down. That completes the journey. And if you want long-lasting peace and prosperity for your people, you have to adapt to the new struggle

23

to make the new gains, as you cement what would now be the old gains. You have to celebrate the millimetres that become metres as you fight to convert them to kilometres. You have to stay focused and admit that often these struggles are generational and that the gains are never instantaneous.

Freedom is what it's cut out to be – exhilarating, uplifting, truly liberating, beautiful. And even though often perplexing and infuriating, freedom carves a permanent smile on your face, makes you happy, knowing it is possible to reach the sky and touch the stars. It adds inches to your height and helps you walk tall and proud. What I did not know is that the fight never ends and at the point of your most important victory in this never-ending battle, the enemy intensifies his effort. It is here that all can be lost or gained. In a world full of greed that is often ruled by people who have practised brutality for generations in order never to share, there can be no rest for seekers of a better world. The sooner we internalise that the war between good and evil is perpetual, the more settled will be our stride and the bigger the chances of a permanent victory. Depressing at first but when you have scaled Mount Everest, the highest mountain on planet earth, every mountain after is never as daunting.

ARE WHITE SOUTH AFRICANS NICE PEOPLE?

Let's start by defining the word "nice", shall we? To a black South African like me, nice would mean, first and foremost, not racist. Racist would mean assigning anything negative to me simply because I am black. And everything does flow from there, does it not? I could say being nice means being courteous, for instance. But we all know that a racist will never be courteous to the target of his/her racism, don't we?

Based on this definition of the word "nice", my short answer to this tricky question is "No". Most white South Africans are not nice people. But do I have any scientific research to back up this claim? Sadly, the answer to that question is "No". So then, on what do I base this contentious answer regarding my fellow

24

citizens? Well, the explanation is complicated in its simplicity. It's based on a little research and a little intuition that comes from that little research.

First, the research part. I don't know a single black South African person who does not have a horror story that involves a white South African person. These horror stories range from being beaten to a pulp for no reason other than being black and walking through town at night to having a chef coming out and asking people at every single table at his restaurant how they are enjoying their meals only to skip the only table full of black people, and then say he did not see them when asked why he did what he did! On the surface that tells me that a lot of white South African people constantly do nasty things to black South African people for no other reason than the fact that they are black. And that's not nice.

Do black South African people dish out the same negative encounters to their white counterparts? I don't think so. Most white South African people I have known always have nice stories to tell about their black counterparts. They will tell you how black South Africans are always smiling. They will tell you how hospitable they are and welcoming. I mean, if you listen to a lot of white South Africans talk about their encounters with black South Africans you would swear that black people did no wrong! And those amongst them who will tell you the horror stories they have amassed over time in their dealings with black people, i.e. hijackings, robberies, murders, will be the first to admit that black people have the same stories and more that they have amassed at the hands of black criminals. If you press these same white South Africans further they would admit that black is not the colour of all South African criminals.

Now for the intuition. I am always extremely uncomfortable when surrounded and outnumbered by white South Africans. This happens even when they look like they are genuinely trying to be nice. Now, intuition is a funny thing to base important answers on. I mean, it's so subjective! So take this with a pinch of salt if you want. But I intuit that I am this uncomfortable when I'm outnumbered by my fellow white citizens because I always feel like they do not want me there. The headlines say "Welcome", nice to have you here. But the small print says "What the hell is he doing here?" "Are they going to take over everything?" That's not nice.

But ask me if there is such a thing as a nice white South African. Then my quick answer is "Yes! By God, yes." At the end of the day we are all human, aren't we? It would be totally naïve and stupid of me to say white South Africans lack the human capacity to be nice to black South Africans. In fact, it would be racist of me. So now if white South Africans are capable of looking into the eyes of their black counterparts and seeing an equal, how come so many of them can't, won't or don't?

My answer is embodied in one word: training. White South Africans, like many white people around the world, I presume, were trained over many centuries to believe in racist bigotry. How could they possibly have wiped out all those people around the world and taken everything those people owned if they believed them to be equals? The construct of racism was an important one for conquering the other and the collection of wealth. In a sense, as far as race relations go, that's all most of them know and are comfortable with because change is painful, difficult and demanding. The few amongst them who are truly and genuinely "nice" have had to make a concerted effort to undo all those centuries of training. That's a tough ask, isn't it? But it's a beautiful thing to observe when they do make the effort. You suddenly see this glowing light in their eyes as the burden of hate is lifted off their shoulders. You almost sense a near tangible relief in the air around them. It really is amazing to watch.

But you might argue that black people have also been taught over many centuries to believe what white people have been trained to believe, i.e. that they, black people, are inferior and white people are superior. So why are black people making faster progress towards undoing this horrible lesson? My short answer

26

to that is that those who are uncomfortable and oppressed are generally more likely to fight for and want change than those who are comfortable and oppressive. Black people were not comfortable with the status quo; white people were and to a large degree still are. Make the deduction.

So now should we be comfortable and say we understand, poor white South African, you were trained wrong and we black South Africans shall suffer your racism quietly? My quick answer to that is "NOOOOOOOOOOO! Damn it! If I am going to go against every sinew in my body and hold back with this great Herculean effort the overwhelming desire to throw you in the sea or slit your throat at night because of the horrors you have visited upon me over the centuries, by jove, you are going to make an effort to be 'nice' to me. I will not tolerate your racism for a single second beyond this point. Never. So play your part, pitch in, so that we can have a civil resolution to this impasse that's got my people poor and diseased while yours grow fat due to all the excess."

You might ask, what does pitching in mean? What does playing your part mean exactly? In a nutshell, it means doing all the things that all the nice white South Africans I know do. And that's quite simple in its difficulty. Do what's counter intuitive to you when you encounter someone like me or shall I say someone unlike you. Work with the simple counter intuitive thought and feeling that in front of you is a human being of equal and sometimes higher value than you. Why do I add the phrase "higher value"? That's not difficult. No person, whatever the colour of that person's skin, can be totally your equal, totally your superior or totally your inferior. What makes us equal is that we are simultaneously equal to, inferior to and superior to each other. Give that a little thought.

CAN YOU REALLY OWN A WHOLE HUMAN BEING?

Here's a little story you will find amusing. I am at my maternal

27

family Christmas gathering. It's a beautiful event. Everyone is getting to know everyone and how they actually connect. This is a beautiful thing, you see, because in this way we are all very unlikely to fall in love with family and possibly give birth to deformed, inbred babies. It's a beautiful thing, too, because it reaffirms our African-ness as we celebrate the importance of not only having an extended family but knowing and embracing it. Beautiful!

And here I am listening to a conversation between my female cousin and my other cousin, the male A who is much younger than the female N. Cousin A asks Cousin N who she is, where she comes from, who her parents are and how she connects to the family really (in tsotsi-taal, we say he asked her "*iPass ne special* – i.e. everything). Cousin N, a successful, highly educated businesswoman who is much older and much more successful than my less successful, much younger and inebriated-looking Cousin A answers all the questions frankly and enthusiastically. After all, this is what the gathering is about – know thy family.

Once she had answered all the questions to male Cousin A's satisfaction she naturally, with the same level of enthusiasm employed in answering these questions, started asking male Cousin A the same questions he had asked her, because they genuinely had not known each other up until that point and she wanted to know who he was too. And here is where the whole conversation starts to take a less enthusiastic and open tone and a much more quietly aggressive tone. Without actually saying anything, male Cousin A let it be known that this woman had a cheek to be doing this. Male Cousin A might not be as successful as female Cousin N. Hell, he might even be a drunk on the way down as she soberly climbs higher but he has been to the bush and been initiated and she hasn't. At least not in the way that he was! He's a man and she's a child. How dare she question him directly? Why could she not wait for someone else to introduce him properly to her with respect and proper tradition?

Well, whether or not my female Cousin N could hear these simultaneously quiet and yet loud protests from my male Cousin

A, she ploughed on and got all her answers, shook his hand and genuinely pointed out how happy she was that they had met. So now you begin to see how early and subtly this male dominance over women can manifest.

How amusing is that?

Now here's another amusing anecdote. A man is travelling with his wife through Johannesburg city centre when he sees his mistress, girlfriend they call them here, *emzansi*, walking with another man. Even though this husband is with his wife and doesn't know who the man walking with his mistress is, he stops his car, jumps out, rushes to his mistress and slaps her across the face. Unfortunately, the man his mistress is with is some devastatingly accomplished karate expert, so he pummels the s#&!t out of him. Finally, after some truly embarrassing punches, kicks and slaps, the humiliated husband manages to quickly get away and back in his car, start it and flee the scene. After prolonged quiet in the car, the wife, naturally, asks what all that was about, to which the beaten husband mumbles: "*Hah aar man, u ya ngikolota.* (No, no, no, no, no, she owes me)".

End of anecdote.

And so you see that male disrespect for women has no boundaries. A man will lose his head and humiliate himself simply because he suspects a woman he knows intimately needs to be "disciplined".

How amusing is that?

How about this less amusing anecdote? A man buys his mistress a flat. He comes to visit at some ungodly hour and does not find her there. He calls her on the cellular telephone that he might have bought her and finds it off. He leaves. He then comes back the next day and beats the living daylights out of her without caring to know where she might have been!

How sick is that?

And so you come to realise that many men in this country believe that they own the women who allow them to have sexual relationships with them! And if these women happen to accept their gifts, God forbid that they attend to an emergency at the wrong hour because they might just get killed by these men, who are generally two-timing other women to be with them when they, the men, choose to be with them, the women!

Exactly how sick is that?

Now here's a true story that won't make you laugh at all. A woman in Meadowlands on Ndlovu Road finds herself four boyfriends. One supposedly takes care of her hair and make-up bills, the second boyfriend buys her clothes, the third is apparently fantastic in bed and the last one has a very nice car. It so happens that one day while the one boyfriend is dropping her off, the second one arrives without an appointment and waits for this car he doesn't know to move. She then sits in the one boyfriend's car scared to get out in case there's a scene. But while she waits, the boyfriend with whom she has an appointment for that evening arrives almost simultaneously with the fourth one who has brought his friends to show her off. This was apparently an amazingly beautiful woman.

To cut a long, sad story short, one of the more hot-headed boyfriends then approaches the car with this woman in it and demands to know what's going on. All four boyfriends now realise that they are all simultaneously going out with this woman and have therefore been "played" by her etc. Having established this, they take her and first burn her scalp by smearing hair chemicals on her head and leaving them there for much longer than the prescribed period – That's for all the make-up the one boyfriend bought her I guess. Then they rape her in turns – this is so she knows who's got the power I guess. That done, they drag her behind one of the cars until she dies – I guess now they are saying this is for the car you liked one of us for. Pieces of her body are found in different parts of Soweto and no one is arrested.

Here's the zinger: a woman tells me this story as an example of what justifiably happens when a woman tries to have more boyfriends than one. No doubt these alleged killers are still running free because the society around them, including the police, believes that this is justified. And so we have a society that teaches women that they need men for everything. But most black men in this country can't afford everything a woman might need. We all know how little most black men get paid if they are employed and that most black men actually have no work. By extension, this means that if you are taught that you need men for all your needs and the society you are in generally has poor men, you will need more men to satisfy all your needs. So why do we teach women something and then kill them for doing it to perfection?

The biggest joke about this horrendously sick double-standard, of course, is that the likelihood is that those four men were able to go out with the same woman for so long without realising it because they too have other women that they use to satisfy those needs that they might have that she couldn't satisfy! But I have never heard of four women dragging some man to death because they discovered he was four-timing them! And maybe it's about time. Legend has it that Mozambican men do not dare beat up their girlfriends or wives because soon after liberation, if a man beat on his wife or girlfriend, four strong soldier women were sent to that man. On arrival they put their AK47s down and physically beat the s*%!t out of the abusive man. This went on until respecting women was a culture in that country. I like that. But it's not going to happen in South Africa. So here's a story that will amuse you female Mandingos, and there might be a lesson in here for you because Selebi* and his police are letting men get away with the murder of women in this country, literally, considering that statistics say every six days a man in Gauteng, not all of South Africa, Gauteng, kills an ex-wife or girlfriend. That's more than 60 women a year killed by men who are idiotic, with low self-esteem, and insecure! And there are four men supposedly running free in Soweto after allegedly publicly murdering a woman because they believe it's the right

* Full name: Jackie Selebi. Position held in South Africa: National Police Commissioner. Position held internationally: President of Interpol.

31

of men alone to have more than one sexual partner!

Here's the story, female Mandingos. A woman repeatedly receives heavy beatings from her husband until one day she can't take it any more. So one night she waits for her husband to fall asleep. Then she gets up to boil a pot full of water. That done, she exposes her husband's feet and pours the entire pot of boiling water on them. When he's done screaming, she calmly tells him that next time he has an urge to beat her up, he must kill her. If he doesn't, she adds, he must remember that on this particular night, she chose only his feet and that because she's still alive, she might do something even worse next time around. That man never lifted so much as a finger against that woman for the rest of their long marriage.

And so you come to realise that men are not going to change without some help from women – sometimes this takes cruel courage.

To you male Mandingos, who battle with this sickness called woman abuse, seek help. It is freely available. Let's get rid of this scourge together. To Selebi, if you are listening, investigate and see how true the story of the murdered Sowetan woman is. If it is, find those men who committed that heinous murder in Meadowlands and make an example of them. The fact that they are supposedly running around free is not helping our cause at all. In fact, it's doing the opposite.

CAN YOU PLAY THIS GAME?

I remember waiting for someone who was late for a meeting with me one day. It was one of those situations where the one person thought the appointment was for the next day and the other thought it was on that day. So I was a day early or they would have been a day late. That doesn't matter. What matters is that we had the same venue in both our diaries and as she was on the way to the agreed venue, her office, when I called to discover the mix-up, we agreed that I should just wait and the meeting would commence when she arrived. And so there I was, waiting.

And I wrote this poem:

The Waiting Game

Time has a funny way
Of creeping slowly when you wait
And when time is creeping slowly
Everything in the world seems like it's standing still

Except the insides of an impatient being's chest
So repeat after me as a test
I am a patient being
I am a patient being
I am a patient being

Can you feel your psyche
Assume this countenance
Can you feel your breathing
Slow down a sec'
Can you feel the insides of your chest
Calm down a touch
Can you feel the pores of your skin
Open up and take in the air

Now contemplate the world around you
Because it's never more beautiful
Than when it's standing still
As time creeps by
So that you can take a look at its figure
And contemplate its every feature

Soon, time will take off again
At a helluva speed
And there'll be nothing to see
As the world whizzes past

33

Stand still
Be beautiful
Take in the world

Eric Miyeni 2002

The person I had the appointment with finally arrived sweating and apologetic and, well, we had a great meeting. It went swiftly and the time I had allocated for it was not exceeded. A poem was born.

Later that evening I went to host my weekly Tuesday poetry sessions (Poetic Tuesdays) in Yeoville, Johannesburg. To kick off, as we often do at these sessions, I opened the floor for discussion. On that evening I read out this poem that you just read above and asked the audience to contribute their thoughts on time and how Africans are perceived to be perennial latecomers who have no respect for time.

The first contribution to this discussion blew my mind. A young Mandingo woman raised her hand and said that there are two kinds of time. The one, she said, is monochromatic time, the other, she said, is polychromatic time. As you probably know "mono" means one and "poly" means many. She said that the Western world generally works on monochromatic time, i.e. an hour is divided into minutes, which are divided into seconds, which are further divided into milliseconds, and so on and so forth. This, she further said, makes the Western world overly impatient because every passing second is seen as a lost opportunity. Time, to the West, she said, is a commodity that is scarce and must be packed with useful activity.

On the other hand, she said, the developing world, like Africa, generally works on polychromatic time. This, she said, is the acknowledgement that in every passing second there are as many things happening that are useful as there are living beings and objects on planet Earth. And it's all taken care of. For example, while someone is dying, another is being born. While you are speeding to meet a deadline, another person is on honeymoon. And, yes, your friend might be late for an appointment and you can choose to stew because monochromatic time says that your friend is wasting your time, a valuable commodity, or you can do something else while you wait, even if it means taking in the world around you for a second and observing its beauty.

A Mandingo brother then stood up and said that the West has always lost the important battles with the developing world because the developing world always adds polychromatic time as a fourth dimension to the war effort. For instance, in Vietnam, the Americans used air, water and earth space to fight the Vietcong. But in addition to this, the Vietcong added polychromatic time. They simply said, "We do not have to win this war in this generation, but every generation will carry on fighting until we win." The Americans eventually lost and withdrew. That's essentially how we South Africans finally beat apartheid. It's not about the second we are living in. It is about all the seconds in the universe.

I don't know if President Mbeki is aware of this concept, but I vow that if he is not aware of it on the conscious level, he is conscious of it on the subliminal and unconscious level because of his approach on the Zimbabwe issue – and thank God for that. You see, my lesson from the discussion born of the poetic visitation I had made me realise another facet to the concept of polychromatic time. The more people you add to an activity, the more time it takes. Zimbabwe will come right. Iraq will disarm. The world will be a peaceful place. But because we cannot "impose" our will on others and must seek to cooperate with others and take in their fears, their concerns, their needs and respect them as part of the solution-seeking process, we need more time. A second becomes an hour as an hour becomes a day, which becomes a week, and it's okay, because when one person dies another is born and so the process will continue even when we are dead.

Earth's survival is not about instant victories and heroes' badges now. It is about permanent solutions that work for all people. We must pull back a bit from this "time is scarce" mentality of the West to the "time is abundant" mentality of the more evolved and wiser developing and ancient worlds that you and I are ruled by, Mandingo.

Variations on the Colour Black

BLACK MONEY, BLACK HANDS!

On Sunday the 27th, in the month of January this year of our Lord, as the Christians would say, 2002, at about six in the evening, I felt a cloud of depression hang over and hover a bit, then descend and cover me like a thick blanket on a hot African summer day. At first I thought this had to do with the weather. It was a bit chilly for a summer evening and the sky was menacingly dark, like a big Gauteng storm was brewing and gathering strength to strike. I quickly found myself fumbling about under the depression blanket, frantically trying to emerge from the subsequent darkness. But before I could succeed, I was depressed.

I blamed the weather, you see, because my surroundings, at least on the surface, could not be the cause of this depression. I was at my most favourite hang out in the world, Time Square in Yeoville, Johannesburg (surely they should change that name – who was Johannes?). I was surrounded by black people, who are my favourite people in the world – warts and all. The little-known and now late musician Zola was tinkering on his new guitar and cajoling us to put more money in his money bowl, the place was full and the people were merry, thanks to this wonderful Sunday outdoor musical event.

Despite this, though, the more I looked at these people who are my brothers and sisters, the more depressed I got and the more I wanted to get away. So I went to join the guys by the park and play dice, you know. After being accused of gambling to simply while away time while the people at this outdoor gambling spot were genuinely trying to make money, I protested that whoever said that would get me beaten up. I said that I too wanted some money, then I promptly left. Back at Jo'burg's Time Square, I could not shake off the depression. In fact, the more I soaked in the scene, the more depressed I seemed to get. I took my car and drove around to think. Then I got it.

If you compare Time Square to Parkhurst or Melville, you will note that the difference is in the way people dress, the cars they park outside, the amount of alcohol they drink, and how much food they actually eat per sit down session, to name a few differentiators. The Time Square people will generally have walked to this favourite hang-out of theirs, barring the odd few who have cars ranging from old Beetles to the latest Volvos. That's if they did not bum a lift or take an expensive taxi to avoid muggers. The Parkhurst and Melville visitors will park anything from the latest Polo Player to a top-of-the-range Ferrari, with a few Porsches sprinkled in between, depending on the age of the *joller*. Generally speaking, no one would have walked to the *jol*. The Time Square people will be more shabbily dressed, you know, torn T-shirts or other old threads. Their clothes will be nicely put together as a rule, but they will be old overall. The Parkhurst–Melville crowd will be in the latest Diesel threads to dress down and the latest Armani shirts for a more conservative look. The Time Square crowd will generally be black, it will drink more per sit down session and eat a lot less food than the Parkhurst–Melville crowd.

The one crowd, my crowd, my people, my brothers and sisters, basically has a lot less money than the Parkhurst-Melville crowd. It is as clear as the sky on a bright summer morning in Africa. And this lack of money amongst us blacks, I realised, was the true cause of my sudden depression. Once I could lift my head above the darkness though, I thought, why not try and find a few reasons why money eludes us South African blacks today, even while we rule the country, and then explore how we can maybe stop this trend and reverse this tradition of constantly having little cash, even while we command six-figure annual salaries. So I wrote this piece, Mandingos, for better or for worse, but totally out of love for all of us.

The first barrier we must cross is the notion that money is bad. I always say to my friends that the notion that money is bad is not a poor person's concept. What better way to keep the most money in the fewest hands than to convince the majority that money is bad? If money were so bad, why would the Catholic Church collect so much of it every weekend? No. Money is good. It pays for education. It feeds families. When you have more than enough of it, it pays for you to see places you would otherwise never see in your lifetime and enjoy luxuries otherwise unattainable. If you are a goody two-shoes and scoff at luxury while you espouse the notion of a better world for all, you can use your money to run an orphanage, give bursaries to some needy children or whatever charitable cause you prefer. Look at it this way: Bill Gates is rumoured to have a billion-dollar fund to educate black people worldwide! Give yourself the option to afford to be kind. Aspire to be rich. Poverty is not hip. Now how can we get black hands on some serious money for black agendas?

Let's start with BIIIG black business. First off, all BIIIG black business must begin to realise that company ownership is overrated. If you own 100% of a company, it means you are 100% responsible for all its liabilities. This is the only reason why the white boys will say that it's okay, you blacks own the majority of the company, just let us be the majority operators. Often they justify this by saying the black component of the partnership has no experience and this is agreed to by the blacks – boom! The whites start to run the show. But you see, when you do not operate and you own the majority of the company in question, you are at the mercy of the operators. In this case, the operators are white people who are essentially hostile to black people and want them out of the business arena! Do the maths! So to start off, operate. Work for your money. There are no short cuts. That's why I always say I would rather work for a 100% white-owned company that is over 50% black operated than work for a 100% black-owned operation that is over 50% white run. The ideal, of course, is a 100% black-run and -operated outfit. That's called truly having your financial destiny in your hands.

Now, let's move on to those who work for others. This applies to any employee level in any company. It applies equally to parastatals, private companies and government departments. Ask yourself this question: what are you working for? Then tell yourself this: you are working to be financially free. You are working to buy yourself time. So if you work for three years, you should be able to lose your job and still be able to maintain the same standard of living for at least a year while you look for other opportunities. So now three years has bought you a year of financial freedom! At the moment, virtually all of us are broke the minute we get fired! And this applies no matter how long we have been working! No job lasts forever. So treat your current job like it will be gone tomorrow and buy time. Buying time is called saving. If more black people lived by this principle, we would have more liquid cash in black hands and serious generational improvements all round in terms of standards of living in the country. Think about it.

They say it is more difficult to save your first R100 than it is to save your first R1000. It's true. If you have R100 in your pocket, it is very easy to spend R55 thereof. But if you have R1000, it is more difficult to spend R550 thereof. Is that not weird, considering that both amounts equal 55% of the money in your pocket? More black people should save more in order to feel the power of a growing bank balance. It gets easier to save as your money grows. So, save save, save. Save your money and watch it grow!

Spend your money with fellow black people. A Jewish friend of mine who is a strong ANC supporter and working activist once said to me, "You know, I can't believe it, hey. Here I am thinking

I am liberated, and yet I look at all my personal suppliers – they are all Jewish! My dentist, my accountant, my lawyer, every one of them is Jewish! She was horrified. I was impressed. We can learn from that. We need to get away from the kind of self-hate that says black dentists will mess up our teeth, so we need white ones – even though both black and white ones now qualify at the same schools. Let's try and keep our money circulating longer in black hands by passing business to each other. If the first black gynaecologist messes up, try the next black one. Don't condemn all by holding your fellow blacks to standards unattainable. Everyone makes mistakes, including black people.

Only buy sale goods if you have the cash to spare. I have always found it astounding that people find this argument convincing enough to make them spend money: WAS R3000. NOW R2500. BUY NOW AND SAVE R500! The logic goes something to the effect that if I spend R2500 I will save R500! As Malcolm X says, you are being hoodwinked. You are being bamboozled. You are being had. Know this: you cannot save money by spending it. When you find yourself being attracted to act on a message like this, ask yourself if you can afford to spend R2500. That is the proper question. Don't ask yourself if you want to save R500 by spending R2500! That question is like asking if you can move one metre forward by moving five metres backwards! It's very seductive to believe that this is possible. But the truth, my friends, is that it is not possible.

Finally, if you have designs to start your own business, don't begin by getting a loan from the bank. This is the most expensive form of start-up capital. Draw a business plan, then save the money required to start the business. Putting your own money at risk can improve your business acumen many times over. Borrowed money can easily disappear through your business hands like sand through the hourglass. The thing about putting up your own money is that you do not want to see it rush the hell out without results. And that is the ultimate in business intelligence. If you have to, borrow from friends and family. It's a cheaper way to borrow money and honour won't allow you to fail your loved ones.

I am sure you can add more ideas to this thinking. For instance, renting property versus buying property, which is more financially sound? Buying that zooty car or buying a townhouse, which should you go for first? Saving money then buying cash versus buying on credit, which costs less? We need to explore these questions if we are to enjoy the political freedoms we fought so hard for and won. And it is not hard to learn all the necessary lessons around money. There are tons of books on the subject at bookshops around the country. You can also go on some fantastic courses to achieve the same goal. So let's all go for it.

All I really want is to go to my favourite hang out, Time Square in Johannesburg, *eGoli*, *a Joni* (pronounced "ah jorny", meaning Johannesburg in Shangaan) and see the most expensive cars, clothes, etc., and know that it was actually no sweat to my black brothers and sisters because they know about money and now have it aplenty for themselves and the generations to follow.

BLACK LEGACY

My close friend and business partner, a wonderful fellow by the name of Al Zoya, recently introduced me to a very dear soul. A businessman, now business associate and, I believe, soon to be a dear friend. This dear soul teases me by calling himself a disadvantaged Greek South African because I send him *O'Mandingo!* e-mails which say they are For Black People By Black People (FBP BBP). Over the years, this dear soul built a fortune you and I can only imagine. Al and I were at his recently completed, magnificent seven-bedroom house in the hills of Constantia in Cape Town, as the first guests outside of his family to be entertained there. It was wonderful.

A story that he told, a story that stuck in my head and made me think about black legacy, was the one about his first and most

42

important business lesson. His uncle's fish and chip shop had a boat in its window that he loved. One day he told his uncle that he would love to own the boat. The uncle said sure, just come and work at the shop over the holiday and the boat is yours. He worked and worked and worked and finally, the holiday was over, and most important of all, he owned the boat. The lesson in this is simple but critical, money is a means to an end. You do not have to obsess about it.

Another great soul who tells a similar story is a fellow by the name of Robert Kiyosaki, the Japanese American who gave the world the *Rich Dad Poor Dad* series of financial management books, which I believe should be read by anyone who is serious about financial freedom – the ultimate freedom. Mr Kiyosaki talks about his rich dad teaching him to work for no pay in order to be rich! A strange concept. But have you noticed how many white kids volunteer to work for no pay on their way up to running corporations? Again, the lesson here is simple, money is not the be-all and end-all of prosperity.

I also suspect that in these stories is the lesson that teaches the importance of leaving a good legacy in one's wake. When money is not your primary concern, you tend to be more concerned about the kind of legacy you leave behind. You tend to be more patient about making money even as you make it quicker than those whose main and only quest is making money! You tend to be more content in your life's work.

Mandela will leave the world a legacy of truth and reconciliation. I believe Mbeki will leave the world with a legacy of third-world efficiency and calm in the face of a hostile and well-established opposition. What legacy do you believe Dr Motlana will leave South Africa? Remember him? He belonged to the first fast, furious and visible black empowerment group to hit South Africa. What will you remember Mzi Khumalo for? But remember Mr Richard Maponya, a man who started with a bicycle delivering milk and ended up with the first black supermarket in Soweto at the height of apartheid! His legacy is simple: anyone, black or white, can rise to the highest echelons no matter what the obstacles if s/he so desires. You all know Jomo Sono. He started playing soccer in his bare feet. Now we all remember him as one of the best soccer players in the world and the great Pele, no less, described him so. We know what Oppenheimer did, don't we? He left us one of the strongest union movements in the world because of his blatant exploitation of black people in the mines. Donald Gordon of Liberty Life fame on the other hand will be remembered by many for donating R100 million to the medical establishment of South Africa through his Gordon Foundation.

Now most of you Mandingos are working for someone else. The likelihood is that that someone else is white. That's understandable, considering South Africa's financial inequalities. Now let me tell you a story. It will open your eyes to how blocking your ability to establish a legacy can be used against you in a working environment that is hostile to your presence to enable you to see it coming and fight to stop it, so that your bosses don't eradicate this all important tool for your prosperity and freedom.

I have been servicing my car at Sandown Motors in Village Close, Sandton, for a while now. For years, my Service Advisors there were white men. And they did a superb job, it must be said. I had no complaints. Then one day I walked in and – lo and behold – Sandown Motors had a black Service Advisor! I'll never forget his name, Mr Charles Phoshoko, a wonderful guy. He became my Service Advisor and I swear to the heavens I did not feel the difference in service levels. By all accounts, he was as good at serving me and my car as the white guys were. He looked after my car for at least two services. Then I walked in for my third service and there was Mr Phoshoko directing who should get into which car to be delivered wherever they were going after booking their cars in for a splendid Sandown Motors service! He had been demoted.

I asked him what the hell was going on, you know? I was curious and a bit disturbed. The long and the short of it was that his white boss had overloaded him with work. At any given time he had five more things to do than his white counterparts and, as every human being is wont to do under those circumstances, he started dropping the ball. This was used against him. When he explained why he was dropping the ball, his white boss did not care. He had the ammunition he needed to demote the man and, as a result, there was my guy on the same floor with his former white colleagues, demoted to directing the shuttle service. You know what I still find amazing? Mr Phoshoko never denied messing up. Not even to me, an outsider who had no way of finding out the truth. He just honestly pointed out what made him mess up and how unfair it was.

Do you see what Sandown Motors did to this black man? Sandown Motors, which is 75% owned by Daimler Chrysler*, a company supposedly in the forefront of employment equity in South Africa, decided that no black person was suited to be a Service Advisor and so systematically blocked his way towards building a legacy of efficiency. And when they had done that, they demoted him.

Remember this, wherever you are working, a legacy is your primary concern. You want everyone to remember how good you were at what you did. Not how much you earned. But the flipside is that you want to protect with ruthless ferocity your ability to build that legacy. You know what they say in the game of power: if you want to destroy a man, destroy his reputation. A good legacy is a good reputation. Protect it with your life. Know this: the dear soul of which I spoke, the "disadvantaged" Greek South African business associate, is known throughout his industry of choice as one of the most innovative pioneers of new systems. That's his legacy. No one really cares about his fortune except to acknowledge that he deserves it. Remember that Jomo Sono is a good and astute businessman who has systematically made himself a small fortune. But everyone remembers him for his great talent

* http://www.daimlerchrysler.co.za/corporate1/OurPast.asp. Accessed 10 February 2006.

and his outspoken honesty. That's his legacy. On the other hand, Hitler is remembered for his hatred of Jewish people. That's his legacy. Now what legacy are you going to build and leave behind? Is it good, like Maponya's? Or bad, like Hitler's? And while you are at it, remember that your legacy determines how well those who come behind you are received!

God knows, black people need to build good solid legacies for the future prosperity of all Africans.

BLACK PRIVILEGE!

One of my dearest friends and a Mandingo of note is Samantha Stern, a white woman from New York in the United States of America. After receiving the *O'Mandingo!* newsletter entitled "Skin Colour!!" (13 January 2002), she responded by sending me an essay by Professor Robert Jensen, a white member of the Department of Journalism, University of Texas, Austin, USA.

An extract from this amazingly frank and well-written article published in the *Baltimore Sun* in 1998 goes like this: "I am as white as white gets in this country (America). I am of northern European heritage and I was raised in North Dakota, one of the whitest states in the country. I grew up in a virtually all-white world surrounded by racism, both personal and institutional. Because I didn't live near a reservation, I didn't even have exposure to the state's only numerically significant non-white population, American Indians.

"I have struggled to resist that racist training and the racism of my culture. I like to think I have changed, even though I routinely trip over the lingering effects of that internalised racism and the institutional racism around me. But no matter how much I 'fix' myself, one thing never changes – I walk through the world with white privilege.

"What does that mean? Perhaps, most importantly, when I seek admission to a university, apply for a job, or hunt for an apartment, I don't look threatening. Almost all of the people evaluating me look like me – they are white. They see in me a reflection of themselves – and in a racist world, that is an advantage. I smile. I am white. I am one of them. I am not dangerous. Even when I voice critical opinions, I am cut some slack. After all, I'm white."

That article made me think. And while I was thinking about it, I ended up in the Johannesburg International Airport branch of ABSA bank trying to deposit R6000 into one of ABSA's client accounts in Cape Town. The first thing I noticed was that the queuing for the tellers was arranged in such a way that you could easily have two queues going at the same time. But as people would have it, they queued in such a way that there was only one queue to make sure everyone who came first did not end up being served last because one queue moved quicker than the other. This is just a pure result of the basic fairness that people have deep inside, be they black, white, green or blue. I joined the back of the queue for the first time that day and waited my turn.

But as luck would have it I somehow ended up having to go back to the same ABSA Bank again about ten or so minutes later that day to complete the same transaction. I did not have one thing or the other to conclude the transaction the first time around. This was entirely my fault. When I finally went back, the longish queue had dwindled to almost nothing. There were just two people at two teller windows, one teller on each side of the possible two-queue teller window arrangement. Again, as before, I positioned myself so that I could take advantage of the very first window to clear. Just like we all did about ten minutes or so before. At this point, a white man walked into the bank, saw me standing the way I was standing and chose to go straight to one of the teller windows in front of me. I stood there slightly perplexed and waited. As the window he chose opened first, he moved to be served ahead of me. I stopped him and told him I was first. He mumbled, angry that I didn't choose a queue and stick to it. I kept quiet and stepped in front of him to be served. Now, for me, the matter was settled. But at the window the white teller immediately took up his fellow white's concluded fight and told me that I really should choose a queue. He did this at the top of his voice so that his fellow white tellers could hear that he was now taking the fight over from a more powerful position, i.e. he could refuse to serve me and insist on me giving way to this other white guy.

I lost it then and said, spitting fire to the white teller: "FUCK YOU!" He said: "What did you say?" I said: "FUCK YOU!" This was not too bright on my part but you know, I could not cope, and so I just lost it. I'm not proud of this performance. In fact, I'm a bit embarrassed by it. Needless to say, his white female boss, the Johannesburg International Airport ABSA Bank branch manager was standing behind him. So he simply turned and asked if he was obliged to serve a customer who swore at him. She told him that, no, he wasn't obliged to and then told me to vacate her bank. I screamed some obscenities to the effect that THIS WHITE PRIVILEGE MUST STOP AND THIS WAS NOT HER BANK AND BLAH BLAH BLAH... A black security officer had just come into the bank and I could see that he was waiting for a signal to handcuff me so he could "serve", you know, and I thought, I can't win. I left the Johannesburg International Airport ABSA Bank branch in a huff only to get help in the Rosebank ABSA Bank branch about 30km away. God! I was pissed off!

What made me so angry? It's simple. A white man became insolent. Another white man took his side against me even though I was in the right. Then a white woman nailed my coffin to conclude the white bashing of a black man, without asking what happened to create the animosity. This is white privilege at its best. You don't have to be right to be awarded privileges if you are white. You just have to be white! It did not help that I had read the honest professor's article just before all this happened to me. That's what made me realise why his article made so many white Americans angry. In a way, it heightens the black person's ability to pick up and define racism even at its most subtle. It also heightens the discomfort of living with this largely unearned privilege that white people navigate each second of their lives within all racist societies.

Most important for me though, in addition to the above, was the realisation that what is lacking in this supposed democracy here in South Africa is black privilege. We do not want white privilege to disappear as *O'Mandingo!* is always at pains to point out. We want this "privilege" to be spread more evenly between all the races. Just like the manager at the British Airways counter demonstrated about twenty minutes before I went to that Johannesburg International Airport ABSA Bank branch at the same airport on the same day.

The British Airways service office at the Johannesburg International Airport has counters on both the south side and the north side. Somehow British Airways customers, like my friend and I, were queuing on the south side, oblivious to the fact that there were more counters on the north side. As a result, the British Airways manager kept telling the customers at the back of the queue to consider going to the north side counters where the queue was shorter. The strange thing was that some of us joined the queue when we reached the north side counters while other people, mainly white people, would go straight to an open counter, as if there was no queue and they were served. After observing this for a while, I interrupted the white British Airways worker who was allowing this to happen: serving latecomers ahead of early arrivals. She told me that these white people she was serving ahead of us were sent from the other side. I said we were also sent from the other side. She said she would attend to me and I should wait. I said no, she should attend to me first. At this stage, the British Airways office manager heard the commotion and came to ask what was going on. After getting the whole story, she told the white people that they should queue like everyone else and that the woman worker should serve my friend and I first. The white people then moaned in anger, asking what the point of moving them from the south side counters was if it was not for them to get immediate service on the north side counters. In other words, where the hell was their white privilege? The manager simply and calmly told them that the point was for them to join the shorter queue and get quicker service that way. The point, she said, was not to make sure that they did not queue at all. And that was that. We were served first, and rightly so.

Spreading privilege more evenly amongst the races, as this fantastic British Airways manager demonstrated, means working with a deep sense of integrity and fairness. It's not about people. It's about principles. Principles don't lie. They don't shift and change to suit the weather or the mood of the people living by them. And they are as fair as fair can get.

Now what else can be done to balance this abundant white privilege against the scarcity of black privilege in this country? We want more black people to be affirmed. Everyone goes on about the unfairness of affirmative action when black people get affirmed, but the truth is that every time any individual is promoted to a position higher than the one s/he held before, they are being affirmed – be they whatever colour. No one can tell with certainty that they will perform to the standard required. It's a risk. What we are saying is that more risk should be taken with more black people. We are saying the system should bestow more faith on black folk. We should be trusted more. We can't continue to have white affirmative action, which is now seen as not being affirmative action, actually more like normal progression. Very normal. A white guy comes in, learns the ropes from a black guy who has been doing the job for the last five or more years and then comes back a year later as the black guy's boss. What is that if it isn't affirmative action? Let's just spread this more evenly to avoid a Zimbabwe situation. That's all.

Having asked the establishment to push through affirmative action and be fairer in its distribution of privilege, what can black people do to increase "black privilege"?

May I suggest networking?
At the moment, we have an ability to network around meat and
booze for no reason other than to eat meat and drink alcohol!
This ability that we have to network for the sole purpose of
consuming other people's products is so superior that, in my
opinion, it is equal to no other in the world. I have been amazed
by the discovery of the latent power at a black braai that no one
else seemed aware of because no one asked. I think this is left
over from our apartheid days. Asking people what they did for
a living was frowned upon by black people back then because,
hey, you might discover that I'm a garbage collector! God forbid!
But those days are gone now. Some of us are CEOs in charge of
multi-million rand enterprises. Some of us are in government
deciding how to spend a few billion rands per annum. And a lot
of us have an untested ability to help those on top deliver on the
affirmative action mandate. Why the hell don't we talk? Why
don't we network more? Why don't we have braais and parties
for that purpose? To do business. To cut deals. Shake the world.
Create more black privilege to balance the playing field.

May I suggest a little less self-hate?
Give your people a bit more slack. Don't be so hard on yourself
by being so hard on your own people.

May I suggest a passion for excellence?
Do everything you do like your life totally depended on it and do
it better than the best you can offer.

May I suggest a respect for money?
Freedom without money is no freedom at all. So respect every
cent you make and spend it wisely if you can't save and grow it.

May I suggest patience, above all?
The longer it takes, the longer it lasts. Don't rush for that
fancy car. Take your time so that when you do buy it, it's not a

significant dent in your pocket. Build that company slowly, which is the proper way. You know, when you save money, it's hard in the beginning. Then you reach a critical point where your money grows so fast and so easily... and when you have the money power, privilege just follows. The bank manager invites you out. You do not knock on his door begging. Now that's privilege. Hey, I say try it. Try a little patience in the mix, okay?

And that's all for now. I'm sure you can add a lot more to this list to develop more black privilege to level the playing field and move more black people above the poverty line forever. Peace.

THE ONLY BLACK AT A DINNER PARTY!

There's something very seductive about being one of a kind. Like being the only black this or the other. I remember when I was growing up, if you were the first black this or that or the only black this or the other, you were top of the pops.

Take this scenario: you are the only black person at a dinner party. All eyes are on you. At first it is very intimidating. Whenever you speak, the whole dinner party goes quiet to hear what you are going to say. You get sized up, questioned, turned this way and that, examined, are you real? Then it gets exciting. Where did you learn to speak like that? Where did you go to school? Can you be one of us? You are so special! By God, blacks like you exist? Man! You are the star. You are the centre of attention. You are special. This is all very seductive. Then it gets boring. Please, not the same dumb questions again!

But you are still the star.

Then you rock up at the next after the seventh dinner party, for example, and damn it, they invited another black. Now you find yourself sizing this new black up. Is he or she going to be a bigger star than me? Are his or her views going to carry more weight than mine? Does that mean I'm yesterday's news? Damn it, why did they invite this other black? Does that mean I'm not good enough for these wonderful white people all of a sudden?

I remember being invited to this launch affair for a condom brand some years back. There was this high-profile black businessman there. The minute he arrived, which was late (he was a very busy man then, but everyone, including white people, understood this and waited patiently; a pioneer in black business advancement and so on and so forth, very rich today, very important man), I immediately felt the need to approach him and say: sir, thank you for your pioneering spirit, you have inspired us younger folk and we are ready to carry on where you have led us, thank you.

I moved to the circle of whites that was surrounding him and waited patiently. Being the only other black there, he saw me. I waited. I coughed a bit. Waited. He ignored me until one of the whites in the circle around him said to him that he thought I was waiting to speak to him. The very important black businessman turned around to face me and I started my rehearsed speech to thank him and, halfway through it, he said sure, turned away from me and said something like "as I was saying" to his white circle, and I just stood there, quite embarrassed, as you can imagine.

Then it hit me. This important black man had been the only black for so long that his importance was now partially defined by being the only black in white circles. To him, I was a nuisance that was stealing his thunder and he was not going to allow that. Later I saw many pictures of him in the company of big industry players and, yes, he was the only black there. I felt sad for him and all of us black people. Again we had been divided and were being ruled. If you can make one black so important as to lock out other blacks, then, hey, why do the dirty work? There's no racism here. All you have is black on black psychological violence.

Mandingo, it is now the most stupid thing to believe that being the only black this or the other is a good thing and a healthy source of self-worth. On the contrary, being the only black anything points to the oppression of your race. It points to the many doors that are being locked to this day. So when you get that important position and you are the only black there, remember that your biggest task is to increase the number of blacks there as quickly and effectively as possible. The days of wanting white slaves to feel important are behind us now. They are so dated. Train up a black secretary for God's sake. Fire ten of them to get to the perfect black one, if you must. But don't set standards that are too high for your own people and end up surrounded by whites eating off your misguided sense of self-worth. Hire and employ the services of as many black people and organisations as you can. Part of the sacrifice of this new and important economic struggle will entail being let down by your own people until you find the right ones to work with and help enrich.

Whatever you do, don't be suckered into feeling important about being the only black at a dinner party. It's a bit twisted. You are a lot brighter than that. As a white friend of mine once put it, the most effective form of affirmative action happens when black people employ or do business with other black people. How true and beautiful is that?

It's your job to empower your people, Mandingo, so do it.

Unsolicited Advice

GOD WITHIN!

I saw God the other day. He was a builder. I saw him plastering a wall at the coffee shop Nino's in Rosebank, Johannesburg, at about eight-thirty at night. I stopped for a good five minutes and watched him plaster that wall. For that length of time, nothing mattered in the world. Not the conflict in the Congo. Not HIV/AIDS. Put it this way, if a truck came shuttling down on me at that very moment I would have hardly looked up, even if the driver were hooting. God was busy, you see? And I was watching him.

When I was a kid, I experienced this God on earth and working in front of my very own eyes feeling every time my father cleared the kitchen table and used it as an easel to paint. I love my soccer. And as a kid growing up in Soweto, there was no better time to be outdoors than in summer when your street had a soccer "chuylence" against another street and you were in the team representing your street. We would play until you could hardly see the made-of-plastic-paper-and-rags ball in the dark. We would play until our mothers screamed us back into the house to bath, eat and go to sleep, in order to be fresh for church or school the next day. We would stop playing only when we had to. Even then, we would do it grudgingly.

But when God was working in my kitchen, you could never drag me out to the street even if you said there was ice cream for free to go with the soccer street challenge. The only time I heard someone accurately describe what the feeling of watching my father paint was like was on CNN's *Larry King Live*. Paloma Picasso told Larry King on that programme that watching her father paint was like magic, one minute there was a blank canvas

55

and when you looked again there was an explosion of colour! Nothing could be more fascinating for a kid. My father was not a Picasso. As a matter of fact, he was a Miyeni. Anthony Njakeni Miyeni, to be exact. But when he painted or drew, it was like he was following lines that were already on the blank canvas. He was fast. He was furious. He was totally possessed. He was God possessed. He made everything other than his painting disappear into complete insignificance. Watching him work was truly magical.

I remembered this as I watched God plaster that wall at Nino's the other night. He was wearing well-polished, pointy black shoes. He had neatly pressed black pants on. Over his non–builder shirt, he wore a bluish overcoat. He was squatting as he plastered that wall. He was a white man, poor looking. But the way he plastered that wall was with so much love, so much care, so much precision, you could have sworn he owned Nino's. A black man was watching as he worked. The black man was dressed to plaster. But there he was, watching like I was. You got the feeling that God arrived and said, let me give you a hand here. Let me show you how it's done. And then went to work.

It occurred to me there and then, as that white man's image reminded me of my late black father, that there is no better way to make colour acceptable than to do what you do extremely well. There is no quicker way to shut down prejudice than to be an expert at what you do. There is no quicker way to bring out the God in you than to do what you do with intense honesty, love, focus, passion, concentration and total spiritual commitment.

You see, Mandingo, God exists in all of us. Bring him out to play.

GET THE HELL OUT OF SOWETO!

Every time I go to visit family in Soweto, I am very conscious of when to leave. The minute I see it getting dark, I start getting nervous. And if I have a woman in my car, I become an even bigger nervous wreck. The joke is that I grew up in Soweto. Even after I had left for the rural areas, I still spent many of my school holidays there. But man, Soweto scares me to death now. I have simply heard too many stories of hijackings, rapes and murders to feel safe there.

A lot of people would argue that I'm a sell-out. How could I feel that way about home? How could I even write this about home? Considering that, often, as a young kid going to school there on a Monday, I would pass dead bodies on the way after weekends of mayhem, considering that I would witness at least one fatal weekend knife-fight a month growing up there, considering that I would watch men hit their girlfriends on the head with bricks and kick their crotches in broad daylight and in full view of everyone who could bear to watch, I guess it is understandable that people would think I should consider Soweto home. Surely I should be used to this lifestyle. It is how it is, and I grew up with it. After all, millions of people live this way and still manage to crack jokes and laugh.

But that's the hook you see. When you are inside an unnatural environment, it seems natural because you don't have another environment to compare it to. Someone I know made the example the other day of a fly that's trapped in a closed glass jar. First, the fly will try to fly out. After a while, it will reckon there's no way out and then settle in. Even if you open the glass jar lid, the fly won't attempt to escape again until it dies. It has learned that this is the only environment cut out for it. Inescapable.

I went out of Soweto to live in other parts of South Africa and suddenly the Soweto lifestyle did not seem natural or right. In rural South Africa, the air was cleaner and the people were friendlier and more on the loving side. Fights in the rural places I lived in were a rarity and people respected each other, their elders and brought up their children as a community. In the white parts of the then-divided South Africa, the streets were clean, the people seemed more disciplined and no one seemed to piss in the streets or litter everywhere. There seemed to be a certain positive order to the lives people lived outside of compounds like Soweto, now considered hip by people who, in fact, should aspire to getting the hell out!

The hardest thing anyone can do is swim out of a sewer. For one thing, the oxygen supply is limited and oxygen is a large source of the energy that that person will need to swim the length of the sewer in the first place. And so a lot of us suffocate and die, long before we can see the end of the filthy tunnel. What is worrying though is that a large number of us don't even try to swim out. Instead, we assume that the sewer is our lot. On the odd occasion that we decide that it isn't, we often give up our escape too early and then hide behind statements like "I can't turn my back on my home". And so townships are elevated to levels way above their station.

But townships were never our homes, Mandingo! This is where the butchers that were the architects of the horror that was apartheid sent us to die of disease, filth and self-hate. When we built something that we could call our own, like District Six or Sophiatown, with all the flaws of these places, they tore it down and forced us out.

And now?

Well, here we are proclaiming that places like Soweto are our homes, that no one should say anything bad about them, that we love them, that even if we wanted to, we can't get out, that these places are our lot. But we are dying there, Mandingo! There's not enough space there. The air is thick with pollution! The environment there drives us so mad that we prey on each other and progress is limited. How can you succeed and reach heights beyond dreams when you have to worry about driving at night, let alone walking at night? How can you be a success when you are constantly worried about the possibility of someone raping your wife, mother or daughter? How can you win when you carry so much fear amongst your own?

And so I say to you, Mandingo, get the hell out of Soweto, leave Khayelitsha, run away from Umlazi, you don't want to be stuck in Seshego, get out of Mabopane! We fought apartheid so that all of South Africa can be a home to all South Africans. The jar is now open. We must not settle down and believe that because the townships are the places where we were born, we must make our homes there. We are built for bigger and better lives, Mandingo, and we can achieve those now. Let's do it.

I would love to feel free and safe whenever I visit Soweto. But this won't happen until most of the people living there have moved out to bigger, better places with bigger, better houses and leaving fewer people who would then have, in the same space, bigger, better spaces to build bigger and better houses than are possible now. Let's work to get our people employed. Let's work to get our people rich. Let's work to get our people to a point where they can afford to leave places like Soweto and settle in places like Melville and Sandton in Johannesburg, Constantia and Observatory in Cape Town, Morningside and Berea in Durban, and so on and so forth. Let's work to be economically free to live anywhere we choose to live in South Africa, Mandingo.

Now that we are politically free, let us be free to roam our country equally freely. That's it, Mandingo. Have a great week ahead. Work to break the mental shackles that bind us. Be free.

PERFECTION

I was having a chat with a friend of mine about a job she might take up in the near future and she talked a bit about the workshops she would like to run for her staff if she were allowed to. She said that the first workshop she would run would be on perfection, just so her staff could be taught how fulfilling it is to get something just right. That got me thinking, you see, because for most of us it is easier to say: "I'm not perfect" than it is to say: "I am perfect".

This can be a handicap to success.

We are taught from an early age that we are not supposed to be vain, that we must be humble, that we must never bang our

59

own drum. So to hear someone say they are perfect at this or the other thing brings out this feeling in us that we are in the presence of someone who has some terrible affliction of the soul. To even think of ourselves as perfect in one way or the other or at this or the other makes most of us feel a bit uncomfortable in our own presence, let alone in the presence of others. And so we spend our lives pointing out to people what our flaws are, and generally downplaying what is great about who we are, just in case people start to think that we are full of ourselves.

How can you be perfect when you spend your time downplaying perfection? Consider this: whether or not you downplay your perfection, you are already perfect. But if you downplay your perfection, your success will come with the greatest of difficulty! The real problem for most of us is that we believe that it is difficult to attain consistent perfection at everything we choose to do even though deep down we know that we are perfect, and therefore perfectly poised to attain perfection consistently in our lives.

Let's take a look at the word perfect for a moment. The *New Oxford English Dictionary* defines the word perfect as "having all the required or desirable elements; as good as it is possible to be". What this means is that no matter what the world thinks of your current partner or job or looks or style of dress, if, when you look at these things, they have that which, to you, seem to be all the "desirable" or "required" elements, then they are "perfect". Attaining and seeing perfection requires a certain degree of independence in your thinking. If you say you will arrive at a certain place at a certain time and you do, that is a perfect achievement. The required or desirable elements are that you said and committed to doing something, i.e. arrive somewhere specific at a certain time. When you do just that, you have created a perfect moment in your life. Don't mind that most people believe that in Africa ten o'clock means twelve o'clock. Be independent.

In a sense then, it is easy to achieve perfection all the time because first of all the *New Oxford English Dictionary* defines the word perfection as: "The condition, state, or quality of being free or as free as possible from all flaws or defects". We already know that perfect means having all the required or desirable elements. So to consistently achieve perfection (having a condition that is free from or as free as possible from flaws) you must choose the required elements to get something done and then make sure they are all there at the right time and you will have perfection in your life. Don't set up a meeting at six in the morning when you know you have a tendency to oversleep. Don't marry someone skinny for money when you know you prefer someone with a big build who has money. There's a subtle difference there.

The thing about imperfect moments, like being late, is that they take up a lot of your valuable time because after an imperfect moment you will spend a lot of time trying to repair the damage done. So, for instance, if you promise to take a child to a certain place on a certain day and you fail to do so, it might take you years to repair the damage done because the level of trust erosion created by that simple imperfection is very deep. So another strategy for achieving perfection daily in your life is never to promise what you cannot deliver. You need to be honest with yourself and those around you to be a perfectionist.

And I guess some of us will go: "God! Who needs to be a perfectionist! What a burden". But a perfectionist, according to the *New Oxford English Dictionary*, is "Someone who refuses to accept any standard short of perfection". It really could not be easier than that. The only danger lies in achieving perfection by setting very low standards. For instance, you can say to yourself that, in your perfect world, being thirty minutes late is not a train smash and so consider yourself to be on time every time you arrive twenty minutes late for your meetings. Sure, you will have perfection because the requirements you set for a perfect execution include a thirty-minute leeway. The imperfection in that perfect scenario is that it does not take into consideration that you live with other human beings on planet Earth and that,

61

when you set a time, you do so for yourself and others. There is a standard for all of us, but you are allowed to create your own standards, if you like. But when you do so, you will have to market your own standard vigorously and thus bring in the outside world too if your perfect world is at a much lower or different standard. You would need to market it so that it is well known in all your circles that you have a thirty-minute leeway in your timetable. This way, everyone who sets up a meeting with you works with that in mind. This is a much harder way to achieve perfection. Just be on time. You say two o'clock, rock up at two o'clock. That is a perfect achievement. Otherwise, agree to arrive at two-fifteen. Then rock up at two-fifteen, exactly. Perfect.

Now extend this to every aspect of your life. The beauty about being a perfectionist is that, not only is it easy to do, but as my friend pointed out to me and sparked this article, you get immense personal satisfaction and tranquillity from it. You could be rushing yourself silly, but when you enter through that door and you look at your watch and it's exactly two-twenty, just like you said it would be when you arrive, man what a feeling. In soccer, it would be like a perfectly taken free kick that results in a goal. Perfect. In music, it would be like hitting the right note at the right time. Perfect. In business, it would like shaking hands on a deal that has all parties truly committed and happy about the outcome. Perfect.

Attaining consistent perfection also takes the ability to know your strengths and play to them. Don't spend your life trying to be a singer when you know very well that you are tone deaf! Don't spend your valuable time trying to lead when what you are truly good at is being the power behind the throne. Don't insist on being a striker when your true gift is defending. When you do this, you are playing to your weaknesses and the most perfect thing you will achieve is perfect failure. You are wasting valuable time. You could be a phenomenal businessman but here you are trying to be a nurse. You could be a brilliant teacher but here you are trying to be a truck driver. You could be a fantastic carpenter and here you are trying to be a microbiologist. You could be a magical negotiator and here you are trying to be a race-car driver. Playing to your strengths gives you the best shot at attaining perfection consistently every day of your life. Being a perfectionist gives you the best shot at achieving the highest and most fulfilling successes in your life. And being successful is a beautiful thing, Mandingo. You want to be exactly that: highly successful.

Attaining perfection also involves playing what I call "The when is...?" game. When is the perfect time to spend your money? Answer: when you are in total control of it. Even after you have signed the contract, delivered the perfect job on the contract and the cheque has been deposited into your bank account, do not spend that money until the cheque has been cleared. The cheque could bounce, you know! Imperfect. Wait until you are in possession of and in total control of your money before you spend it or attempt to grow it. When is the perfect time to stop eating? Answer: when you are full. Not when the plate is empty. When is the perfect time to make a judgement call? Answer: when you have listened and heard all sides to the story you are passing judgement on. Not when your best friend says that's what happened. Play "The when is..." game, Mandingo.

Often perfection is not something that you have to work hard at. On the contrary, you need to simply look around to see, feel, and touch perfection because it is in the flight of a bird, the smile of your loved one, a naughty wink from a stranger, your laugh when you love the joke told. Often perfection is consistently achieved when you come to the perfect conclusion that you are, in actual fact, perfect, that you have, in this body that carries you around on a daily basis, a perfectly functioning support system that only you can let down. Not the other way around.

That's it, Mandingo. Be a perfectionist.

SKIN COLOUR

I am totally fascinated by this "Who are you, who am I?" question that many intelligent people consider unanswerable and therefore a useless pursuit. Have you noticed how it seems to jump up highest when we are in a state of flux, at a crossroads or something? Also, you can rest assured that it will crop up whenever you think you have arrived and have become something. You can be sure too that it will arise whenever you have really messed up. These are exciting times and central to existence is this question: who are you really?

One of the most exciting times in a young person's life comes when they suddenly feel a sense of superiority, a feeling of having paid their dues and being poised to make others do the same, a point at which they can now choose to either be merciful or ruthless. If you have been through educational institutions, you will know that this feeling of liberation comes suddenly, when you are in your second year of a new phase in your educational progress. Grade nine (Standard seven), the second year of high school. Your second year of university. The day you are, for the first time, not the most recently employed at your new job.

In the first year, you are the rookie who is expected to be the butt of every senior's jokes. In the second year, you are not the rookie but you are close enough to the newly arrived to have them seek your counsel. This gives you that first feeling of power in this new phase of your life. At this stage, funnily enough, you are also most vulnerable to being made to feel quite small. It's kind of like you have arrived but you haven't. You are not at the beginning and yet you are not at the end. It's like being the middle child.

Who are you really?

In my second year at university, a group of us second-year students were taking some first-year students through the university, showing them where things were and how to get to them, telling them what the best behaviour was, who to confide in, how to deal with lecturers, what to look out for in order not to fail, etc. We were generally being the know-it-all group to gain power over the rookies and have our own slaves, if you like, before the seniors came and devoured everyone. At some stage during this process of orientation power play, we entered one of the residences because amongst us junior-seniors was this one girl who wanted to show off her room. This would, of course, be done under the guise of teaching the junior-juniors in the group what the best state to keep your room in was.

As we entered the show-off's residence, a white girl came around the corner. At that point, the show-off girl ran with arms akimbo towards this white girl and screamed as if they hadn't seen each other in a hundred years and then continued to talk while our group sort of waited around to be shown her magnificent room. This carried on until our group started a conversation of its own to while away the time while waiting for madam to conclude her friendly chat. Then the weirdest thing, at least in my mind, happened.

Miss Show-Off suddenly turned around to face us and shouted, "Shut up, you blacks!" And before any of us could react, she turned straight back to her white friend and continued talking like nothing had happened, laughing and generally having a ball. When she turned around a few minutes later, the group of blacks was still there somehow. It had miraculously not disappeared. Needless to say, the little power we had worked so hard to attain went with her comment and the newly arrived just thought, what pretentious idiots. We lost out on building a strong power position over the junior-juniors. But everyone went through the motions. We observed her neatly kept room and commented on the lovely matching floral this and that and then dispersed. The magic was gone.

Now Miss Show-Off was right. We were a group of black people and that kind of group is commonly referred to as "blacks". So why did this bother my black group and me so? Why did it suddenly raise this "Who are you?" so acutely? I thought about this and the next time I saw her I sat her down and shared my thoughts. None of us were disturbed or in any

65

way ashamed of being "blacks". What was disturbing about her sudden outburst, I pointed out, was that it seemed like she felt that, although she was the darkest amongst us, she was not a "black". Her sudden outburst, referring to us as "blacks" who must "shut up!" in the presence of her white friend (who, it turned out, had been at lunch with Miss Show-Off the very day of the evening when Miss Show-Off jumped at her like a long lost favourite cousin), seemed to mean she did not see herself as a "black". There was our group, uncivilised, loud and black. And there was her, a friend of the white, civilised, quiet and maybe by extension actually, not black.

I told her that this was disturbing to me personally because it was like watching someone with a big nose denying that they actually had a nose. It made her look ridiculous and sound totally out of touch with who she was as a person. I told her she can't help being black as much as she can't help having a nose, being a woman or having the parents she has and that she had better make peace with these simple things as quickly as she could if she was to find inner peace and thrive as a human being. I mean, we all know how hard Michael Jackson tried. He's a brilliant musician but most would agree that what he's done to his skin colour makes him humiliatingly monstrous and freaky to say the least. Anyway, that was then.

Years later I was sitting in my magnificent corporate office where I worked as a managing creative director of an advertising agency. I had, by many standards, arrived. No crossroads here. I was the boss. It was at this time that a white man walked in to do business with me. We talked about this and that, as is the custom before cutting a deal. We were sizing each other up and deciding if we wanted to be in each other's business corners. To really win me over, this white man looked me dead in the eye and said, "Eric, you know, when I look at you I don't see colour. I just see another human being sitting there. Colour does not matter to me. I don't see it." I turned to this well-meaning white man and said, "Robert, when I look at you, I see a white man. I see your colour and in addition to that I see and embrace your humanity."

It's quite amazing that this event did not immediately send me back to my second year at varsity and Miss Show-Off, but it gave me the same feeling of incredulity. Miss Show-Off was denying a big part of who she is to ingratiate herself to her white friend and this white man was denying the existence of a big part of who I am to ingratiate himself to me. Heads you lose, tails they win. In both instances, blackness, my skin colour, is given an invisibility cloak.

I don't buy that, you see. I am the added parts of everything that makes up my mind, my body and my soul. The skin is not only my largest sex organ, as they say; it is my biggest organ, period. It is placed outside of every physical thing that makes up who I am. So how can you not see it? As one of the best poets I've ever watched perform on stage, Lemn Sissay, writes in one of my favourite poems, *Colour Blind*, amongst the many beautiful ones he's written:

If you can see the bluest eye
If you can see the reddest hair
If you can see the colours that reflect
In the rainbow that hangs in the air
If you can see the inky blue of evening
Why is it that you say you are colour blind
When you see me?

Some will argue that seeing colour is the root of all racism and that ignoring it completely will be our salvation. I say to those who say this that the one is just an extreme replacement of the other and in extremities lies very little progress. As people, we must bend where necessary without losing our ability to be firm. Deny anyone a big part of whom they are and it is a matter of time before they force you to acknowledge it with brutal, unyielding force. The man who walked into my office and denied me my colour in a salute cloaked in kindness is white, a family man,

67

Jewish and a businessman. I see all this. I acknowledge all this. I embrace all this. I would not refuse to do business with this man because of this and I would never do business with him because of this either. I would do business with him because our mutual business interests can be satisfied by a joint business venture.

To say to a Venda man, I do not see your being Venda at all is like saying you do not see the man. It is like saying the man does not exist. What you want to say with confidence is that you know and acknowledge without prejudice that the man is Venda and then move into a fruitful partnership with him. It would even be better if you went a step ahead and demonstrated some knowledge of the Venda culture or language.

For South Africa to shift beyond the big divide, we must see who each one of us is totally and embrace the differences about who we are completely and then forge partnerships. But it starts with the individual. See yourself completely and accept everything that you cannot change for the better about who you are totally, do the same for your brother and sister and then follow that up by doing it for your fellow citizens. I must see a white person's whiteness and embrace it. A white person must see my blackness and embrace it. No abuse. No prejudice. Otherwise we render each other invisible and thus make of each other non-entities that can be ignored.

Who you are is not a denial of any of the parts that make up your body, mind and soul, least of all your skin colour. Who you are is all these things acknowledged and affirmed by yourself and others without prejudice.

HIGH MAINTENANCE!
What you want to be, my good friend, is a low-maintenance individual. Low-maintenance individuals, you see, are no one's burden. They build their own empires. They are completely at ease with who they are. You walk up to this kind of individual and you say something like "You are a no one, you have no life!" And this individual looks at you like you are mad. You know

why? It is because what you are saying is being checked against what this individual knows about himself or herself and it is being found wanting. That's why. This is who you want to be.

When a low-maintenance individual walks into a room, they will have their head held high, they will have a bit of a spring in their step and their back will be upright, straight. When they ask you how you are doing, their smile will make you say "I'm fine" and you'll mean it because even if you have problems they seem to fade into nothingness in the presence of that individual's confidence. These individuals seem to smile from way deep inside, where everything is absolutely perfect. These are low-maintenance individuals.

When you try to look for a gift for a low-maintenance individual, you always seem to run short of ideas because they seem to have it all. These kinds of individuals seem to be conversant on any topic because knowledge and the quest thereof are second nature to them. They love to read and engage with relevant information. They have opinions, well thought out and well articulated. They know their stuff. When you hire a low-maintenance individual, you can rest easy. You do not have to worry about whether or not what you hired them to do will be done. They will deliver. But most important of all, they will deliver like it was the easiest thing on earth to do. They paddle quietly but hard. This is the kind of individual you want to be.

Low-maintenance individuals pay their own way. They do so without any hint of stress. When they join your table, you never have to worry about how the bill will be settled. They never assume that someone else will pay. Often, they assume the whole bill will be theirs to settle, so if they get invited by anyone anywhere, whether it's their parent, boyfriend, girlfriend, friend, colleague, boss or anyone else, they will be the first to say "I don't have the money", if they don't have it. Otherwise, they will be the first to pay their portion of the bill. They never assume the world owes them a meal or anything for that matter. They pay their own way and are proud of it.

Low-maintenance individuals are their own spiritual healers. They go through trauma like the rest of us. But when the trauma needs dealing with, they rely on themselves first before burdening the world. You will never hear them blame history even when they have more knowledge of the history that traumatised them than you will ever imagine. These individuals seem to say "Yes I'm human, yes, I suffer, yes, I have an even more painful history but God, do I have a future to shape!" Low-maintenance individuals know how hard it has been and is at times but they are so busy designing a better tomorrow that the pain of yesterday seldom trips them up on the ladder of success. They fall like all of us, but unlike most of us, they always rise with a smile to tackle the world and win. Low-maintenance individuals have a super psychological make-up. This is who you want to be.

Low-maintenance individuals simply love themselves. They love who they are. Often they are not as pretty as you and I. Often they are not as intelligent as you and I. Often they are not as tall as you and I. Often they have a harder background than you and I. But, God, do they win us over quickly with their super confidence! It's like nothing can ever faze them because every comment, every criticism, every slight, is there to make them better. They stick in your mind these individuals and they stay there. Often you can't figure out why you miss them so much. And when you think deeply, you find that it is their presence that you crave. They calm the seas and make the world seem such a lovely place. These are low-maintenance individuals.

Low-maintenance people have integrity. They follow through on their word. You will never catch them lying, cheating or lashing out in anger just to hide their insecurities and the simple fact that they too are human. They revel in being human. They are truly comfortable in their skin, and so are the first to acknowledge that they made a mistake. They are the quickest to say "thank you". And they never make you fight for an "I'm sorry" statement when they've done you wrong. Their "thank you" and "sorry" statements are like the truest gifts because they are always completely genuine. These individuals know that their place in the world is unique and secure and, therefore, they seldom worry about camouflaging their downfalls. They are super beings.

Low-maintenance individuals are generous. But they give of their own time, their own money and their own possessions. You will never catch them giving to John what belongs to Jane and calling that generosity. Low-maintenance individuals are always on time. You see, they respect every promise they make and every person to whom they make that promise. You never have to wait around for then after setting an appointment, unless there's a monumental reason for it. Low-maintenance individuals love to build their own things from scratch. You never have to worry about what they will ask of you next because they love to do things for themselves. And when they do ask something of you, you are more than pleased to help because it is such a rare and special occasion. Low-maintenance individuals are considerate, so they are larger than life, but they take up little room in other people's lives. Low-maintenance individuals are positively driven. That's why they light up a room. They suck very little energy from people around them. Low-maintenance individuals are proud. They will never take it lying down, but they know which fights are worthy of a good fight. That's why they find it easy to walk away when the fight is of no value. Low-maintenance individuals don't like piggyback rides. Often they give piggyback rides, but while they are doing it, they give walking lessons to those they are carrying. Low-maintenance individuals are life givers. They are at the very source of life, be it the life of a business, a party, a marriage, a friendship, you name it, if it needs life, you will find low-maintenance individuals at the very heart of the life it needs.

Low-maintenance individuals are you, Mandingo. This is who you are. Just reach down and bring this gold in you up to the surface. There are four steps to mining this gold mine. Read. Try to read this piece at least once a month to remember who

71

you are and what you are capable of. Believe. Believe in yourself. Act. Act out this belief. Act like you own the world, because we all do and you are we and we are you. *Umuntu ngu muntu nga bantu*. Share. Share with others. Share your powers, Mandingo, because the more low-maintenance people there are amongst us, the easier it will be for us to climb higher. And God knows, we need to climb up. And we need to do so on our own steam.

Be a low-maintenance individual Mandingo.

TO SPRINT OR NOT TO SPRINT, THAT'S THE QUESTION!

Africa never sprints, but she always gets there on time. This might seem like a contradiction in terms because the world is in a rush. Everyone wants to get there ahead of everyone else. And so you might ask "How can Africa be on time when she's moving in the slow lane?" As a matter of fact, has she not been left behind precisely because she never sprints?

Conventional wisdom says "yes" to the latter question. Africa is being left behind because she is too slow. Africa never sprints and so is always late. This logic seems to make sense. There is such a thing as African time after all, isn't there? When northerners from Europe and America plan meetings with us, they make room for about an hour's delay or they end up tearing their hair out because we will arrive an hour late, if not later. And so everyone agrees, Africa never sprints and so is always late. Whenever she arrives at the banquet, everyone else has had their share and more, and is already on the way out to yet another banquet to which Africa will, yet again, be late!

Let's examine this conventional logic to see if it really holds true from another angle. We can start by examining what Africa is late for. We missed the industrial revolution. We were late for that, and so the northerners built all these empires based on their ability to sprint ahead and catch the industrial wave. So, no, Africa is not a massive car-manufacturing continent. But, in being late for that, we also missed the devastation of acid rain.

We are not in danger of a Chernobyl nuclear disaster where more than thirty northerners were instantly killed and over a thousand evacuated. With the industrial revolution, the northerners made a lot of money, but they sacrificed their environment. Who can put financial value to that loss?

And so we arrive at what this means for Africa today. In a nutshell, we are at the forefront of nations that will benefit from eco-tourism. The only place you can go to for the serenity of nature is not in any leading industrial nation. The G8 do not have this. They killed it sprinting to make artificial monetary gains through the industrial revolution, you see. They have zoos where you and I have wild life in the true sense of wild life. Kenya has the Serengeti, South Africa has the Kruger National Park (God, when will they change that name?) and the G8 have zoos. Look at it this way: America got analogue cellular telephones as they marched fast into the information age. They built major networks to capitalise on this. They spent huge amounts of money to do this, and now they must somehow undo it all to catch up, even though they sprinted ahead! But Africa entered the fray after digital replaced analogue. And so we go back where we began; Africa never sprints, but she always gets there on time.

When the northerners in Europe built their cities, they never saw a time when a city would need four-way lanes to breathe. But any country with no roads can build from scratch and do a better job by just observing the mistakes of all the sprinting northerners. Why do you think South Africa is renowned for having one of the best road infrastructures in the world? The simple answer is that we were late to build our roads. It is yet another reason why Cape Town roads are cramped and Johannesburg roads are open.

Yes, we have a crime problem. But we will not deal with it superficially with zero-tolerance xenophobia and racism-driven systems. We will not repress our people to gain artificial serenity in our streets. We will take our time, consult our people, examine the root causes of crime and try to eliminate them. We will pray for and work hard to change the fundamental belief systems of our people to gain a truly lasting and sustainable crime-free Africa. And so, yes, New York will gain quick crime-free results in a sprint to gain the mayor recognition before he steps off at the end of his term. But with all that zero tolerance sprint, the twin towers will still fall! What's the use?

The problem most people have in defining arriving on time is clouded by their definition of when the right time is to get rich. In the north, Europeans rush for quick monetary gains at the expense of all else most of the time. If you read page 23 of the June 10 to June 17 edition of *Fortune* magazine (or go to www.fortune.com and look for Geoffrey Colvin's article "When Scandal Isn't Sexy"), you will find a one-page story that talks about a business scandal that makes the sickening Enron debacle seem like a hugely forgivable non-event. The financial disaster you will read about there is also sprint-mentality driven. Apparently the telecom industry in the United States of America assumed that with the advent of the information age there would be so much information being moved around that, to capitalise on this possible boom, it invested trillions (note, not millions, not billions, trillions) of dollars in fibre-optic cabling. In this rush to make this imminent wealth, no one stopped to say "Guys, why don't we watch the market for a while and see if this information overload theory holds true?" No one said, "Guys, let's jog, we'll still get there." If they had said it, I'm sure they would have been shut down by shouts of "WHAT IF SOMEONE GETS THERE FIRST?"! As though it were a disease to sometimes stand on the sidelines and watch. So they rushed and got there, but the information overload they anticipated never materialised and so over 500 000 jobs were lost and more people were released onto the streets of America to fend for themselves without income. How do you think that country can ever solve its serial killer and similar crimes syndrome when it sprints with such irresponsibility?

On the other hand, Africa's fibre-optic cabling will be driven by market demands. It will be much slower, but when Africa gets there, she will be on time yet again with a perfect product for her people. My Uncle Dingaan, who used to drive me mad with his slow driving from Elim Hospital in the north of Limpopo to Johannesburg when I was a young kid, used to calm the tension in the car by repeating the Shangaan saying "*Ku tsutsuma swi tlula hi ku famba kunene* (Walking beats running)". Some people would get to Johannesburg before us, but often we would pass people dying on the side of the road as my uncle repeated the saying one more time: *Ku tsutsuma swi tlula hi ku famba kunene.*

We Africans are not in a rush, you see, because deep down we know that there is always enough time. As Africans we understand very well that life is not a 100-metre dash. We know that life is a centuries-long marathon. We know that we do not have to achieve it all in one term of office. We know that success is judged best by generational gain and that the best success takes time and needs patience. It would do northerners good to heed their own saying: patience is a virtue.

Don't be slow, Mandingo. But never let anyone rush you unnecessarily. It is always better to do it right than to do it fast. Speed and perfection seldom mix well. In the movie business, they have a phrase for it. They say "Hurry up and wait". More often than not, nature connives to slow you down when you sprint too fast. We did give the northerners rock and roll but our endearing beat is that of a calm heart. Never forget that. Peace.

THANK GOD FOR THE AMERICANS

I'm sitting with two college graduates – one American, one Sudanese. Their names are Zachary Yorke and Lumumba Stanislaus-Kaw, respectively. The Sudanese has a degree in Philosophy and Mathematical Economics and another in Jurisprudence, both from Oxford University in England, and he is a registered Doctor of Philosophy candidate. The American has a B.A. (Fine Arts) degree from Amherst College. He also majored in Anthropology and was a course short of having majored in Open Economy Macro Economics and Social Psychology. Both have asked me to read some papers they have written. Lumumba's piece is about the production of poverty on the African continent, a preamble to an entire study. Zachary's, on the other hand, is a collection of pieces on his observations of the art scene on his travels throughout South Africa.

Lumumba, without provocation, announces to me that he wants the audience for his book to be anyone who can read English, whatever their academic qualification. Zachary's pieces, on the other hand, move in and out of being rigorously academic and totally accessible. I tell both that I firmly believe that knowledge in the early days was designed to be the preserve of the few. This tradition of leaving the masses in the dark and ruling them through fear and lack of knowledge has managed to last all the way from the beginning of knowledge preservation and dissemination to today. And so, highly educated people often feel that the more inaccessible their theories, the more complex their style of deconstructing their arguments, the more intelligent they sound and the more respect they garner from their peers.

This peer pressure is at the forefront of this obfuscation of knowledge. There is such a thing as academia. There is such a thing as academic discourse. There are such people as the academic police. These police are found, to a large degree, within the confines of such institutions as Oxford and Amherst. Often these police instil in their protégés this ancient style of writing academic theses. This ancient tradition owes its allegiance to the few. And so, often, you find that these wonderful graduates end up producing written work that is impenetrable.

It's one thing to grapple with a difficult paper because the issues it discusses are difficult and new, which means language, as it exists at the time of writing, is inadequate. It is another thing altogether when the paper is peppered with obscure words and difficult sentence constructs. I find this to be the difference between Wole Soyinka's work (difficult though grappling with everyday issues) and Chinua Achebe's (accessible even as it gives complex insights).

I give no apologies for being a champion of easy-to-understand and highly accessible writing. And this is where I want to thank the Americans. With all their nonsensical and brutal interventions around the world, all their arrogance, all their inability to choose the right leader at the right time, all their racist hatred of the other, you must give them praise for making knowledge much more accessible in the English-speaking world. Most "*X for Dummies*" books I know are American written. So you have *Nietzsche for Dummies*, *Sushi for Dummies*, *Chess for Dummies* books written by Americans without the pretense of academia. When you are done reading *Chess for Dummies*, you will have the same grasp of chess fundamentals as any chess Grand Master. You might never play like a Grand Master, but you will have the same grasp of the fundamental principles of the game as s/he does.

And then, of course, you have business books that range from Robert Kiyosaki's *Rich Dad* series to the ex-Stanford School of Business Professor Jim Collins' books *Good to Great* and *Built to Last*. These books do not have the words "... for dummies" on the cover but they might as well be written for "dummies" because they make it so easy to grasp the concepts that drive good businesses. Get hold of a book called *E=mc² A Biography of the World's Most Famous Equation* to get my meaning. The author, David Bodanis, decided to write the book when some actress, I think it was Cameron Diaz, was asked at the end of an interview if there was one thing she would like to know and she answered, yes, what is the meaning of $E=mc^2$? The author said he realised at that moment that there were many people who knew this Albert Einstein formula but very few who understood its meaning or true impact. So he wrote the book, not to impress his professors (the knowledge police) or dazzle his peers, but to make "anyone who can read English, whatever their academic qualifications" understand the concept. I bought that book for my son, who was about thirteen or so at the time, and he read it cover to cover and understood it.

To my knowledge, no nation has done more in recent history than the Americans to demystify knowledge (for centuries the preserve of the few and privileged). For that, I salute them. Imagine if this nation could put all its ingenuity behind building a great world for all who live in it! But, alas, George W. Bush is still in with a chance to go back to the White House as president of the USA. And who's to tell how Kerry will differ. In fact, if you asked Michael Moore (Author of *Dude, Where's My Country?* and producer of the Academy Award winning documentary *Bowling for Columbine*), he would tell you there is no difference really between the Democrats and Republicans in America.

Scary!

But back to my academic friends Zac and Lumumba. I am excited to say that for Zac, an American, it has taken a trip to Africa to embrace what some of his compatriots started a little while back, i.e. writing to be understood by as many people as possible. In Lumumba's attempt, I see a glimpse of a future where African academics demystify what northern countries do to bamboozle Africans in order to loot their coffers. I see an academic paper that has a built-in potential to be revolutionary for the betterment of Africa by Africans. I see an accessible explanation of economics, its constructs, its use and, ultimately, its understanding, which then becomes a tool for Africa's salvation. But will he get a publisher? Maybe Moeletsi Mbeki will take up the challenge. After all, he published Prof. Sampie Terreblanche's economic analysis of the widening gap between the rich and the poor in South Africa. Yeah, maybe I should tell Lumumba to forward his paper to Moeletsi Mbeki.

Maybe you, Mandingo, will be the publisher. Who knows? Peace.

HUMAN VALUE

I have always found it absolutely intriguing that the poorest man on earth has pride. Have you noted how the most stupid guy in your group also has pride? What you might call the button "not" to push! Pride it would seem has a way of residing within people from all strata of society. You find pride amongst the poorest and amongst the richest. The most gifted athletes and the most crippled human beings have pride somewhere deep inside. Pride, it would seem, sees no colour either. It has citizenship in the hearts of all race groups and in all nationalities on earth.

Now why is that?

We at *O'Mandingo!* have come to the conclusion that pride is resident inside every human being because pride is the human measure of human value. Every human being, therefore, was given this thing called pride by the creator so that each and every one of us can intrinsically know his/her value. Okay, so some amongst us have more pride than others, it would seem. And that can be unpalatable. But imagine for a second a world without pride.

There would be no reason to bath would there? Why would you want an elaborate sewer system if you did not care, which is what lack of pride is? Not caring. Why, for God's sake?! Just leave the stench to fester, thank you very much! Who cares? Do you think there would be computers? Yes, there is the flipside, which is that the middle eastern conflict would not be raging still if there was no pride at stake, for instance. In this regard, pride in the sense of one group believing that it is more valuable than the other. Pride, they say, is a horrible thing. We think they meant to say that pride "can be" a horrible thing. Imagine for a minute, a world without pride… would we know as we do today that inside the Milky Way are over a thousand other planets with life on them, just like earth? Hey? Would we have seen the surface of the planet Jupiter? Would we even know that Jupiter exists?

Pride is resident inside all human beings without discrimination because it is the only indicator of human value. Most human beings just know, they don't question this, they don't care how it came to be, they just know that they should not be talked to in a certain way. That's it. Something inside them tells them they have a value above what is being dished out to them, if indeed what is being dished out to them is without respect. Have you noticed how kids refuse to give away something that they have unless you really beg sometimes or find another way of making them feel valuable before being given the thing in question? They don't know why, but something bigger than mom and dad tells them that they have a value that says no one must just take something that they own. In this case, ownership meaning I'm holding it, therefore it is mine. Forget that it was bought for the kid next door, who is now howling to get it back. Pride. They have pride and pride constantly reminds them that they have a value. And so, they demand, just like we all demand, and need respect to survive.

Why do human beings need a constant reminder of their value then? Let's flip the question on its head somewhat and ask this: why does racism fuel itself with the mission to make the other feel valueless? Why do white racists insist on saying that black people have no value? Why do xenophobic blacks insist on saying that fellow blacks who come from countries other than the one they are resident in are valueless? Why do South African xenophobic citizens insist on using derogatory terms to describe fellow Africans who are not from South Africa before insisting that they be shipped back to where they came from? Why is it so important to insist on the lack of value of the other in order to propagate the philosophy of exclusion? This insistence on a lack of value on the part of the other that drives maladies like xenophobia and racism is important to those who belong to these types of movements, because when people forget their true value they are easy to control.

We need pride, the constant reminder of human value, because when people forget what they are worth and start behaving like robots, they are eaten alive, and when people die a big part of our planet's potential goes with them. You see, the world is highly competitive and often people devalue other people in order to get ahead. If you are black in a hostile white environment, you know what we are talking about. If you are Jewish and know your history of persecution, you know what we are talking about. If you are a lower-caste Indian amongst higher-caste Indians, you know what we are talking about. If you are a dark-skinned coloured person amongst light-skinned coloured persons, you know what we are talking about. If you are a poor Caucasian amongst rich Caucasians, you know what we are talking about. If you are of peasant stock amongst royalty, you know what we are talking about. See? In short, if you belong to the majority of the world's population, you know what we are talking about. Now, if we are going to depend on the world to know our value, we might just end up with 95% of the world's population believing that they are nobodies and being pulled around and apart by the 5% who currently own everything. You see, we need pride, the human value barometer, to save the world from itself.

Now what is this value that pride measures? When you are left naked and cold, with no food, and you refuse to let go but insist on continuing to live, what are you protecting? What is the value of a human being when s/he has absolutely no worldly possessions whatsoever? What is the measure of all that a suicide reduces to nothing when the suicidal person takes his/her life? Why are we so traumatised by human death? That's what we believe pride measures. Now what is that value?

A scientist at CERN Laboratory measured what it would cost to produce a machine that could duplicate all the functions of the human eye. You will be amazed by what he found out. But first, let us tell you what CERN Laboratory is. CERN Laboratory is a European laboratory concept first proposed in 1949 at the European Cultural Conference at Lausanne by French physicist and Nobel prize-winner Louis de Broglie. The proposal to form this laboratory was made in an attempt to redress the brain-drain effect on the European scientific community, triggered

81

by the Hitler tribal wars. CERN Laboratory, in a nutshell, is not a Mickey Mouse concept. It employs some of the best scientific brains in the world and is, in fact, at the forefront of nuclear science and its technological breakthroughs.

Now, let's get back to the findings of a researcher at the CERN Laboratory. The scientist found that to duplicate all the functions of a human eye, using the latest cutting-edge technology at the time, would take a machine the size of an average room in a house costing over 50 million English pounds to manufacture and rising! That's what your eye is worth. Fifty million pounds sterling! Now, do some research and try to find out what your ear can actually do. You will discover what we can simply define as a marvel of intricate creation. And this, dear Mandingo, is what your pride wants you never to forget. You are an immeasurably valuable machine, and no one must ever forget that, least of all you.

So walk tall, Mandingo. Walk with pride. Let no man or woman force you to forget your value. But keep in check this pride thing, because if you go overboard, you can reduce your value no end. You have a fantastic machine for a human body but, like most machines, you need to know how to work it. You need to know how to improve and upgrade it from time to time. You need to practice running the machine, so that you can get all its benefits at the most optimum levels. What is the point of owning a video machine that can wake you up in the morning, phone you when it is time for the news, and record your favourite programmes while you are away if you do not know how to work it?

Your body is no different. Forget all the obvious things that it does for you, even while you sleep, and remember the powers that it possesses, the powers that you can tap into when you are awake. For example, your intuition, the ability to know things without knowing them! Another example, your ability to decipher the meaning behind spoken words. Think of your ability to keep on learning and learning and learning, without ever running out of brain space! Think of all these things, and see how much of this potential you are tapping into. Then start to maximise and multiply your value to your family, your work environment and society as a whole.

You are a valuable machine and your pride won't let you forget that, so don't. And while you are busy remembering, don't forget that it is up to you to tap into the potential that your body can yield.

Finally, in the first of a series of endorsements for products that we believe can add value to your life, *O'Mandingo!* wants to urge you to go and buy yourself a book called *Head First – 10 Ways to Tap into Your Natural Genius* by Tony Buzan. This book will show you what you are worth. It will teach you how to maximise the value that is locked in who you are. In simple terms, it will help you work and walk with pride. You can find it at Estoril Books in Village Walk, Sandton, any Exclusive Books bookshop around the country or at Amazon.com on the Internet. Invest in yourself. Buy this book and read it. It is a fun, easy read as well as a highly enlightening piece of literature.

And as my baby brother Errol always says:

Catch a fire and build Africa. And be good to yourself, whatever the system dishes out to you, you know? Be good to yourself.

LINKS

As I grow older I am more and more convinced that life is essentially about links. I am not a psychologist, but the most miserable people I know are the ones who seem not to have healthy relationships. These are people who do not seem connected to anyone or anything. On the other hand, the happiest people I know are people who seem totally connected to a cause or another human being. Have you ever seen how often people look happy at a wedding, a ceremony that celebrates the connection of two human beings? Have you ever seen a child being separated from someone the child loves?

On the other hand, the unhappiest people I know float around like islands. They have no one to talk to when the lights go out and depressing periods start to take hold of their lives. They have no one to laugh with when the funnies cross their paths. They are alone, and somehow this makes it very hard for them to navigate happily through life. Do you remember how much of a loner the American serial killer Jeffrey Dahmer was? Do you remember the desperate need to connect that manifested in his cannibalistic killer spree?

So I have come to the conclusion that human beings need to be healthily connected to other human beings as much as they need oxygen and food to survive. But to be connected is a complex thing, isn't it? And so, we end up with this conundrum! Breathing is not a complicated process. Neither is eating. But try and get a boyfriend or girlfriend if you are single! Try and keep a good relationship going smoothly if you have one!

Why is something so essential for our survival so complicated to incorporate into our lives?

I think it is because every human being is unique and we have been taught throughout time that conformity is the key to universal harmony. So, fat people must lose weight, while skinny people must put on some weight. It depends on who the dominant group is at the time. Christians must become Muslims while Muslims must become Buddhists who must become Hindus who must become Moonies who must think about following some other religion depending on who is the dominant religious group in the region at the time. Women must be men as men become women. Why can't all these co-exist?

And there in lies the conundrum, in my humble opinion. I think our lives would be made so much better if we were taught to be comfortable with our differences. Whites do not have to be black as blacks become white for the world to function because grey is a dull colour. As you look for a relationship or try to keep the relationships you have going, remember that the people in your life are as unique as you are and as different as you are, and that it is okay. Of course, there will be people who will be so different to you that you will find it completely uncomfortable to have them in your space, just as there will be people who will be so similar to you that it will rub you up the wrong way. It's okay. When that happens, move on. Do not be stuck trying to change these people or spend your life trying to fit into a mould that does not match your shape. But do it graciously by accepting that they are not better or worse beings than you. They are just different.

Men beat up their wives and girlfriends to have power over them in order to force them to be something that they are not because they are uncomfortable with what they are. Men do this also because they are too insecure about who they themselves are and so try to feel better by gaining power through force over the women in their lives. This is a sick power game. Different racial groups try to do this to each other to gain dominant positions. Different ethnic factions within the same racial groups try to do this to each other. Older people try to do this to younger people. And onward this sickness marches to destroy.

He or she is different. It's okay. If you are not comfortable in that space, you do not have to destroy. Move on. There are enough people in the world for you to connect with. It takes all sorts to make the world habitable. Be respectful of "the other" and you will find harmony in your relationships. Be accepting of "the other" even as you walk away because you must and you will be happy in your relationships.

Differences make the world tick right. They are what we must celebrate.

WE APOLOGISE!

There is no doubt that, in the pecking order of racist South Africa, the black woman has been heaped with the most abuse. As learned politicians will never let us forget, and rightly so, the black woman was and often continues to be oppressed as a woman before all other forms of oppression are heaped on her. She's always one bit more traumatised than the black man. But what is even sadder is the fact that, as a woman, she is often most

85

traumatised by the black man. This, we must overcome. When two are powerful, they move better, faster, with more purpose and more swiftly than when one is powerful and spending half that energy making the other less powerful.

On this day, one day after Africa Day, the day on which the 39-year-old Organisation for African Unity was formed, *O'Mandingo!* offers an apology on behalf of all black men to all black women.

I Did You Wrong

I did you wrong
When I read me out loud
While the book open to read was you

I did you wrong
When I said you were strong
In a manner that left you feeling weak

I did you wrong
When I spoke at the top of my voice
And built a barrier to your beautiful words

I did you wrong
When I extended my hand to lift you up
When what you really needed was to sit right down and rest

I did you wrong
When I finished your sentences
Taking away your only right to be who you are in my presence

I did you wrong
When I cracked a joke to stop your tears
When grief was truly your soul's need at that time

I did you wrong
When I over-injected your dreams with my passion
And thus took them away from you and made them mine

I did you wrong
When I looked through who you are
To worship whom you could be

I did you wrong
When I raised my hand
And bruised your spirit with my physical presence

I did you wrong
Because I did not love you right
While I blamed you saying you loved me wrong

I did you wrong
Because I could have taken so much less from you
But I took so much more

I did you wrong
But I hurt me more because you hate me now
And I could have made you love me

I did you wrong
Because in hurting me so
I must have given you more hurt than pain can give

I did you wrong
It is as clear to me as lightning in a thundering night sky

I did you wrong
I know it now and it takes away my desire to wake up and
reach out to kiss the sky

I did you wrong
Because I allowed a little smoke
To stop us from making a bonfire of love to block the
winter winds

I did you wrong
Because I was in such a hurry to watch you grow
I never left you alone to dictate a pace of your own

I did you wrong
Because I loved you with so much heat
I burnt your space to love me back

I did you wrong
Because I loved you so much
I could not be secure enough to trust you with my eyes closed

I did you wrong
Because I said I would take you away to lover's land
But look, I took out the map to hell and played navigator

I did you wrong my love
Because I could love you right, now
But your love is gone and I am here, alone, clutching at
phantoms in the dark

Eric Miyeni

From this day onward, black man, pledge never to abuse the women you love. They are your mothers, the mothers of your children. They are the other half of your very soul.

From this day onward, black woman, pledge never to labour under abuse. You are bigger, you are stronger, you are a queen, don't let us make you forget that. We can only be kings if you remain the queen you were born to be.

ONE TOOL FOR SUCCESS

I am prejudiced. This is a fact. Sometimes it saddens me. But it is as true as night is dark. However, you probably know that it is through prejudice that humankind survives the rough seas on planet Earth, right? I mean that's why candid camera can be so funny at times; most candid camera spoofs are built on people's pre-programming. Have you not yet seen people duck because they heard the sound of a landing Boeing 747 inside a shop inside a mall?! Your pre-programming, your prejudice, makes you duck before you investigate, in case your investigation interferes with your survival and you end up crippled after an aeroplane "silently" broke through the concrete walls of a mall, flew through all the zigzagging mall corridors and came rushing at full speed into the shop you were in and flattened both your legs as it pulled to a halt! Rather look stupid than die, right?

So, yeah, I'm prejudiced because it's good for survival. And I've always thought that if I met a white man who had always been mugged by black men, beaten up by black people, abused by them and seldom, if ever, met a decent black person who treated him right and then he told me that he hated black people on sight, I would completely understand. His prejudice is his survival tool and that tool would probably help him whenever a nasty black was in his vicinity. It's just human nature to use your experience to function on autopilot. Imagine how much time you would waste if you could not do that? You'd be like a child, wouldn't you? You'd look like you were constantly running around trying to figure out what was what, and you'd probably die early from stress-related malfunctions of your vital organs.

When I was growing up, something made me firmly believe that if I were ever to speak a language other than my own, I would do my best to pronounce the words in a manner that sounded as close to the original speakers of that language as possible. I don't remember when or how I came to this belief, but I know that to me, it is now, as it was then, the only way I believe one can show respect for the original speakers of a language. And so when I hear someone butcher another language, another prejudice in me jumps up to be noticed. I cannot stand people who speak badly.

Have you heard those people who speak English and pronounce the Rs like they were gurgling with thick spit at the back of their throat? I hate that! One of the tools for success is communication. Why would anyone interfere with his or her own success by sounding disgusting or totally incoherent? Look, English is a tricky language in that it is widely spread and spoken differently in many different places by different people but, come on, the basics are the same. I used to say that accents can differ but the pronunciation of the words should stay the same, until I realised that the way you pronounce the words is actually your accent! To have the correct accent, i.e. one that is closest to the original speakers of a language, you must learn to listen carefully and then practice like you would practice singing a new song. Now obviously this might pose an impossible challenge for the tone deaf, but these are few, aren't they? Most of us can hear and mimic sound correctly, so why not do it with foreign languages? "Arrogance" is not "arrogancy" you know! Saying "arrogancy" is not only pronouncing a word wrong, it is tantamount to creating a new, meaningless word that makes you sound stupid and incoherent. Try again, okay? Arrogance.

I could never put it better than my dear friend, *O'Mandingo!*'s copy editor, Lara Gochin, put it, so I'll just quote her. She says: "If I hear someone talking with a strong accent, I'm too busy listening to the accent and the way they butcher the vowels, than what they actually have to say. The accent gets in the way of the content – it's like an obstacle to understanding."

My worst, worst, worst prejudice of all is against those people who wear the horrible way in which they pronounce any language that is foreign to them like a badge of honour. As though saying, "this is my identity, this is who I am, take it or leave it". There are things one can be proud of but really now, sounding like a moron or a disgusting freak is not one of them.

But is this prejudice useful? I doubt that very much. So maybe I should just get over it already and shut up. But then again, I will tell you this: you don't want to go into one meeting and have no one want to follow up on whatever important matters you discussed because they could not stand hearing that spit at the back of your throat as you butchered their language. It just comes across as disrespectful, you know. So you check yourself and see if you are worth listening to for any length of time for those people whose language it is that you are speaking. No one wants to constantly be checking what you are trying to say to them because you thought that, for instance, making Zulu sound like Afrikaans, or English sound like Shangaan, was cool. It's too difficult and time consuming. Listen to the original speakers carefully and try to speak as closely as possible to how they speak. It's worth a try, and it's a sign of respect.

SELF-HATE

Let me say, off the bat, that I do believe that true love is possible across any human colour line. I know this to be true because I have felt it for people who history has prepared me to hate. I mean, it's only logical. Human beings have been known to love animals that are wired to eat them! If we are capable of that kind of love, how could we fail to love another human being simply because that human being has a pigment of a different colour?

Now that I have that off my chest, let me tell you a story. Over a year ago, a mixed couple made up of a black man and his white wife asked me to come to their home and give them my views on love across the colour line for a documentary they were filming for the SABC. I agreed because I had known this couple for quite a number of years and even though I did not know their journalistic pedigree, I felt that it was okay to speak candidly with them on the subject. I spent my own money to travel to this couple's house and gave my time freely for this documentary. The interview on this subject lasted no less than thirty minutes. The subject by the way, just like the title of the

91

documentary, was *Black Man, White Woman*. The subject was not about mixed couples in general. As I understood it, I was being interviewed about my personal views on why I think some black men prefer to go out with white women. And one of the theories that I came to surmise as I was being interviewed was that self-hate played some part in this phenomenon. But we'll talk about that later.

The first thing that alarmed me when I viewed the documentary, after receiving an sms to alert me to the screening, was that these people I had known for so long actually spelt my name wrong. Instead of "Miyeni" they wrote "Moyeni" or "Muyeni" or "Myeni" or some other bastardisation of my surname. That's not good journalism. The next thing that disappointed me was that I discovered watching that documentary that I was actually a "Slam Poet". That's the title they put after my bastardised name! I had never delivered a single slam poem in my life and here I was being presented to the world as a slam poet! My friends called to ask when I had become a slam poet! When I next met the female part of this documentary film-making couple, I voiced my disappointment. She apologised. I accepted. We left it at that. Water under the bridge.

Fast forward to more than a year later. I receive an sms insinuating that I'm a racist because I have said that for a black man to be with a white woman is a sign of self-hate. So I sms back to find out where this information comes from and I am told that it is from the local magazine *Femina*. Now I do not read *Femina*. I know I have not given an interview to anyone who told me they wrote for *Femina*. And so I am totally confused. However, I inform the sms sender that this statement can be true sometimes. Next, I get attacked by very dear friends of mine at a restaurant that I frequent; they say I have literally reduced all marriages across the colour line (and this includes marriages of their esteemed comrades in the struggle) to nothing, and insulted those comrades. When I asked if these people had read this article, I discover that the majority haven't. The one person who had actually read the piece then tries to give me what the quote says. What he says somehow reminds me of the black and white couple that I gave an interview to for television over a year earlier. It is a quote that is totally out of context from what I recall.

On the surface, I felt betrayed by this mixed couple I had trusted. And I started making assumptions. One of them was based on the fact that they told me the interview was for a TV documentary and here it was apparently in print. So I assumed that in order to milk more money out of the endeavour, they decided to recycle the interview for a magazine. This assumption got me upset because I felt that it was wrong of them to do this without asking me for my permission or letting me know that this is what they were going to do. And why did they take the most controversial statement out of the more than thirty minutes of the interview and quote it out of context? I was livid! I could not believe that *Femina* had printed this without checking with me to see if I had been properly represented.

It was time to buy this *Femina*. And I guess for the publishers that is all that matters. Journalistic integrity has no room as long as you get as many people as possible to buy your publication. Well, *Femina* had gotten one purchase for one issue out of me, and made an enemy for life in exchange. I came to all these conclusions before I read the article based on the negative pressure I felt from people who had seemingly read the article.

And then I read the piece and discovered that my first assumption was wrong. The couple hadn't recycled the piece for financial gain. A different journalist, Nia Magoulianti-McGregor, had written the piece. And so it appeared that if I had been quoted out of context, Nia Magoulianti-McGregor had done so. Not the couple. For all intents and purposes, they seem to only be responsible for letting this *Femina* journalist see their documentary *Black Man, White Woman*. So the most they could be held accountable for is perpetuating this untruth that I am a poet because she must have lifted that title off of that

93

documentary of theirs. I do write poetry. I don't deny that. But how many people do? Does that make all of us poets? I don't think so. But let's leave that aside.

For the record, let me say that the *Femina* piece that created all this negativity in my life is a beautiful and candid picture of life inside the confines of a mixed relationship as seen by Sipho Singiswa and Gillian Schutte, the married couple that I had given an interview to for *Black Man, White Woman*. It's a touching piece. Honest. Pithy. And to the point. When you are done reading it, you feel like you have had a window into two honest souls. I'll give *Femina*'s Nia Magoullianti-McGregor that.

But I still take issue with that magazine because I am still disturbed by the pink section of that article that is entitled "Across the colour bar: What people are saying on the streets". First of all, I was not interviewed by anyone on any street. To make what I said sound like a voice pop is wrong and misleading. It means there was nothing more to the statement and that it stands in isolation. That's not true. Second of all, I was interviewed on what I think are possible reasons that make black men go out with white women. To make it sound like my comment refers to mixed couples generally is wrong and misleading. The comment that self-hate could play a part in that scenario would not necessarily make sense if the couple in question was made up of a Jamaican woman and a Chinese man, as the racial dynamic might not necessarily be as pronounced as that between a South African black man and a South African white woman. And to assume, based on that statement, like my friends did, that it means I believe there can never be true love across the colour line or that all relationships across the colour line are based on self-hate, well, that's just senseless and illogical.

The statement quoted in *Femina* that is attributed to me goes as follows:

"I think it's got its basis in racial oppression. You know that when a man wants to get to another man, he gets to the wife, whatever her colour. So what better way to get back at the man who's been kicking your ass all these centuries than to sleep with his woman? If you can win a white woman over and you're black, it's only driven by self-hate, now that I think of it."

This statement still makes a lot of sense to me. First off, we live in a patriarchal society that, by and large, treats women as minors who belong to whomever they marry. Women still lose their surnames in our country because by getting married, they disappear and become whom they marry. We are making a lot of progress in this regard because, for instance, we have a much larger number of women in important political positions than many supposedly progressive governments that have had democratic systems for much longer. But we still have female MPs who go home to be beaten by their husbands! In this scenario, a woman is still a man's most prized "possession" and if you flip that picture you see his biggest Achilles heel. So, yes, men do get at each other by getting at each other's wives, even in today's progressive societies. That's why the rape of women is still one of the biggest weapons for the humiliation of enemies in war. Extend that to a racially divided country like ours and you see how black men could easily see colour ahead of emotion when they encounter white women. Ten years is a very short time.

Looked at from another angle, it's not difficult to see how the black man's fascination with white women can be an expression, an externalisation of self-hate, in a racially polarised society like ours has been, is and hopefully won't be for long. Apartheid, like all racist systems, was designed to make white people believe that they are superior to all other races. But what most people refuse to acknowledge is that racist systems also teach all the people that it insists are inferior to white people to believe that they are, indeed, inferior and that whites are, indeed, superior. So when the oppressed race looks in the mirror, it is filled with self-hate. Worse still, when it looks at the white race, it sees a better race, a more superior race. As a result, and coupled with sexism, it is not madness or illogical to see how the "acquisition" of a white woman can indicate the "arrival" of a black man. He

95

feels validated, important, and even superior, because he has, in his possession, the prize possession of the "superior" race.

This is logical but far from explaining the existence of every single mixed-race couple in South Africa, let alone on earth! What it does do is go some way towards explaining some mixed couples who are made up of a black man and a white woman who are both South African.

So let the record show that I do believe in the first sentence of this article. Peace.

DON'T FIGHT THE POWER. BE THE POWER AND MORE!

When the struggle against apartheid in South Africa was at what some would call the most intense in the eighties, some people in my circle at the time thought I was a bit touched in the head when I said marching on the enemy's turf was weaker than marching in your own community. The point I was trying to make was that when we go to some racist town and march to make the racist stop being racist, we are doing something that is weaker than spending that time toughening ourselves and those who are close to us, so that when we meet the racist he loses purely because of the power we have harnessed to be strong in his presence. Do you get my drift?

It's like this, you see, you could spend a lot of your time fighting for better working conditions at your place of employment. Many would consider that great, noble, even warrior-like, heroic. Often, you'll find that no-one else would be fighting the fights you would be fighting. Instead, everyone would be coming up to you to say how they were unfairly treated over here or over there so that you could do something about it. The best that could happen in this scenario would be that you could fight the evil power that they reported to you and still deliver on what that power actually paid you to do, day in day out, month after month, as you collected your salary. The worst that could happen is that your work would start to deteriorate as your struggle credentials got better and better. With this scenario, you see, comrade, no court of law, union or body set up to ensure that workers' rights are not violated is going to help you. You would simply be fired.

The joke is that, even with the best-case scenario, i.e. where you fought and still delivered on the job, there would be a serious down side. You would encounter so much heated hostility from your employers for causing all the trouble in paradise as it were, that you would need to have a really thick skin, be a masochist or totally insensitive to survive on a day-to-day basis. Heads you lose. Tails they win. And there you would be with your scrotum caught in a vice if you were a man.

So what does this mean? Does it mean that we must just lie there and take it, Mandingo, because we can't win against the companies that we work for?

I believe that even for our unions, considered by many in the rest of the world to be amongst the strongest, it quickly became clear that there is a certain inter-dependence between labour and business that can only allow you, the employee, to push so far and then be forced to stop. If you push a guy who owns a company hard enough for whatever demands you think are justified, he can simply close shop and leave all your union members without a job. The opposite also applies in that, as an employee block, you can seriously reduce a company's profits if you decide to down tools. But the reality is that, in the worst case scenario, where the company has to close shop, the guy at the top, the guy who built the company, the guy you are dependent upon to buy your labour because he created a need for it, is going to rise faster after the fall, and suffer a lot less during the fall, than the fitter and turner or clerk or manager or whatever employee he hired while he had the company. Jobs are hard to come by. Building companies is a whole different and much higher platform of business engagement. Employees are a lot less powerful in that equation.

So what's to be done?

I remember those many years back when I was a university

student. I attended a meeting where black students were planning a march on campus to protest that the university was giving them too little money for their political society to operate on. They were saying that the criterion for the allocation of funds to students at that university was racially biased and so they were going to march and cause havoc to change that status quo. It was 1985 and they were getting an annual allocation of R2 300, or some figure around there, when there were societies on campus, like the Photography Society, that were getting up to R3000 for the same period. It did not matter that the Photography Society was open to anyone on campus to join, black or white. What mattered was that, at the time, this society had mainly white students as members. This was proof of the racism in the allocation of funds at our university.

Trust me here, I know our university was racially biased at the time. That was as much a concern to me as it was to any black student on that campus. So I did not mean to be a spoil-sport when I stood up to speak. I simply could not understand the logic behind the thinking that it was appropriate to go to the very same enemy you were fighting to ask for help to fight that same enemy! Do you get what I mean here? How can I justify coming to you, my enemy, to ask you to give me more resources to fight you! But there was a bigger problem I wanted to address. So I stood up and asked the meeting this: How do you gain independence through dependence? The house went a bit quiet and then I told them that I belonged to a very white society where I was the only black, i.e. The Anglican Society on campus. I told them that this lily-white society only got R230 or thereabouts a year – ten times less than their society got, which was true. But what was amazing, I said to them, was that this Christian society always showed a profit on its grant at the end of every year. It would organise tea parties, hold prayers, etc., and raise funds to add to its grant, and here we were, strong black people, planning a march instead of organising our own fundraising events and building on the R2 300 that we got for simply existing on campus.

The march did not take place, but I'm not sure if the point about staying independent as you fight for independence sunk in because I don't remember attending any fund-raising events organised by that society. It was too much work, you see. You have to balance the books at the end of the year. You have to account for every penny that comes in and explain how it went out. It's much easier to whip a crowd into a frenzy in order to get a freebie. That way, the university increases your grant and, come year-end, you just go back with your hat and it fills it again. After all, the grant was for a year. No institution in its right mind would expect you to have a penny left, let alone show a profit! So, no, I did not attend any fundraising drives by this society. But I know I was not that popular with its leaders at the time.

In my opinion, you see, the university might have gotten the message, changed its racist criterion, and even given those black students more money. But what would that have done for the protesting students? The university would have been taught a beautiful lesson and maybe even learnt it. But I believe that the students would have stayed exactly where they started, only this time they would have more money for their leadership to use or misuse. The opportunity to learn about raising finance, being accountable because of that, and staying independent in order to have a respected voice would have been lost for good. And who could guarantee that that leadership was going to put that money to good use? We know that with money it is easy come, easy go, don't we?

Let's jump forward to today. And I maintain that that lesson still holds much ground after all these years. You don't like the racism at your company. You don't like their salary structure. You don't like the way they treat their staff and customers. Fine. Just don't waste your time trying to change the company, please. It's not yours. You'll just end up without a job, after making many enemies in the industry your company is in. Try this instead: learn everything there is to learn about the business your company and, by extension, you are in. Build bridges in that business arena by being the opposite of what the company is to its clients and employees. Save as much of your salary as you can and put that money away like crazy. Remember, having money in the bank buys you time. You can use that time to build without financial pressure.

Then one day, step aside and open your own company where you run policy and policy implementation. Now go head to head with your previous employers. After all, they created a market for you by being so bad. Now beat the hell out of them in the marketplace. Beat them because you work ten times harder and smarter and care ten times as much about what you do. Beat them, Mandingo, because you are simply the best at what you do. Beat them this way, because this is the best kind of revenge when you really think about it. Isn't it?

Now, I never said there is no room for the guy who likes to fix other people's companies. There's room for a worker's struggle. All I'm saying is that unlike before, we can do more than strike. We can do more than fix other people's shop floors. We can start our own companies and openly compete. We can open our own shops and introduce better labour relations, as we make more profit. We do not have to fight the power any more. We can be the power and more.

That's why I say to you, don't fight the power, Mandingo. Be the power and more. You know you can. Now do it. Be the power and more.

The Berlin Series

THE END GAME

As I looked at those buildings in Berlin, Germany, that still bear bullet holes from the second European war, as I remembered how hard the Germans have had to work after the devastation that Hitler led their country into, this thought occurred to me: Every sensible book that deals with the phenomenon of power will tell you that when you have fully beaten your opponent, you must finish him off without hesitation, and do a thorough job of it. That's why when Hitler decided to conquer Europe, he was ruthless. He was not going to leave anyone to come back at him. And that's why, when Europe and America decided to take him (Hitler) out, they really did a thorough job of ruining Germany. Some will say that's the way of war. And others will ask: is there no better way to win a war?

Chess, a war game, is divided into three sections: opening moves, the middle game, and the end game. To win a chess game, your opening and middle games have to be strong. But no matter how strong your opening and middle games are, if your end game is weak, your opponent tends to come back at you and devour you. So, when it's time to take out the king, you must take him out good and proper. You have your opening moves, followed by the middle game, and then there's the end game. And that must be ruthless.

I want to confess that my end game is weak. Deep down I don't like to see people in pain. I don't like the feeling that most people carry with them after a devastating loss. On the other hand, I do not care that much for winning. There will always be another game and I can always win that. And if I don't, so what? It's about the whole game, is it not? It's not just about the

101

end game. It's about the journey, stupid! Not the destination. Is that not what they say? And so, because of this attitude, you will never catch me cheating to get ahead. That's a good thing. You will almost always catch me wishing that my opponent would come up with a genuinely good move, so that the game can be elevated to a higher level. That's a relatively good thing. I almost always wish to come up with a good move myself. That's a good thing, too. I don't want myself or my opponent to make a silly move because I think that spoils the game. I want both of us to play well. The only time you will catch me upset because I lost is when I lose to someone who does not give a damn about the game and the players but would give his right eye for a win at all costs. I think this attitude that I have towards the game is good. But couple that attitude with the fact that my end game is weak, then you realise that I have a problem. I tend to lose a lot of chess games.

This got me to thinking. How did I get to be this way? What if Africa's problems in general stem from the weakness of our end game and this benevolence towards our opponents? Should we revisit our end game and practise to play it western style - if you are going to take someone out, take them out real good, for good. Is that how Africa should behave to get ahead now that we know the white northerners are not interested in our NEPAD (New Partnership for Africa's Development). We were looking for $64 billion and they offered just short of $2 billion. Should we play to castrate in order to get ahead?

Scarcity thinking drives white northerners. They believe that there is too little to go around in the world, and so one had better grab as much as one can as fast as possible before everyone else grabs and there's nothing left to grab! Scarcity thinking says there just isn't enough in the world. This means that, if you get anything, you must cling hard to it, as there is always someone with nothing trying to take it from you. This means that if you see an opportunity, you must run and grab it at such a ferocious speed that you beat everyone else who will be running and grabbing just as hard and ferociously as you. And God forbid that, when you have grabbed as much as you can, you should close both eyes when you sleep because you will most certainly wake up with nothing if you do that!

As you can see, scarcity thinking leads to very strenuous living. This is the thinking that drives western business and western democracies. That's why you have the Enron and Worldcom debacles. In scarcity worlds, you are not allowed to slip up. If you make a billion dollars this quarter, you are not allowed to make $999 million the next quarter because that sends alarm bells all over scarcity land and so CEOs make up numbers to keep scarcity land happy that whatever scarce wealth has been collected is not about to disappear. On the surface, scarcity thinking makes your end game strong, at least in the short term. You bully hard. And you bully to win.

But I grew up poor amongst the poor. This is where scarcity thinking should be most prevalent. After all, when you are poor, you truly have nothing, and the little that you have you should hold most precious. But to be honest, I could bring any of my friends to my house and they would always be offered food. And if I went to their homes, I would not be allowed to leave without eating something. And if I tried to decline an offer of food, I would easily be labelled too proud. And that's not a good thing. The thinking guiding these interactions was based on abundance thinking. Abundance thinking says there is enough for everyone in the world, and so there is no need to hog everything and live strenuous lives, trying to grab as much as possible while blocking everyone else from grabbing for themselves. And if things get finished today, it is the way of the gods; there will be more later when the gods deem it fit.

Some might argue that Africa's woes stem to a large degree from centuries of internalising and living with the theory of abundance as opposed to scarcity. At least on the surface and in the short term, when scarcity thinking meets abundance thinking, abundance thinking loses badly. It is to be expected if you think about it. The white man came to Africa and found us pretty relaxed about everything. He wanted a piece of land. We said okay, how about over there? He wanted to teach certain things, to which we said why not, go ahead, friend, we can always add to our knowledge. In the meantime, this white man had often been banished from his homeland and pronounced something akin to an animal. His only redemption was going back rich to make other people back home rich. There was no time to enjoy the ride or to play the game for the sake of it. He was going to take the black man out and out for good, if he could. Then grab as much as he could and cling to it for dear life as he sailed back home in glory to seek reacceptance into the circle of humanity as defined by scarcity land. And so he finished off most of the Aborigines, the native Americans, and the Khoi. He just did not think there would be enough for him and all these other people, you see. So, he took them out.

Should Africa strengthen her end game in this manner? Should we be truly ruthless in our encounter with other humans of differing hues, as they are to us? Or does abundance thinking actually represent a stronger end game in the long run? A scarcity-driven end game would have called for all black South Africans to slaughter as many white South Africans as possible, if not all of them. It would have called for us to take the whites out for good and clear space for ourselves to grab and hang on to whatever they owned, before we took them out. The logic here would have been based on the belief that there couldn't possibly be enough for all of us, and so one of the groups would have had to make way. And as the whites had tried to make blacks make way for good, it would have been their turn to make way, for good.

But, you know, we went with abundance thinking. We said, like our ancestors before us said, like the poor families on my street in Meadowlands, Soweto, said, like Africa has said for centuries, we said, actually there is enough for everyone here. Let's work together to make it available for everyone because what is a rich world if the majority in it are poor? What possible future can humanity have if the different peoples of the earth cannot look each other in the eye and see sisters and brothers?

Statistics show that humanity now has the capability to end all traces of poverty on earth in one generation. But scarcity thinking is preventing the world from achieving this noble goal. The western European idea of no success without a neighbour's failure prevented the G8 from giving concrete support to NEPAD. But Africa must see an opportunity in this. It is time for us to put our money where our mouths are. We must find ways in Africa by Africans to make NEPAD work. It will be harder. It will take longer. But when it arrives, it will be perfect for us. With this success we can push ahead with such noble ideals as abundance thinking. Noble ideals that made places like South Africa stabilise after apartheid and forge ahead in a new type of political partnership, as they roll the same thinking over to economic partnerships for true progress.

The best end game does not leave you covered in blood and battling to get rid of the stench of hate surrounding your victory. The best end game gives you panache in victory. It leaves you elegant in victory. It makes your opponent want to cry in happiness for having fought such a true and noble champion. It makes your opponent thankful for having had the chance to share a stage with you. It makes your enemy want to applaud and scream out loud, BRAVO!

I may not win that many chess games, but the few that I do win, I win elegantly, my brothers and sisters. Yes, they took out the Taliban and made a lot of blood money doing it. But goodness, would you like to be the guy credited with the devastation that now envelops Afghanistan? Does the end really justify the means?

I say it's better to win with style, Mandingo.

NOW SOCCER IS THE OPIUM OF THE MASSES

I walk into this church in Berlin and I am overwhelmed by its grandeur. This is not even one of the bigger churches around Berlin, I'm told. It's not the most spectacular, although it has had its glory days. And maybe, because of that, it has survived both world war onslaughts on the Germans. It's easier to hide when you are small. But this small is massive, man. I don't think there's a church in South Africa that can match this Protestant Zionist Church in sheer scale and grandeur. Even the street on which it is located is named after it. It is currently being restored, but even so, it would take centre stage in South Africa. And today it is open. A rather serious looking *"pfarerr"* (German for "Father") is presiding by the entrance. For a moment, I think he is not paying much attention to anything. But, when I drop my forty Euro cents into the bowl on the table opposite where he's sitting, he looks up from what could be the scriptures he's reading, and gives me a stern nod. Money, it seems, is hard to come by amongst church owners today.

It is this kind of church that makes me realise how well marketed religion has been up to now. Even though I don't think it is anywhere near as amazing as the Sistine chapel, which bears Michaelangelo's genius in Italy, this little big church in Berlin *klaps* me on the forehead nevertheless. Some Christian buildings are phenomenal, you know! There is no cost-cutting here. And the followers fork out the money themselves and, when the structures are up, it is like God realised on earth: a visual heaven on earth, a feast for the eyes, a great marketing tool. Then there's the Christian word-of-mouth. As you might know, generally speaking, there is no better marketing channel than word-of-mouth. When I talk, I talk to friends and family, people who trust me, people who have watched me grow, people I've had fights and delights with. When I talk and you talk, Mandingo, if we are selling, we will close deals quickly and we will close many of them. The only proviso is that we are not the ones collecting the money for what we are selling! For your

106

word-of-mouth marketing to be effective, the speaker must have no ulterior motive except the good of the one h/she is talking to. Christianity and most other religions are sold like this. This is for your own good, they say. Fear hell and you'll end up in heaven. That's the basic hook. But get the people to sell this to each other. The marketing is absolutely brilliant. It's beautiful.

And then there are the symbols. Check out the cross. How's that for a symbol? You must agree, it beats the BMW grid by far in sheer power and simplicity and is maybe matched by the Star of David in the Judaic faith. Then you get the uniforms. Grey or black with a white collar. Or colourful and elaborate, as in the Pope's gear. And then there are those who bring the word to you for your eternal survival. These are gifted orators. These will mesmerise you and handhold you straight to deliverance. That's religion marketing. And I am sure those who are deep into Islam, Judaism, Buddhism, Hinduism and all the other organised religions will argue the same for the marketing of their respective religions. But my reference point is Christianity because that's what I grew up with. And today Christian marketing is taking a knock because of bad publicity. What are we to do when leaders on the path to heaven sexually molest our children along the way? What are we to do when their superiors shuffle them around to hide this fact? What are we to do when the clergy declares that it is beyond the law, as prescribed by man, and will answer only to God, even as preachers in its ranks keep dipping into hell to satisfy their desires? Would you say that's why Christianity has moved into conventional marketing with advertisements on billboards along some Johannesburg roads? Is that a good sign or is it a desperate bid to survive?

When the Brazilian team took the World Cup away from an outclassed German team, some of them wrote "Jesus" on their t-shirts while others revealed t-shirts with "Jesus Loves You" already printed on them. This was spontaneous marketing. I don't think those players even think they are in the Christian marketing department. They were simply expressing their love for Jesus, for God, and paving their way to heaven. Don't you love the way they go forehead, chest, and one shoulder to the next before blowing a kiss to heaven? This hand manoeuvre has outclassed and outlasted the high five by decades. It endures to this day and will surely continue to do so late into the future.

Religion, Karl Marx once said, is the opium of the masses. When nothing gives, you can always look to the heavens and find peace. It is marketed like this, too. God will comfort you. Just reach out to him. We of Christian bent would bend our knees and kneel down before doing this. But comfort will come just like it does, I presume, after you have inhaled opium. And when pain strikes one more time, well, just kneel again, and take a puff as you get a whiff of heaven to soothe your soul. And onward Christianity marches.

But I have a sneaking suspicion that soccer is fast taking over from religion as the soothing ointment for the masses. There was a moment as the Brazilian team was marching to the final when I thought Brazil might benefit as a country if Brazilian soccer were to fall all the way down to becoming the worst in the world. It seems that, for as long as the legends of Pele (the poor boy made good), Ronaldo (another poor boy made good) and the others (who, one has to assume, are not from wealthy homes) stay alive, then the Brazilian authorities don't have to close the open sewers in the Brazilian *favelas* (squatter-like homes) of the Brazilian poor, who are the majority of the population in Brazil. As long as Brazil keeps doing well as a soccer giant, the Brazilian authorities can push back yet again the plan to level the Brazilian playing field and narrow the horrendously wide gap between rich and poor.

Most marketing exercises are a ruse to hide real defects in whatever the marketer is selling. How different is soccer at the moment? You see, the Germans wanted to win but, hey, they lost. Do you think they wept uncontrollably for days because of this? No, Mandingo. They did not. At worst they looked a bit sheepish in defeat. I was there. I saw them. The few who did cry were young, drunk or poor. That's because most Germans have much more important games to win. These games take up most of their waking hours, you see. So they simply went back to perfecting their winning ways at the important games at which they are already winning. Games like commerce. Games like international politics. The FIFA Soccer World Cup would have been a "nice to have". It would have been a bonus. In any event they had already beaten some African country called South Africa to host it in 2006 and make some real money.

But for Brazilians in the *favelas*, it is different. They need that win. They need that opium to keep the dream of getting out of the *favelas* alive. That means getting out one day and owning a Ferrari for a whole year and driving it maybe once in that period before selling it, like Rivaldo, the Brazilian soccer superstar, once did. Religion is not bad for the masses. Soccer is not bad for the masses. But like opium, if it is the only thing on which you hang your future, you might just live in hell on earth and still end up in hell in the after life. So you must be careful. No country should excel at one game. No country should believe it can lull its poor into slumber forever by simply marketing opium of one kind or another.

After a while, the pain pierces straight through the prayer and we curse God.

Check out the games you are winning, Mandingo. Select the most important and get better at playing them.

I HAVE SEEN THE NEW JOHANNESBURG. IT'S IN EAST BERLIN!

I have never been into sightseeing. When I travel, I like to meet people. I like to mix with the locals, you know, the natives. I like to get a grip on the underbelly through the local inhabitants. I like to sit at the local coffee shops, the local bars, inhale the local smells and talk. Connecting souls. For the first five days of my stay in Berlin, I couldn't get a whiff of the local flavour. For one thing, I was deaf and dumb because I could not speak any

German at all. Not knowing any German and all. The other thing is the Berlin habit of traveling in packs. Everywhere you look, people are either in packs of more than two or in twos. Whenever you see a lone ranger, you can safely assume that that person is either from somewhere other than Berlin or waiting for someone. Berliners also have a certain way of looking at people who are not in a pack of sorts. It's a suspicious kind of look. Something like "Hmmm, I wonder if he eats humans? Why is he alone? Why has he no friends? Hmmm, something fishy is going on there. He's not connected. Something's wrong with this dude..." and more of that sort of head mumbling. You can tell all these thoughts are racing through their brains just by looking at the way they look at you. And when they've done this assessment and written you off, you will be amazed by the change of expression on these very same faces when someone comes by and greets you. "Hmmm", you see the expressions say, "So he's not alone. Maybe he does not eat humans after all. Hmmm, I like the way he smiles. I wish he could come over and say..."

So I did not meet that many Berliners in my first five days there. I was nervous as hell because of all the skinhead neo-nazi rumours and, as I pointed out earlier, Berliners seemed to suspect that there was something wrong with me because I was not in a pack. Add that I'm not good at warming up to strangers myself and you have a pretty dismal chance of Eric meeting locals in Berlin. So I had an adequate amount of time to get acquainted with the buildings. You know how non-judgemental those are. They simply don't have heads to mumble with.

A Mandingo named PF once wrote to *O'Mandingo!* to ask: "What about the Johannesburg CBD?" when we ran "Melrose Ouch!", the story on the Melrose Arch development which pointed out how white people were using mainly black money to run away from black people. When you take a look at Berlin, especially East Berlin, the first thing you notice is how old buildings are being restored to their former glory. You notice how young people are running clothing shops on the ground floors of these very old buildings. You notice the number of bars and coffee shops springing up in every corner. You see what South African whites are trying to do superficially by creating places like Melrose Arch in Johannesburg happening organically in almost every block in East Berlin. Upstairs people are living. Downstairs people are doing business. And they are young, Mandingo, like you and I.

So why aren't we taking over the Johannesburg CBD while it's still cheap? Why aren't we ganging up to buy buildings in the CBD, fixing them up, renting them out and opening shops downstairs to service the people we lease the living space upstairs to? Why, Mandingo? There are eight-storey buildings going for as low as R750 000 in the CBD! For ten Mandingos, that's R75 000 each! Wouldn't it be a thing of beauty if ten of you took a lease on such a building and paid R25 000 each towards the deposit and then raised a business loan to fix the place up and market it? If there were eight of you, you could even live in that building and own a floor each! Would that not be a better thing to do than to chase whites wherever they go and then get overcharged in the process? Now why aren't we doing it, Mandingo? Why do we not own chunks of the CBD? Young Germans do in Berlin.

Mbongeni Ngema has created a furore about Indians and their ownership of West Street in Durban. He seems upset that these Indian people have the right to refuse anyone who wants to rent the space from them and insinuates that the people often refused are black like you and I, Mandingo. Now, Mbongeni, might be right in his allegations. But is owning our own West Street not the best way to deal with this sort of discrimination? When people refuse you entry to their home, is the best response not to have a home where you too can choose who to invite in and who not to?

I say to you, now, the Johannesburg CBD is ready for us to create a place of our own, otherwise we will be discussing yet another song a few years down the line whining about blacks being refused to trade by yet another group that owns the very places we ignored when we could have bought them on the cheap. We will of course whine like this and feel seriously aggrieved when, in reality, while others were building future heavens on earth, we were seriously concerned with heaven now, wasting money on overpriced products like cars, clothes and buying suchlike rubbish on credit.

To understand how easy it is to get into the property market and make a profit while you create a future heaven, read Robert Kiyosaki's books *Rich Dad Poor Dad*, Mandingo. It's useful. Peace.

BLACK EXCELLENCE MAKES ME CRY

Tonight, black excellence shines

Black excellence makes me cry
I first discovered this when South Africa
Was freed from the big lie
But I found the sentence to describe it thus
Over two hours or so watching Buena Vista Social club

Black excellence makes me cry
That's because it always comes late
Like it did for Ibrahim Ferrer
When finally he played Carnegie Hall
Aged seventy, maybe more

It makes me cry this black excellence
It should make me scream to the rafters with joy
But it fills me beyond measure with sadness
Because its pregnancy lasts even longer for the mother, black pride
Than all pregnancies in the jungle of animals, elephantine

When it really stands out this black excellence
It really makes me weep and holler to the heavens
Why is it that it must take some human beings
A mile to move one inch
In a world that can tell the difference
Between a kilometre and a millimetre?

Eric Miyeni 2000

It's 2002 now. And like most men I know, I seldom cry. It hit me some time back that this is not healthy, because I believe that there is no such thing as a useless emotion. If you don't exercise all your emotions, those that are neglected come out in funny ways. Sometimes you even hurt people because of these bottled-up emotions.

But then apartheid fell and I started to cry a bit more easily. I remember when I first noticed this. I was sitting alone in my lounge when the Springboks ran out to play their first game in the first-ever Rugby World Cup to be held on African soil. They came out of the dugout full of purpose and I just cried. It wasn't about the Springboks. It wasn't about rugby. It wasn't about pain. I cried because I was overwhelmed with the emotion of freedom. The Springboks were free to run out and openly compete with the world's best and we had made this possible. That just choked me up.

I also noticed that excellence in post-apartheid South Africa makes me cry. Whenever I watch a human being do something extraordinary, I get choked up and tears well up in my eyes. So when I watched Josiah Thugwane come around the corner to take gold at the Atlanta Olympic games, I cried. I also got tears in my eyes when I saw the South Koreans link hands with the Turks and salute the crowd as one team after their third-place clash in this year's FIFA World Cup finals in Korea/Japan. If the G8 had truly endorsed Africa's NEPAD plan, I probably would have cried.

And so, you get to see that I find myself overwhelmed with emotion whenever I witness humans achieve something quite normal for humans to achieve but which happens rarely. Warmth and friendship amongst different nations do this to me. Achievement against heavy odds chokes me up. On the other hand, unfairness does not make me cry. Racism does not make me weep. These unnecessary hindrances make me angry and heavily determined to win despite them. But achievement in the face of these obstacles makes me cry. It's almost like I can't hold back the relief I feel because evil did not win. So I cry. It's almost like a short journey that was unnecessarily lengthened finally ended and the traveller reached the destination despite the length and so I get choked up and it's like, thank God, the person made it!

This feeling has no colour to it. I hate to see anyone unnecessarily dragged down. And by the same token, I love watching someone drive themselves to excellence despite all the obstacles that are laid in their path, whoever that person might be. I got choked up when Anastacia sang at the FIFA World Cup 2002 Korea/Japan closing ceremony because what could be more perfect for a performer than to play to over a billion people in one performance. That has to register somewhere as a perfect moment. And when Cafu (the captain of the Brazilian national soccer squad) lifted that world cup and gave us that toothy grin... now you see, that got to me.

During the heydays of apartheid, we had to be strong and show it. Our society was driven by stoicism. White men did not cry. Black men did not cry. The only people who seemed to allow themselves to do this were women across the colour line. And I think they are healthier beings for it. White men could not cry because then the black men would think them weak, and so would their wives, right? Black men could not cry because it takes a lot of fortitude to endure racism. There's no room for cry babies if you are going to survive a hostile white man who has all the power and does not cry either. You must at least match him in your ability to bottle up your sissy emotions. And so, men on both sides of the divide sat quietly with no emotions showing, so that they could survive each other. Often they beat up their wives and girlfriends as a way of letting off steam. And now it's our culture.

But apartheid has fallen. Not only are we free to achieve in ways that were not possible before, we are free to express our emotions in healthier ways too. Just as I have found my well of tears, you need to find yours, Mandingo. Dig into that well and, now and again, bring up a few tears and let them flow. And let someone cuddle you now and again.

You will feel much better for it.

THE BLACKS OF BERLIN

I met a black Mozambican in Berlin. I knew him way back when he was a Mozambican in South Africa and Yeoville was the hip place to be if you were young, white and progressive in your thought patterns. A drummer. He played drums back then and he does the same now, today, in Berlin. He had the same dreadlocks but now they were longer. The same smile. The same accent. The same complaints. Money complaints. Gig complaints. Jobs for musicians are hard to come by in Berlin complaints. It seems that the Euro has made it harder, he says. When it was the Deutchmark, he seems to be saying, things were a lot better. But the Euro! It's making the money hide somewhere and he can't find it.

The other black I met was a Brazilian. This was on the day when Brazil beat Turkey to advance to a first-ever meeting in a World Cup final with Deutschland. With seven World Cup championship wins between them, Germany had never played Brazil in a World Cup clash before. Consider that if Senegal had not faltered, Africa would have been up there and, for the first time ever in a World Cup final, all continents would have been represented in the semi-final clashes and, you will agree, history was what the FIFA 2002 World Cup was made of. The final was not going to be an

115

exception. The Brazilian said something in Brazilian Portuguese indicating a happy mood and then asked for one cigarette. I gave him one and he sauntered off into the distance. Money for him, it seems, was also hard to come by in Deutschland.

At my favourite bar in Berlin, Prenzlauerberger, was a big tall, well-built black man. He had an air about him. Like he owned the joint. I think someone told me that that bar was owned by a black dude but I couldn't for the life of me remember for sure if this was the bar as I looked at this tall black man with an air of royalty about him, talking to all the mainly white Deutschlander clientele with absolute ease. Whenever there was a crowd at the bar and the bartender seemed inundated, he stepped in and helped to relieve the tension and got deeply thanked before stepping back out of the bar area to attend to someone else outside the bar. He was always present. It seemed to me that the Euro was not hiding the Deutschmarks from him. I liked being in that bar, Bergstub'l.

The wonderful thing about blacks in Berlin is that they always acknowledge each other. They never stop to chat or get close, but it's like they are saying, hey, I see you there, I like it, how is it? It's like they are protecting each other against the majority without being aggressive to anyone else. It's a comforting feeling. For a South African black, it's uncomfortable at first. Mandela said reconciliation. Tutu gave us the phrase "rainbow nation". All this makes it hard to acknowledge other blacks without feeling guilty about the whites who are left out.

It's a funny burden to have to travel with because blacks worldwide need to know where each of us is standing and doing in order to collaborate as a group to achieve more. But South Africa's reconciliation politics can blind you from this important growth step with unnecessary guilt. We are made to feel that if there is no white person involved or being acknowledged in whatever we are doing, then what we are doing must be hostile and wrong. At the same time, white South Africans are, by and large, free to do anything to the exclusion of black South Africans.

Reconciliation, you see, is a black South African's cross to bear for bringing down apartheid. And so, as I was adjusting to the acknowledgement that Deutschland blacks give to each other, I got no acknowledgement from the one black I thought to be the most valuable amongst all that I was acknowledged by. The owner of Bergstub'l seemed to be saying, as he probably thought I was saying, there will be one bull in this kraal.

Is that not weird? When members of other nation groups succeed, they seek other successful people in their nation groups to team up with. But when we black people succeed, we seem to want as few black people around us as possible. This has to change if we are to turn the tide of poverty and misery that Africa faces today. We must want more black bulls in the enclosure. Not only do we need bright sparks and bright ideas, we need them in bigger numbers. The days of feeling important because you were the only black person at a dinner party are over, because being the only black person at a dinner party is only good for allowing the white majority at that dinner party to believe that they are not that bad. In fact, it halts progress because every time you appear, the only black there, they feel validated that they have materially contributed to something amazingly progressive, when all they have done is make you feel a sense of idiotic pride in being alone amongst whites because of your self-hate. If you do not hate yourself, you will want to head back to your people as soon as you feel outnumbered. You will want to organise your own dinner parties and host successful black people. That's the truth. If you really hate yourself, you will be annoyed at the first sign that there are more of you in the same position of affluence. You will find it hard to applaud.

But if you do not hate yourself, you will find yourself breaking into a wide grin every time you see someone like you excel at whatever they do. You will find yourself loving having more of you in whatever place you find yourself. That's it.

Anyway, I finally got to meet my black kingly prince and, it was confirmed, he owned Bergstub'l. He was a fine man. A

Senegalese who spoke perfect German, perfect French and passable English. Maybe he was just sizing me up. Maybe it wasn't about two black bulls in one white kraal. Because, now he hands me an invitation to an exclusive party. And trust me when I say Berlin parties can be extremely exclusive. I can't make the party because I'm leaving Germany a week before it happens and he smiles and offers to take back the invitation. You see, not just anyone was going to get that invitation. It was to be an exclusive party and I had cracked it. And he runs the show. And I love that.

Mandingo, look around you and see how widely you smile when you see black people who are successful. See how much pride you feel when you come across black people who are on the rise. Forget their attitude. Forget what vibe, negative or otherwise, they give. Are you proud and positively moved by the fact that they are moving forward, succeeding? Black. Are you? Because that is the self-love test. Loving your own.

IN MONCHENGLADBACH
In Monchengladbach I see an old white man, fat but poor, hunched up with three plastic bags for designer travel bags. He battles to see as he squints at the approaching train to see if it is the right one, so that he can get in. *Ja!* It is. He gathers his rubbish-bag luggage and drags himself to the train door. The train swallows him and takes off.

A bunch of kids rock up near my train and take over the scene from the old man. He could be their grandfather. One of the kids is really pretty in her pink pants and white cap swung to the side. In America they would probably call her a wigger – a white "nigger". If she can keep her weight down, she will remain a stunner. There are five of these kids, three boys and the two girls, including the pretty-in-pink-pants vibrant one. They share two skateboards between them. Like the old man before them, they are poor. But unlike the old man, they are listless, as is often the case with the youth. The three boys range in age from about eight to fifteen. The girls are like fourteen and fifteen. The thirteen-year-old boy brings out a pack of cigarettes and distributes them amongst the group. They all smoke, except the eight-year-old. There are limits, you know.

Then another group of much older kids jumps into the train. Yes, they are cleanly dressed, but they are not that much richer than the outside kids. You can tell by the clothes they wear. Clothes, even when clean, always give the poor away. You simply can't hide your poverty under cheap garments. One of the richer poor kids now inside the train I'm in addresses the poorer outside kids through the window. I don't understand German, but I think he's telling the pretty one in pink pants to come inside because I hear her say something like "*dis moss geschlossen*" and I know "*geschlossen*" means closed. The train doors had just closed. The richer poor boy inside the train talks some more but, as the train pulls off, he spits at the two girls and I think he catches one of them because, although I can't see, I hear the shrieks of disgust as we pull away. Inside the train, the richer poor group laughs. The spitter has this high-pitched hiss of a laugh and he laughs harder than everyone else. These are white kids messing with other white kids. Do you think they would do this to each other if there were black or Turkish kids around to mess with? And so you get the feeling that you are watching neo-nazi seeds being planted as these poor, unsupervised kids, whose parents are too busy being poor to supervise and guide them let alone afford nannies to look after them and guide them in their absence, are little monsters in the making.

It's all very depressing. As the train leaves Monchegladbach behind, I see a small but magnificent church in the distance trying to pierce the sky with its tiers and I wonder if God is complicit in all this. Or if, as the church would have us believe, his presence amongst the poor is to soothe the pain as the poor punish each other to pass the time, because what else is there to do when you are stuck in a sewer?

Have you noticed how ugly scenes seem always to find a permanent living space amongst the poor? In Berlin's

Prenslauerberger, everything is as serene as God's voice. Most people there seem to be making money or to have descended from money. They don't need to perform desperate acts to feed themselves or feel important. Out here in the German hinterlands, I'm beginning to feel like someone might just grab my computer and run when the train stops. I feel like they might even consider just outright ordering me to hand it over before they tell me to !*&^! off back to Africa or wherever the *^%& I come from. This is the kind of hostility that the West claims in its daily writings about "third world" places like Johannesburg in South Africa. But skin colour alone does not seem like a strong enough shield from ugly acts.

Germany, like South Africa, has to get rid of its poor if it is to find true peace, lasting stability and a clean break from throwbacks into the unwanted past. There seems to have existed, up to this point around the supposedly civilised world, the mistaken belief that the majority must be poor for the minority rich to stay rich. But most human acts of the worst barbarism seem to stem from the existence of a poor class. No one robs a bank for the first time for the fun of it, because human beings by nature hate confined spaces. Jail is only fun for the neurotic. The majority of humans are sane. No one ever got too drunk and beat up another person because his – the drunkard's – life was too perfect and so needed to be messed up a bit. And so the chances of my getting mugged were near zero in Berlin, but the chances of me losing my life were higher in the smaller depressed towns of Germany. Incidentally, that brings some places in Germany down to the level of Hillbrow in Johannesburg. With poor people around, no life or possession is guaranteed. After all is said and done, we are all animals and our most basic instinct is to survive at all costs. That is why by law, if we are both sinking at sea and there's one buoy that can carry one person to safety, I am allowed to kill you to claim the buoy for myself.

As we do our best to reclaim a place for Africa on the world stage, we must be careful not to create an illusion of success that is based on the opulence in which only a few can live. We must attempt the seemingly impossible task of bringing every African up as Africa improves. Some will argue correctly that the survival of humankind rests on this basic kindness. Greed and selfishness will be the death of us all. A poor man can watch for only so long before he takes things into his own hands with no regard for the laws he helped pass to regulate the system he's living in. Why would anyone uphold a system that seems designed to keep him down? Logic says bring the system down, but start with some scapegoats as you practise taking down those who seem to be benefiting alone. The poor white kids are practising hate deeds on each other in the German hinterlands. Soon they will move to people unlike themselves. Then they will take down those who are like them on the surface but better off and different in all other respects. And so the house of cards starts to tumble down as the angry wind blows. Hitler was not a rich man when he started marketing hate speech. He died even poorer in spirit, but when he was done getting poor, so was all of Germany, and the building had to begin again, from scratch!

Our house must be built on sterner stuff, Mandingo.

I LIKE THE GERMANS!

Germans are not outgoing people, you know. This I can say about the ones I encountered in Berlin. However, let me quickly point out that it was not easy to find a native Berliner in Berlin. I met a Frankfurter, a guy from Hanover, a Dresden native, a sweetie from Dusseldorf and, finally, a Berliner who had aspirations of becoming a fashion designer and sounded like she would be pretty good at it too. So, all in all, it would be fair to say I encountered a microcosm of Germany in Berlin. If you consider that east meets west in Berlin, you can understand why. So *ja*, I can say Germans, not just Berliners, are not the most open and outgoing people I have met. This can be a shock to the system if you are an African. We Africans are very open people and some might argue that we are still paying for that openness. But I believe that it is the best route for the world and that it is coming back in vogue, this African open-arms approach to strangers. I mean, we all agree that the world needs to get a little friendlier. The Middle East is not a good example to follow.

The Germans can do with a little openness.

But I like the Germans. They are like our Afrikaners. They even have people amongst them with the surname Meyer. They are conservative. They keep their distance. But when they open up, they say what they think openly and frankly. And when they open their arms to you, you can put your head in their bosom with peace and smile in relaxation. You always know where you stand with them. And like I said to my East Berlin fashion designer discovery's boyfriend when he said he hates the neo-nazi German types, human beings will always find a scapegoat when they have no food on the table. Black South Africans, with their reconciliation, are pulling xenophobia moves against fellow Africans for similar reasons. If you put food on the table of every household in your country, keep the playing field level for all to participate equally, and genuinely work towards the eradication of poverty and towards the good of humanity, then you need not worry about unsightly uprisings. But if you lock people out of a system in which you alone benefit, you might end up on the wrong side of an active holocaust.

I like the Germans. Their flag is earthy but vibrantly joyous. Who but the Germans would think to combine black, red and gold? They need to dance more on the soccer field, but you can never call them losers. And I love the way the women in Berlin walk. They have such a swagger to their stride. They have such a nonchalant freedom to their hip movements. I could watch them walk forever and two months. Okay, so German cuisine takes some getting used to, but it's not built around raw fish eggs. It's not rare dog meat. And I don't think you'll catch a German going mad over frog legs. And the way they prepare their cabbage has to be a lesson in turning a funny vegetable into a delicacy. Okay,

so the French have a better sounding language and you don't
have to breathe for the French when they speak like you feel
you must when the Germans rattle off long complicated words
like "*entgegengenommen*" in long complicated sentences without
stopping to take in some air.

But I like the Germans. For one thing, they've had debts to
pay, but they stoically bent their heads, stuck the shoulder to
the wheel and paid them without breaking the bank. And all
for doing the dirty work that the whole Western world secretly
wanted done. It's no secret that for centuries, Jewish people
were not welcome in America and Europe. At some point, they
were not even allowed to be members of certain clubs in both
America and Europe. Most fascist groups still include Jews
in the list of people they absolutely hate. Fascist groups, by
the way, are found mainly, if not exclusively, in Europe and
America. But everyone in the so-called West loves Jewish
people today, even as they annihilate the Palestinians. No one
wants to admit that a group that survived a holocaust can be
wrong. In any event if that group can have a holocaust of its
own doing against some other seemingly unimportant group,
then the playing field will be level again and the psychological
debt will have been settled. No one seems to think that this
cycle might have to be repeated at the expense of yet another
group to appease the Palestinians later on! How crazy is that?
But like I say, the Germans have stoically taken the abuse and
paid their debt as they unified East and West Germany while
steadily climbing to become the leading economic powerhouse
in Europe. Their captain at this year's FIFA World Cup was
a Jewish boy called Oliver Kahn and he's the darling of all
Germany. The wounds are healing.

I like the Germans. Their only sin is being honest. When
everyone hated quietly and committed little devious behind-the-
back conniving deeds to express this hatred, the Germans stood
up and did something about it honestly and openly. And today,
even though a lot of them would argue against this logic, they are

a better people than most Europeans for it. They can't hide and being under the spotlight keeps you honest despite yourself. If you want real growth, then stick your neck out honestly and do something about your beliefs. You might be wrong like everyone says the Germans were, but you will never be called a conniving bastard. I like that, for better or worse, you know where you stand with the Germans.

I came to Germany scared that I might die in some dingy alleyway for no reason other than being black and I came back a believer, because to a large degree you can say with absolute accuracy that it is Deutschland *uber alles*. And, Mandingo, you and I can learn from this zest for victory despite a difficult history. Come on, Germans are people like you and I. They smoke too much and drink beer like mad. They have their problems and, yes, some of them are racist like that. But who wants to dwell on that rubbish? I do not travel to collect garbage. I travel to bring back gems. There is a good lesson to be learned from every nation on earth and the Germans are no exception. In fact, to a large degree, they are the rule here. We can learn a lot from them. For instance, we can take a pause from buying their cars and try to see how they got to be so big in that market, so that we can apply those lessons to marketing products of our own.

And think about that Mandingo. Are you a consumer or a supplier? There's a big difference between the two, you see. Generally, consumers are at the mercy of suppliers. If I build a restaurant, you see, I will choose what menu to serve my customers. I will choose what music to play. And I will choose who to make uncomfortable in that restaurant. It's mine. I'm the supplier. If the consumer does not like what I do, h/she can go to hell or to another supplier you see.

The Germans are suppliers. That's why they are so big and respected all over the world. What are you and I, Mandingo? What would you like to be? Now be it. You know you can.

Now for a Little Sport

JOMO RULES!

Matsilele "Jomo" Sono did not abandon his wife halfway through their wedding to go and help Orlando Pirates beat Highlands North in that amazing game back then that, to this day, is believed by many ardent fans of the man to be his signature game of excellence. No. He arranged his wedding to finish by three o'clock on that fateful afternoon, so that he could listen to the game on the radio because we did not have television back then. He did not even plan to go and play. He just wanted to listen to the commentators on the radio as soon as the wedding ended. Then his father-in-law came outside to join him in the car where he was engrossed in the game. Jomo's father-in-law saw how miserable his newly acquired son-in-law was after learning that the score was 2-0 in favour of Highlands North. A family meeting was quickly held, and Jomo was released to go and play.

The rest as they say is legend. Not only did Jomo score two goals, he created another two to help Orlando Pirates win by a two-goal margin. Highlands North were frozen still as Orlando Pirates rampantly marched forward. It seemed to have been written in the stars. Jomo went on to buy Highlands North, the club he demolished 4-2 that day, and rename it Jomo Cosmos, a team that has been a fountain of talent for the South African soccer national squad ever since South Africa re-entered the international sporting arena. The man is a legend.

My girlfriend recently alerted me to the *City Press* People's Bank Success Club. My first encounter with this club happened at The Hilton in Sandton and the main speaker there was Jomo Sono. I loved the venue, but I don't know who told The Hilton hotel people that black people love heat because after a few minutes everyone was sweating like a few pigs it was so hot. By the time the hotel fixed this problem, an hour or so later, the event was reaching its conclusion and I was so irritable I nearly walked out on the great man. But I stayed and I must congratulate People's Bank, Radio Metro and *City Press* for ganging up to open a tiny window into the inner workings of Jomo Sono.

Jomo Sono says we should start calling him the mechanic as he again takes up his seemingly usual position as the Bafana Bafana caretaker head coach. The first time he did this was back in 2000 when he took what many called a makeshift squad to the Africa Cup of Nations in Burkina Faso. He took that squad, assembled just a month before this major soccer event, all the way to the final, where he lost to Egypt. I always suspected that the psychological triumph of beating Morocco, then ranked first in Africa, took the sting out of the team that took on Egypt in the final. They had already won their tournament, and I suspect that Jomo had already won too when they reached that final. After all, everyone back home had said the squad would come back after the first round of games. And so we lost in the final. It was a psychological thing. The expectations of the team back home were so low that reaching the final was winning. You can't lift a championship cup if your psyche is damaged in that way.

I have a feeling that if, God willing, we reach the final in Japan/Korea, we will keep our heads and play to the death. Jomo is in charge and he is an experienced and gifted man heading a gifted squad from a gifted nation with a will to win.

How will Jomo achieve this though?

When I first sat down and listened to Radio Metro's Morio Sanyane interview Jomo at my first *City Press* People's Bank Success Club event, I quickly got irritable. Did they not say that this *City Press* People's Bank Success Club thing was about entrepreneurial know-how? Now why was I listening to two men talk about soccer when I came to learn about financial success? It isn't that I hate soccer. If soccer is a religion, then I am a soccer high priest. If you ask my friends, they will confirm this. It's just that this soccer talk seemed inappropriate for a Success Club about financial matters.

And then the man spoke to me.

Asked why he did not smoke or drink alcohol as a youngster when it was fashionable to do so in Soweto back then, he answered that he smoked, drank, talked, walked and dreamt soccer back then. Asked why his technical team had so many former players, he said he wanted the national team to be around people who lived and talked soccer almost all of the time and understood the game intimately. Asked what kind of team he liked to coach, he said he wanted to coach a passionate team of players who wore their jerseys with pride. Asked about the style of play he wanted the national squad to adopt, he said they must have fun on the pitch. Asked about his stint in America playing alongside greats like Pele, Beckenbauer and the like, he said when he left South Africa to go and play there, he had said to himself he was not coming back home without a signed contract. Asked if he was not worried about the likes of Spain, the first seed in our group in Korea/Japan, he said his players will not be worrying about Spain, they will be playing to their strengths as worrying about the opposition would be suicide. Asked about the most important ingredient for success, he said teamwork. And then he said, "God willing", Bafana Bafana would progress beyond the first round because he wanted South Africa to do better in these World Cup finals than we did last time. Asked about his management style, he said he believed in open and honest communication. He also said that a manager must be a friend, a boss, a fellow employee and a mentor all rolled into one. He said he spent countless hours with his players and so knew them intimately and individually, that's why he can tell if a player is ready for the big stage or not. He added that you will get the best out of the people you work with if they smile and you can see their genuine smiles. Asked about players getting red cards, he said he believed in players with a fighting spirit and a competitive streak. Asked how he had become so phenomenally successful, he said he thrived on challenges.

When the man had finished, I had gotten the best refresher course in How to Become a Success in the Business World through a talk about soccer. It was all there. You must be organised. You must be totally focused on the job at hand. You must know your talent, your gift and hone it. You must have an unwavering will to win. You must concentrate on your strengths and abilities as opposed to your weaknesses or the opposition's qualities. You must have faith. You must have integrity. You must communicate openly and honestly. You must have fun and be free. You must believe in teamwork. You must be passionate. You must always set goals and targets at the outset of your mission. To manage, you must have an eye for talent and a way of nurturing it to great heights. And finally, you must not be daunted by challenges that spring up in your path to success.

And now you know why the whole stadium, including the players on the pitch, stopped when Matsilele "Jomo" Sono arrived at Rand Stadium to save Orlando Pirates on his wedding day. Now you know why Joe Frickleton, the Highlands North coach at the time, said: "He's going to kill us", when he saw Jomo warming up on the sidelines. And now you know why, again, everything stopped, when he joined his teammates on the pitch that day. The day he says he played his best game for Orlando Pirates. And maybe you also know why he bought Highlands North as soon as he could afford to. He was buying one of the best memories in his soccer career. The man is a legend. He has method. He has skill. And he is driven beyond measure.

As I sweated my way into agreeing that this was, after all, a great evening with a truly great man, I wrote him a note on a piece from the *City Press* that came courtesy of the event managers. The note said: "*Tatana* Sono, we are behind you. We have all the faith in your capabilities. And thank you for sharing all that wisdom with us. *Khanimambo*."

I was moved because genius has a way of making my soul

implode with delight sometimes. Success has a way of inspiring me beyond measure. Matsilele "Jomo" Sono, one of us, embodies both genius and success and I had been in his presence for over an hour.

Bon voyage, Bafana Bafana. You have a great boss. And we are behind you all the way.

A Touch of Justice

JUSTICE SHOULD BE FREE

A very rich Caucasian male once hauled me into a boardroom and said to me, off the record, he was going to give away all the confidential information in the contract between my company and the one he worked for to enemies of my company if I did not "play ball" with them – my enemies, his friends who also just happened to be Caucasian. He further said, off the record, that they would then use this information to freeze all my company bank accounts. Following this, he said, off the record, they would sue my company. If this did not go anywhere, he said, off the record, they would bring me up on fraud charges. In short, what he meant was that no matter how often I won, they would keep the fight coming my way until I could not afford to continue fighting. In conclusion, he said, off the record, this had nothing to do with whether or not I was in the wrong in this dispute with my enemies – his friends. In fact, he said, off the record, he believed that I was morally right and justified in my fight with these enemies of mine – his friends. Then he said, off the record, my friend, you can fight all you want, and I'm trying to help you here, you can go all the way to the supreme court, just remember this: the law is an ass.

What I found out soon enough was that not only is the law an ass, but that it costs a helluva packet to get it to show you how donkey-like it really is! I'm a stubborn man sometimes and often I don't sway at all when I believe that my standpoint is the correct one. So I decided to take on the fight. The first thing I had to do before I could even consider myself gloved for the ring of legal blood was put down R50 000! I won't tell you what the final tally of costs in this legal fight came to, but this should give

131

you an idea of what it really costs to get justice. I mean, you don't just get justice! You must fight for it, hard. Second, you can't fight for justice without an army of lawyers. When we entered the courtroom on the first day of our case, an old man, white, trying to plead his case single-handedly preceded us. The acting judge on that day would not take him seriously at all. In the end, this old man was dismissed together with his case because, to hell with it, where were his lawyers? There are rules and procedures, you know! And this old man was creating a glitch in the legal system! He knew nothing of these rules of procedure! In the end, this poor old man resorted to sleeping outside a judge's house and refusing to go until the judge ruled in his favour! I, too, did not get my justified victory in court! It was like Baby Jake Matlala with his hands tied behind his back trying to simultaneously beat both Mike Tyson and Evander Holyfield in a bare-knuckle fight!

It costs a lot of money to get justice. It costs tenacity. It costs time. It takes guts. Simply put, getting justice is very expensive, whichever way you look at it. The net result is that the poor just get squashed, while the rich protect themselves and their friends often against and at the expense of the poor. This is how Western justice, as it sits today, works. Black people worldwide were not so much excited by the fact that O.J. Simpson was innocent as they were excited by the fact that here was a black man who could afford justice in what could arguably pass for the most expensive judicial system in the world! Isn't that the ultimate bastardisation of the law?

Young Caucasian lawyers with hearts of gold often start in the inner cities of their respective cities to help dispense justice to the poor, often black, people who cannot afford the true cost of justice. The legal-aid concept in South Africa fulfils this function. In the end, however, these wonderfully valiant and altruistic youngsters invariably end up packing up with all that experience, all that knowledge, and joining big law firms to help the rich get the justice system to rule in their favour as often as possible, whether or not these very rich people are in the wrong.

At this level of litigation the question, simply put, is who can afford to keep going to court for the longest time possible before giving up the fight? The question is not whose rights have or are being infringed upon here? The question is not who deserves justice here? The question is how deep is your pocket?

Is this how justice should be dispensed in this young, beautiful country of ours? Should justice, like basic healthcare, education, and the necessities of life, such as water and electricity, not be free? I believe that we South Africans should attempt, at least try, to evolve a justice system that is free for all. I believe that justice cannot afford to be, and should never be, like any other commodity that keeps going up and up in price in the marketplace. People who suffer the hardest injustices in the world today are people without the ability to pay for basic necessities like food let alone lawyers to fight their legal causes. The majority of people in this country are poor.

You might argue that the criminal justice system is free because a thief or murderer or rapist or whatever kind of criminal is investigated, charged, prosecuted, sentenced and then kept alive in a cell somewhere away from society at very little or no cost to the sufferers of these criminal infringements.

I'll say to you that this is a good start.

The current and most difficult phase of our struggle has moved into the economic arena. The whole world is now talking about poverty alleviation and the sharing of rich pickings amongst all nations of the world. In this country, in order to bring more and more poor people into the economic arena, we need to level the playing field in terms of economic litigation. We simply cannot afford to have the traditionally rich amongst us continue to use their money to manipulate the justice system for their own selfish ends at the expense of new players who are cash-strapped! If this carries on, we will lose the economic struggle to have no poor people amongst us. Alternatively, we will win this struggle at too huge a cost compared to what we have built so far through our political struggle.

133

My first suggestion to remedy this situation is that our country should set aside a budget to handle economic litigation like it handles criminal litigation. A state lawyer – read prosecutor – should take up the case for the underdog in an economic litigation case. Of course, this must be preceded by proper investigations into the merits of the case. But every time some economic top dog takes on some small player, that small player should have an office to go to, to see if the state can assist in the fight. To see if, indeed, he has a case and whether or not he should fight on for justice despite the shallowness of his pockets.

As things stand today, if I, a university educated man with some business acumen, the will to fight and R50 000 to fight with, cannot get economic justice, how can the poor, uneducated but entrepreneurial among us even begin to have a chance in the present economic system? There is a young white man who tried to take on Absa bank, alleging that their system of selling things via ATMs was his and he had presented it to them previously but they were not interested and then, lo and behold, implemented it. The last I read in the papers was that this young man had to have a minimum of R500 000 in the bank, by law, before the case could go to court! Five hundred thousand rands! By law!

Come on, people!

I believe that justice, and I mean all justice, should be free – for all.

COME WITH ME!

Wouter Basson is free to go. Forget for a minute the mothers, brothers, uncles, fathers, daughters, nieces, cousins, aunts, nephews and friends who thought Basson's trial would give them some closure, and help them come to terms with the deaths of their loved ones. Forget that for a minute. The Wouter Basson trial failed to provide this because Wouter Basson is free to go and there is no sweet revenge.

What do you make of this, huh? For my penny's worth, I think Basson's farcical trial points more to the deficiencies of our justice system than anything else. In Basson's trial lies South Africa's need for serious justice system introspection. How do you spend R40 million, or whatever number of millions the government says it is, and travel the entire universe, talk to over 200 people, and not get a conviction? How does the state put so many resources behind a case and fail to get a conviction? That's the question for our justice system.

How can a prosecutor hope to prove a murder case without showing the body of the murder victim? A dead body is a fundamental necessity in any murder prosecution's case. Why do you think they drag all those serial killers to the shallow graves of their victims? If there is no body, how can you hope to convict? I'll tell you how: with the greatest of difficulty. For all the court knows, in the case of Basson, these supposed murder victims of his could all just be missing persons! Ackerman and Pretorius, the state prosecutors, did not bother to spend part of the R40 million (or whatever amount the government says it is) at their disposal to find the bodies of the people Basson supposedly killed.

How do you spend all this money investigating crimes for which the guy you are accusing has been officially pardoned? In our negotiated settlement, we pardoned the then SADF army personnel for crimes committed in the then South West Africa. And yet Ackerman and Pretoriuos, the Basson trial prosecutors, seem to have discovered this only when counsel for the defence raised it in court! How *dof* is this? After spending all that money and travelling to all those places, they only get to realise inside the courtroom, back in South Africa, that they did not have to look into the South West Africa murders at all! Shock, horror!

And if it is all a case of a really bad judge, then it begs the question: what the hell is our justice system doing allocating such an important case to one of its bad judges? We know we have a serious shortage of black judges having just recently emerged from apartheid. Most of our black lawyer friends would rather get

135

rich outside the state justice department than gain the prestige of being a judge, having mostly been poor for large chunks of their lives and all. Does that mean we do not have a single good white judge in South Africa? Does that mean that the few black judges we have do not have the expertise to handle a case of the nature of the Basson case? How far are we from a colour-blind justice system then, hey? Come on, man, what the hell was our justice system doing allocating a Judge HARTZENBERG to a Basson trial, hey?

Did the government have any tabs on the bill? Or did the government decide we want Basson so badly, just go to town, so to speak, we will pay whatever it takes! Okay, so the government is disputing the R40 million figure, right? Hell, for all I know the bill could be R10 million. Could someone not have said, "Hey, you are now at R5 million, show me what you've got. Oh my, you have nothing! After R5 million! Look, let's rethink this whole thing. Who was supervising the allocation of the R10 million to R40 million spent on this failure to convict Basson? Maybe that head should be on a platter, Mandingo, what do you think? How much money does it take for a prosecution team to know that it does not have proof beyond a reasonable doubt? Did this prosecution team really want Basson convicted? Or was this all a question of old apartheid smoke and mirrors to blind the new South Africa as Basson slipped through the huge cracks in our justice system?

If this prosecution team was really serious about a conviction, why did it not take a lesson from the Americans and the Al Capone conviction? For those who do not know, when the American justice system discovered it could not pin any murders on the mafia boss Al Capone, it shifted gears and looked at his taxes. Through that, Al Capone was put in jail for life for tax evasion.

Basson was caught red-handed once, and that was for dealing in the drug E for ecstasy. Why did the prosecution not put him away for a long while for that? Would you care if this alleged monster were put in jail for avoiding to pay parking fines? You just want him away, don't you? And while he serves his time for the minor offence, you can take your own time to build other cases against him without too much pressure of time, which leads to huge monetary expenditure.

But, no, our justice system had to risk it all in one swing. And now it's all lost. You can't try a guy twice for the same thing, can you? There are major R10 million to R40 million lessons here and I hope our justice system is sobering up fast to learn them, in order to avoid repeating the terrible mistakes made in the prosecution of this trial. For instance, in law, there is what happened, and then there is proving that what happened did, in fact, happen. The latter is a prosecutor's job. Did the prosecution team in this case know the difference?

I'm not so sure because Wouter Basson is free to go, see? He was charged with over 80 crimes, ranging from fraud, defeating the ends of justice, and dealing in illegal drugs to the murder of hundreds of Southern African black people. How hectic is that? We own the justice system now, we who love justice and democracy and all those other lovely things we fought for and are now sharing in equal measure with our previous killer haters, but the Judge Hartzenbergs of this world still run it. And there's the rub. Ownership is over-rated. We need to run things, Mandingo! Damn! We need to run things. And, at the moment, we do not run the justice system. We just own it. The enemies of justice run most of our justice system. We can't win. And that's why Basson beat us. And now we have no just reward for the monies spent to get this guy. There is no closure for the families and friends of his supposed dead victims. What a bummer!

If our democracy is to survive and stand the true test of time, it needs our government to gun for new South Africa critical mass in its justice system ranks. If our democracy is to survive, we need more new South Africa people wanting to work in our justice system for the good of the country more than the pursuit

137

of money. We are not against wealth. In fact, we are very much FOR wealth. But we also understand that for wealth to be made and preserved, all the relevant pillars of our democracy must stand strong. And the justice system needs us as much as the corporate world does right now.

So, if you have a love for the law, or you know someone who does, Mandingo, encourage them to study the law with the view to fixing our justice system and making it work like it should, because the old guard still think it's a game of us versus them and they are creating divisions where we need unity. They are fuelling the fires of hatred where we need understanding. They are taking us back when we should be moving forward.

The march forward is our responsibility. All of us who know, believe in and want this new South Africa that is so much better than the old one. This march forward is yours and mine. Let's take the first step. The journey is going to be much longer than a thousand miles. But it's sure going to be worth every step, because there is nothing as sweet as building a legacy. Even money is most precious when it is the product of a good, if not brilliant, legacy.

So come with me. Let's go.

WHAT'S WRONG WITH OUR POLICE FORCE?

It must have been '91 or '92. I went to a concert at Ellis Park. I don't remember who was playing. Mandela had just been released. De Klerk was making big strides to try and make amends now that apartheid was looking to be the horror that most local whites were only discovering at the time, but that we local blacks had known all our lives. I see this young guy come running with policemen in pursuit. Finally he stops or they catch up with him. Well, he's black and, although I'm black too, I immediately assume that he's guilty of something and I'm embarrassed. I'm thinking, brother, why would you go and steal at a concert? Why would you spoil other people's fun like that? Look now, you're going to spend the weekend in jail.

What do you know? The policemen search the guy and find nothing on him. But there's a crowd now and it has seen how hard they chased after this guy. To let him go is definitely going to be an embarrassment to them. So they start to harass him, looking for another reason to take him away rather than admit that they might have made a mistake and let him go. I wasn't about to be a spectator to this trampling of a man's rights so soon after Mandela's release. So I pipe up and say: "Look, guys, you haven't found anything on this man, why don't you let him go?" "What did you say?" one of the policemen asks. I say, "Look, De Klerk just promised us that you will be service orientated, which is why your name now has the word 'service' at the end. Why don't you let this man go now that you have established that you have nothing on him and go look for real criminals, who must be busy doing criminal things, while you waste time here?"

Now here's the kicker: I see the white cops who were involved in this move back out at the mention of De Klerk's promise to the populace. They are getting ready to move on. But get this: I see the black policemen get really upset and agitated. My prejudice did not prepare me for this! And as I'm trying to make sense of it, one of the black cops says, "If you don't shut up, we will take you in instead." I ask him under what charge. He's stumped because he did not expect that, but just as I think I have now got him, his other black colleague says: "Obstruction of justice." I say "What!" They grab me, one man to each arm, and start dragging me to their van. As they force me in, I get hit with a fist on the back of my neck, only to turn around and find this white policeman preparing to hit me again. He has the power to do this now that his black colleagues have opened the door. In the end, I did not see the concert because this happened right at the beginning before it started. Once I was locked up, they told me they were sending me back where I came from, i.e. Zimbabwe. No, says the other black cop, Malawi. They agree, without even looking at me. When they finally address me, it is to say: "You think you are clever, heh? You think you know the law, *nê*? Now you are getting on a train all the way back to Malawi where you come from! We are going to teach you a lesson, you big mouth!" To get out of there, I had to cry like a baby and plead like a child.

Fast-forward to 2004. Twelve years after 1992. It is early in the morning of Saturday the 18th in the month of September. I am walking a friend home to Westdene from Melville. A police van with two black policemen comes by and stops. Do you live here, we are asked. I answer by saying, no, but we are on our way to where we stay. They drive off. As we come around the next corner, the van swings by again, slow and menacing. We ignore it. It drives by. Further down our walk, the van appears again. This time I walk towards it and I ask if there's a problem. No, says the driver. I say, well, that's good; I was beginning to feel a little harassed. Out jumps the passenger cop. Harassed, huh! He screams. You! He points at my female friend. Get in the van! For what, she asks. You are drunk in public! he screams. Get in the van. I say, hang on a second, what's going on here? You shut up, he commands. Otherwise I'll have you for obstruction. I then bring out my phone and call one of my friends in police high places. He says find out what the cop's name is and let me speak to him. I say what's your name, sir? The policeman refuses to give me his name. At this point, he is manhandling my friend and pulling her towards the van. I will not talk to anyone, he screams. What's your name? I ask again. Why don't you speak to the commissioner here? He won't answer and he won't talk on my phone. I listen to a little advice and then put the phone down and ask this man: "Let's say she's drunk, is it not true that if she's with someone who is sober she is safe and should therefore not be arrested?" "Oh, so you know the law, huh! Listen you," he screams at my female friend, "Get in the van. NOW!" I get in the van with her and we are driven to Brixton police station where she's going to be charged for being drunk in public without a blood or breathalyser test!

Once inside the police station, I ask the rough cop what his name is again. And I think that because there are other cops around aside from his sidekick who has been silent throughout this harassment he tells me that he is Hlungwani. I engage him in his home language. In the end, my friend does not even get the fine she was told she was going to get. Instead, her name goes into the silent cop's notebook and she is told that that is a warning. Hlungwani then tells me that I should never ever try calling anyone when policemen like him are arresting me because, as he put it, say you phone the station commander, he will just tell you straight that there's nothing he can do for you. You know why? he asks me. I shake my head. Because we arrest them too, that's why. So don't even think about calling anyone higher. We arrest everyone.

Now, whether or not this is true is irrelevant. The point is that this policeman believes it. He believes that as an arresting officer he is above the law and ordinary citizens have no recourse when he and his kind are involved. If I'm wrong and it turns out he does not believe this and knows for a fact that this is wrong, he is even more dangerous because he is going around trying to teach ordinary citizens that they have no rights when he is involved. This goes against our constitution, which contains the rights we look to policemen like him to protect and teach us about. Why couldn't he have said: "Look, don't feel harassed, okay, we are just making sure that the streets are safe. Would you like us to escort you anywhere, seeing as it's so late?" Why couldn't he have said that, instead of acting like this was still apartheid South Africa? And why was he insistent upon taking my female friend alone? Would I be wrong in thinking they were planning to scare the hell out of her and rape her? What the hell is wrong with our police force!

Having harassed us enough for the evening, the silent cop is tasked with giving us a lift to wherever we are going. On the way, he says that, on telling Hlungwani that he knew me from television, Hlungwani said that's good because they can use the press against me. How sick is that!

141

Maybe not as sick as the story I'm about to tell you actually. I am standing outside Six, a cocktail bar in Melville. I see a friend of mine I hadn't seen in a few weeks. He has lost weight, so I'm thinking hmmm, staying at home has done him good, this one. He must be doing a lot of exercising. No, he says to me. I just came from jail! What for, I ask. The long and the short of it is that he bought a car from this woman for R69 000. He paid R65 000 and was battling to pay the remaining R4000 because of hard times, when this woman then told him to bring the car back. He pleaded with her, "Look, surely you can't take back the whole car when you know I have so little left to pay. Just give me some time." He thought this was settled, considering that she still had the car papers awaiting his settlement of the debt. But he was wrong.

Soon afterward, he is stopped by some policemen who inform him that the car he is driving has been reported stolen. He ends up in jail. The investigating officer then says to him look, use this lawyer for your bail application. It will cost you R3500. My friend decides that's too much and finds his own lawyer. On the day of his bail application, the investigating officer appears and tells the magistrate that the court can't rule on the bail application as he is still investigating the possibility that my friend is Nigerian! For the next three weeks, this excuse is used every time he has a hearing and, as a result, my friend is left languishing in jail for that period of time. Finally, at his wit's end, he calls this investigating officer and admits to having made a mistake by insisting on his own lawyer. The investigating officer says that he's glad my friend could see his mistake. He takes R1000 from my friend and appears in court to say that the issue of my friend's nationality has been resolved – he is indeed South African. The woman mysteriously drops the charge of a stolen vehicle and my friend is set free. What the devil is wrong with our police system! I mean, how many times do you think these investigating officers are using the s/he's a foreigner ruse in our courts to delay justice and extricate bribes! Why don't our politicians fix this?

It's been twelve years and our police people are still using the same tricks to harass citizens they should protect. If you are not obstructing justice, you are a foreigner who must be deported or both. This is disgusting. Something must be done about this, damn it!

RACE-EXCLUSIVE LOVE

Dumisani, God rest his beautiful soul, had packed so much into his short life that by the time he was killed he had contributed to this new country of ours way beyond what most people his age would even dream of contributing in entire lifetimes. He was geared to be the best film and television producer this country had ever produced. This is evidenced by *Homecoming*, the last film he worked on and that has just started showing on SABC 2. Leigh, God bless her soul, was about to turn 21. She was still at Bond University. We are not sure what she would have become. However, for all we know she could have become the first white female president of this beloved country. But the truth is, she hadn't shown the nation much in terms of her potential yet. Who knows? Given a few more years, no matter what she was studying, she might have turned out to be more successful in her chosen career than Dumisani ever became in his.

I am not in any way suggesting that the one life was more important than the other. At the end of the day, when families lose their loved ones, the pain is the same. And if those lives ended unnaturally, prematurely and violently through the actions of rogue elements, like Dumisani's and Leigh's lives did, the equality of the lives through the losses is even more poignant.

There are those who would argue that the one life is more important than the other, of course. They might say that Dumisani had already become an asset to this country because it takes many years, a lot of money and much hard work to produce a film and television producer of his calibre. And so they would argue that his life was more important. They might add that given that he is black and there are so few blacks in the industry he was working in who are qualified to do what he did, his life was even more important than Leigh's. The more prejudiced amongst us might argue that Dumisani's life was more important than Leigh's because he is black and she is white, case closed.

But on the other hand, there are those who would argue that Leigh's life was more important. These people might argue that women, as per President Thabo Mbeki's lead, are the future of this country and the world and we need as many of them as possible to partner us in creating a better South Africa and a better world. Every female life senselessly lost like Leigh's was lost is a multitude of steps back in our fight against woman abuse, femicide and all the anomalies that go with patriarchal dominance. The more shallow amongst us might simply argue that Leigh's life was more important than Dumisani's because she is white and he is black, period.

I don't fall in either of these camps. I believe that both of these lives were equally important. It is for this reason that I am so amazed at the frenzy and speed with which the best of our investigative resources were put behind the speedy apprehension of a suspect in the one murder case and the absolute silence and near total lack of progress in the other. I want us to examine why this is the case. It can't be because the one murder was easier to solve than the other surely, otherwise Piet Byleveld, the crack serial killer investigator, would not have been called in. It can't be because there was no press coverage for the one while the other got extensive coverage, because they were both covered in the media. So what happened? Why does it seem to me that the South African Police Services decided that Leigh's life was more important than Dumisani's, and then allocated resources with the support of the president's office? Why do I get a sick feeling at the bottom of my stomach that no one in the SAPS really gives a horse's ass whether or not Dumisani's murder gets solved? What's going on here? What's behind this inequality?

I think it starts with our press. Dumisani was killed in his home over two months before Leigh was kidnapped and killed. This absolutely shocking loss of life was reported in the local press, the local black press, to be more precise. In the local white press, it got tiny mentions on the forgettable inside part of those publications. The feeling seemed to be stop, it's enough already. It never got front-page coverage like Leigh's did. In fact, one of the editors in the black press had to fight to have a spread in the cultural pages, as his bosses were insisting that the story was old already.

On the other hand, Leigh's death got front-page coverage in the local media and a bit more of the same internationally. Why do you think that is, Mandingo? I have a few ideas of my own. The most benign of them all is that this case involved kidnapping. Man, that's newsworthy, because in our part of the world it is as rare as the winter sun in Finland. And you know what, Mandingo? I'll be damned if the shallow reason I mentioned in paragraph five above had nothing to do with what made Leigh's story more newsworthy than Dumisani's. Who gives a damn when black men die? It is expected. The more violent our death, the more normal. But a white girl, kidnapped the day before her 21st birthday? Now that will prick ears over nine hours away in England! It will get on CNN and be reported on in Germany. Cousins stick together.

But that's okay. I don't mind that. Black people can learn from that, except we are too busy trying to teach the world that we must ALL love each other the same and get away from this race-exclusive love. What I find abhorrent is that this racist media is driving an institution in our country that should be driven by our better than world-class constitution. What gets me really upset is that sometimes even our esteemed presidency panders and supports this OH MY GOD THEY KILLED A WHITE PERSON AND THE WHITE PEOPLE ARE CLAMOURING FOR REVENGE. LET'S PUT THEM FIRST AND FORGET ABOUT ALL THE BLACK PEOPLE. Can I remind everyone now that every life is sacred in this country? We are not in the first world. This is not America or England. We are not in apartheid South Africa anymore. Or in an Israel that has no room for Palestinians.

I want this rotten system to fix itself and make sure that the best resources are put behind making sure that Dumisani's killer/s lands up in jail. I want the president to ask the tough questions about the police service's sloppiness in investigating incidences around black lives. I want Selebi to prioritise South Africa as he basks in his new role as head of Interpol.

Three Places in South Africa

KAAPSTAD, A TALE OF TWO CITIES

It's 1998 and I'm in Kaapstad at the height of Euro 98, that big European soccer spectacular that comes around every two years, just like the Africa Cup of Nations. Hey, I love soccer. I could almost love the British for giving the world this sport. I could almost forgive them for colonising my continent and giving us all the different, many and varied bloodbath repercussions, including those in the Middle East, because of this soccer gift. But you know, that's a tall order.

But I'm in Kaapstad, right? And I convince my brother to join me for a number of Euro 98 games. I had been told that there was this one bar where they had a big screen TV and if you arrived early you could sit ringside, so to speak. We get there to find this three-metre long couch right in front of the big screen TV. We sit on the corner of the couch. We are early and it feels good. We are going to see the beautiful game... beautifully. Then the bar packs up, you know? The average age is about twenty, twenty-two. It's young people. White people. This is the supposed future that is not racist. I mean these kids are now schooling with black kids blah blah blah blah, right?

The place packs up with this "new" type of white. It gets so full that to get a drink in the bar is like a good ten-minute squeeze. And guess what? My brother and I are still the only people sitting on the edge of this three-metre long couch. But this place is full of young, white kids who see the world differently to the way their parents do, right? It gets to a point where I'm so uncomfortable with people pushing and shoving each other behind me and above my head but opting to endure the discomfort rather than sit with us that I could actually scream. Then I feel a tap on my shoulder. I turn around and this white boy asks if there's anyone sitting on the rest of the couch. You know, with utter, utter relief, I say to this boy: "No, you know, no one's sitting here. And you won't believe this but the boy then says: "Well, then, you won't mind if I take the cushions." And he grabs the cushions and disappears back where he came from! My brother and I are now sitting on the edge of a three-metre long couch with two thirds of the cushions missing!

So now you can say, like I can, Kaapstad is a racist town.

Move up two years to 2000. I decide to hell with it, you know, I don't care what the Kaapstad attitude is, I will walk like the world is a beautiful place. I will smile. I will be warm. I don't care what this yields, but I will carry myself like I have absolutely no baggage. And guess what? I do this, right? And I get the best service everywhere I go in Kaapstad. In restaurants, waitrons go so far as to touch my arm when checking if everything is all right with the meal. At beaches, people mistake me for someone they know, then say: "No you know, it must be your friendly face." And I'm not acting here. I'm just being a happy me who's left all his burdens behind before engaging the world. I spend my two weeks in Kaapstad in absolute heaven, so to speak. I do not experience a single racist incident.

So, now you can say, like I can, Kaapstad is what you make of it.

Visit 2001. I go to Baraza in Camp's Bay, Kaapstad. It is the height of fashion. I mean, it's Levi's jeans and Armani sunglasses. The girls are styling. The boys are cooking on designer gas. The beautiful people are sipping on sundowners, looking cool. The foreigners are staying at the Hilton, some other fancy five-star hotels or in their own apartment somewhere overlooking the sea. The topics are designer things orientated. They are what do you do, meaning how much money do you make to buy what designer bits, type of topics. The music is light House, beautiful. You watch the sun set over the Atlantic Ocean, I think it is… the cold ocean. The human contact is… well, let's say, between groups, it has taken on the ocean temperature. But if you are in a group, any group, you will feel that it is decidedly warmer. The prevailing attitude is, if you are not in my group stay over there. Kaapstad is cliquey, I hear. This is proof. But here, you feel no colour to this cliquey-ness. It's just that we did not make our money the same way. We did not go to the same school. We have yet to do a deal together. I don't know you. Yes, you belong. God, I love your sunglasses but, look, stick to your clique for now, and I'll stick to mine.

The very next evening I go to Stones in Observatory, Kaapstad. The jeans are torn and dirty. The drink of choice is beer across the board. You offer a white guy a drink and he honestly looks you in the eye, says thank you for the beer and explains that actually he can't reciprocate the gesture. Honest. When you get drunk, the bartenders try and steal your money. The girls are trying to show off their belly buttons, but the stomach fat is getting in the way. The boys look like they are running out of veins for drug needles. The foreigners are backpackers. The music is rock and roll. The main activity is playing pool. The topics are esoteric. Everyone seems to know everyone's star sign. The human contact is… well, let's say that it is way warmer than Atlantic Camp's Bay. This feels more like one big group of people. There are no oceans of cliques to see even while there are groups of friends hovering around separate pool tables.

I look across and I see this girl who I talked to briefly the night before at Baraza in Camp's Bay. I turn to my newly acquired drinking buddy, who happens to share a star sign with me and can't reciprocate the drinks offer gesture, and I say to him: "What are the chances that two strangers, one female and white, the other male and black, can independently choose to go to two places as different and far apart as Baraza and Stones on two consecutive nights?" I tell him I don't really care whether it's

149

synchronicity, destiny, coincidence or fate. I find something very special in all events of this nature. I approach the girl, and in no time I discover that her very first and most passionate romance was with a guy who was born on the same day as me! She herself shares a star sign with my drinking buddy and I. But she's a leap year baby. Born on February 29, she celebrates her birthday once every four years! But she's a Piscean, so we form a Pisces tribe around the bar. No colour situation here. Her name is Sarah.

Then I feel drawn to this other woman sitting quite a distance from us. She's wearing this red, one-shoulder top, and I think she's a bit drawn to me too. She approaches the bar at some point, choosing to buy her drinks from very near where I'm sitting, so I start to speak to her. And she tells me her name is… can you take this? Sarah! Just like our leap year baby! Isn't that something? I mean what are the chances of experiencing this many serendipitous occasions in one night?

So, now you can say, like I can, Kaapstad is a magical place.

But where are the blacks, man? Wait, before we go there, first of all, can some *Kaapenaar* please tell me: "How do you manage to drive badly at 40km per hour? I mean, I've seen people do this in Gugulethu and I've seen their white counterparts do it in town! And I'm not talking old people here who dish out their own brand of driver nightmares, like indicating to the right and then turning left! I'm talking young people driving badly at speeds below 60km per hour! Now that's a shock to the system of a Jo'burg dweller. How do you manage that? How do your taxi-drivers manage to drive so badly at such low speeds? Do you guys have any proper driving schools down there? Should we have a word with the national department of transport?

Anyway, leave that alone. Seriously, though, where are the blacks? I know they form less than 13% of the population down there, but then where are the coloured people who form over 70% of the population down there? I am making the definite distinction between black and coloured, because that's how issues of race are understood in Kaapstad, right? I mean, I was once confronted by a pitch-black parking-attendant *Kaapenaar* with a heavy coloured accent. He said to me, "You people drive nice *kaars*, *nê*? I decided to go cocky on him and put him on the spot. So I asked him, what do you mean, "you people"? And without skipping a bit, this man, who is way darker than me, shot back, I mean you blacks. Like it was the most natural thing. What can I say, except, only in Kaapstad.

But how is that, huh? Everywhere you go in Kaapstad, it's just white people having fun! Where are the natives? Where are the native-coloniser cocktails? I mean, it's their town! Where are they? Is it lack of money? Is it racism? Is it that apartheid was so strong the barriers are still in their heads and just won't fall off? Is it that old syndrome of sticking to what one knows? Do black and coloured *Kaapenaars* find change too traumatic, even when it's for the better? What are these people doing stuck in the townships when all is open for them to enjoy? Why does it take Jo'burg blacks to bust Kaapstad open when there are black brothers and sisters down there? I mean Kaapstad is sexy, *boet*. They should come out and enjoy it like their fellow white *Kaapenaars*.

They should come out. I mean, Kaapstad is so sexy that people tend to forget that it is actually an Afrikaans town. It is easier to believe that it is English or something. But Kaapstad isn't. It is Afrikaans. For starters, the over 70% that I spoke about earlier, speak mainly Afrikaans. The street names around the town tell you that you are in an Afrikaans environment. And yet, we all agree, it is a sexy town with things, such lovely things to do, places – oh how fantastic the places are – to go to and people – and I mean sexy coastal people – to see. It's a sexy town and it is Afrikaans. And those English racists in Natal will have you believe that the Afrikaner has no style, that the *boere* are still the enemy to this day!

Will someone tell the racist Natal English types how disgusting and lame this habit of Afrikaner bashing is? They are still trying to divide and rule, you know, create a few more potential bloodbaths for the future! To the Afrikaners, they say we are the kaffirs causing all the trouble. To us, they say the Afrikaners are the *boere*, who must be blamed for everything racist. Meanwhile we know how unsexy, unstylish, racist and fuddy-duddy Durban is. I have a sneaking suspicion that this is due to all that Natal English hypocrisy that oozes through the gin and tonic and afternoon tea belief that one day I, Member of the British Empire (MBE), will be back home living in Buckingham Palace! Will someone scream it out loud that the monarchy has indeed gone out of style and even taken a chance at falling from grace, for God's sake! What's wrong with these people?

But now you can say, like I can, Durban's gin and tonic has too huge a dose of hypocrisy.

Kaapstad on the other hand is complex. It is racist but inviting. It is Afrikaans but stylish. It is the destination of choice for the international rich, famous and royal, and yet it is home to some of the poorest communities in South Africa. It is lily white, but its population is over 80% black. It is the home of the National Party, but Tony Leon of the Democratic Party somehow believed that it was his back yard. It is a city, but it feels more natural to call it a town. Now that's complicated. Hey, maybe that's why the *Kaapenaar* darkies stay away, they just can't figure it out, let alone figure out their position in it. I don't know.

But I do know that this complexity is part of the reason why I keep going back. I know also that, most of all, I like the honesty inherent in this Kaapstad complexity. This is why I'll pick Kaapstad over Durban on any given day, including Sunday. There is an Afrikaans honesty to all its *kak* and beauty *jy weet*. Whatever goes down, I can always tell where I stand. And that means a lot to a black boy like me. In Durban, on the other hand, they smile with their front teeth as they say, while they grind their back teeth.

So now you can say, like I can, the "*boere*" have done a nice job down there in Kaapstad. The black *Kaapenaar*, and this time I mean Jo'burg "black", i.e. everyone who is not white, must just come out and enjoy it.

YEOVILLE, WHAT A PLACE!

The most beautiful aspect of Yeoville is that it never ceases to inspire debate. From the time when it was Jewish strong to today when it is black strong, this place has always made people wonder why they are so strongly drawn to or repulsed by it. So much so that, this past weekend, it warranted a full page in one of the Sunday papers in what must pass as some of the worst journalism and writing that this country has seen.

When Jewish people were the majority in Yeoville, the place seemed so inclusive it bordered on self-destruction. I mean, if you allow everyone in, how can there be a limit to the scum you attract? And you know what? You might end up with a predominantly black suburb! You know what that means, don't you? Oops! There goes the neighbourhood!

Well, guess what? This horror did eventually come to pass. The neighbourhood, at least from the white and Jewish perspective, did go. And most of these people did leave for whiter places like Melville, to name one. But this did not happen without some sort of white protest struggle. So, a lot of blacks were bashed for being black and in Yeoville. Service levels suddenly dropped when we walked in and took our places at the bars or restaurants. Every flat we wanted to occupy was suddenly "taken", and then open again the week after because the advertisement reappeared in the paper, and then "taken" again when we phoned one more time. It was hard. But in the end, we took Yeoville over. And now, it is black strong and that is official. This, however, has come at a cost additional to the racist humiliation we endured to gain the victory.

As someone who has lived in or near Yeoville and always come here to relax and talk shop with friends or get drunk and try to get laid for over ten years now, I miss the beautiful little bookshops and the varied coffee shops. Sometimes I even miss some of the whites that used to hang out here. They helped make the place seem like the epitome of "non-racialism". I miss Mama's, the pizza place that tried to hang on when all but a few whites had fled, but which had to give up in the end because of the robberies, I miss Rumours, the jazz bar that hosted the late blues-singing, piano-playing American, Champion Jack Dupree, once, then turned into The Politburo discotheque, then... nothing. I miss The Coffee Society, a coffee shop cum theatre that offered highly innovative plays under the banner of The New Black Sun. In short, I miss all the white-run businesses that Yeoville boasted in its heyday. I miss The Harbour Café, a meeting place for artistic wannabe's with a penchant for over-indulgence and an abundance of kind acceptance for all and sundry.

Today, it must be said, the same drug dealers hang out at the same corner selling the same merchandise as before, plus a few new products. Most of the businesses on Rocky Street seem to sell alcohol and nothing, if not very little, else. Standard Bank took over a whole block, then pulled out. CNA abandoned the neighbourhood. Nedbank became People's Bank and the Yeoville Mardi Gras died. Yeoville has irrevocably changed. The only places left to talk about, really, are Time Square Café from during the day to late evenings all week long and Tandoor on some late nights. Both businesses are white-run and -owned. The new entrants to Yeoville, if we leave out the places that specialise only in alcohol peddling, are Ekhaya across the road from Time Square Café and Zim, about two houses down from Ekhaya. These two businesses can best be described as decent shebeens or taverns. They are both black-owned and run.

What makes black Yeoville a lesser proposition than white Yeoville, in my opinion, is that most black people don't know how to start, then profitably run businesses that make a popular suburban business street tick. We don't know how to manage and run coffee shops. We don't know much about running art shops and second-hand book shops, to name a few businesses that are essential for a neighbourhood to be a favourite middle- to upper-class hang out, like Melville, Parkhurst and Greenside for whites, to name three areas that differ remarkably from black Yeoville. To compound the problem, those few whites, who decide to make money off blacks in black neighbourhoods like Yeoville, simply downgrade everything to liquor outlets and cheap second-hand-like new clothing stores. And, invariably, the blacks in those neighbourhoods don't disappoint and these businesses flourish.

Who's to blame for this? We can start by blaming the status quo. Whatever wealth Gauteng might carry, moneyed blacks are few and far between. That's number one. So it is a huge risk for anyone to invest heavily in a classy coffee shop when the majority of people in that neighbourhood are battling to make ends meet. After all, what is a coffee shop outing if it isn't a luxury of sorts, a costly one at that? The risk factor is compounded even more if you have never run that sort of business before! So, no, Yeoville can't even begin to compete with Melville when it comes to being trendy. We have taken over Yeoville, but it will be a while before our pockets are deep enough and our business knowledge healthy enough for us to shape it into a trend-setting neighbourhood.

Be that as it may, Time Square Café remains the most popular hang-out for professional blacks who love Yeoville. And I would like to argue that contrary to what you might have grasped amidst the confusion of thought and lack of backing for the statements written in the article I mentioned at the beginning of this lament, we go to Time Square Café, because one, we love and relish black company; two, it is the only decent coffee shop left in the neighbourhood; three, you will be hard pressed to find a place, anywhere in the world, with more stimulating, intelligent and brave discourse; four, you will meet anyone from anywhere in South Africa and abroad here, from South America past North America via all of Europe down south to Swaziland from North Africa; five, no one here cares what you drive, who you work for, how much money you make or whose mother's son or daughter you are.

What we do care about is what you have to offer as an individual. Under this criterion, everyone is welcome, from transvestites to whites. It does not matter whether you are skinny and short or fat and tall. We do not care whether you are an Oxford graduate with a degree in genetics or an uneducated businessman with millions of dollars in the bank. We don't care if you are poor. It doesn't matter to us if you regularly have breakfast with President Mbeki for fun. What we do care about is whether you have a soul. And boy, do we shake you when you first arrive to find the seat of that soul of yours! But when we do find it, and you've been brave enough to reveal it, you will have friends for life, jokes galore, and of course, if you happen to have a racist white boss and you'd like to talk about that situation, we will listen, and when asked, and if we can, we will help.

That's us. Yeoville lovers. Time Square Café chillers. Beat us down if you want. This is who we are.

Unusual Business

MELROSE OUCH!

I went to see Melrose Arch the other day. Melrose Arch is the new development in Johannesburg's "leafy suburb of Melrose", as I recall the brochure to have said. The development is accessible off Corlett Drive and Athol-Oaklands Road, just off the M1. My sisters, my brothers, it is beautiful. The concept behind the development is truly world class and ground breaking. The place is a mini city within a city. And it is designed to create the old local suburban business-street feel, like the old Rockey Street in Yeoville and 7th street in Melville today. Those who live in Melrose Arch can work there, eat out there, shop there, jol there and enjoy the African sky right there. The Melrose Arch brochures tell us that this is how the world is moving to avoid traffic congestion. Once you reside in Melrose Arch, you don't need to drive, unless, by necessity, you have to leave Melrose Arch. Everything you need is within walking distance. The concept is retro made modern. It's a real groove.

This is the face of Melrose Arch. But if you and I are going to grow and be strong, Mandingo, we must learn to read the numbers behind the façades. Let me give you an example. I'm sitting inside JB's Corner, a restaurant inside Melrose Arch, and this young man is explaining something to this older woman, who appears to either be his mother or business partner. Either way, she carried the demeanour of someone who put up the money. The young man is explaining how he's going to create a counter here to sell whatever from and how he's going to break down this wall there to get that effect. The woman listens, then asks, like it is the most natural question on earth, if this is going to get

157

him more room for people around the bar. Is he getting more people around the bar? Read: how much money is the space you are creating going to generate? The more people you can get in a bar/restaurant, the better your chances of making money. JB's Corner is the façade, you see. The real deal is in the numbers behind the façade. And this older lady understands it, like you understand breathing, i.e. as the most natural thing on earth.

Let's forget the look of Melrose Arch and the concepts behind it, the glamour and all the smoke and mirrors in front of it. Let's examine the numbers behind the façade instead. Every piece of publicity material you read concerning Melrose Arch tells you that the developer behind this modern day retro mini city is Sentinel Mining Industry Retirement Fund (formally known as The Mineworkers' Pension Fund). What this means is that miners' retirement funds are being used to build this development. Then you must ask yourself this: who persuaded the Sentinel Mining Industry Retirement Fund board of trustees that this was a good investment? Now ask yourself who has been entrusted with growing this miners' pension fund by 20% or more, year in year out? And your finger will point to a company called Investec.

Investec is a super company by all financial accounts. It started out with eight guys and now, barely twenty years later, it employs more than three thousand people worldwide. It manages assets in excess of R170 billion, of which R103 billion is from overseas. Of the R67 billion or so left over, only about R9 billion is from the management of pension funds, such as the Sentinel Mining Industry Retirement Fund in South Africa. The rest of the R67 billion is mainly from white corporate South Africa. This is a typical white-money syndrome, making mainly white people rich in a white company. Who would blame the company for wanting to go off shore where there are more white people? In any event, Investec said to the miners' representatives, this Melrose Arch thing is good, do it. Put money in it. But how did they manage to convince these guys to agree to this?

The answer to this question is not hidden. In fact, the Investec Property Management office that is managing Melrose Arch for the Sentinel Mining Industry Retirement Fund (read Sentinel Mining Industry Retirement Fund trustees know nothing about property management and so will not make a cent in that area) at Melrose Arch boasts huge banners that proclaim that Melrose Arch was built to escape the rot that was taking over the Johannesburg CBD. One of the listed reasons for this rot is hawkers. Another one is crime and whatever else made white people say to every other white person back then "Desert the CBD, NOW!"

So that's who said use the money for this purpose and these are the reasons they used to make their point and so Melrose Arch gets built. Now let's examine this. As we speak, R1 billion has been spent to build phase one of Melrose Arch. And by God! These people have done a fantastic job. The security is so jacked that the cameras make you feel like you are living in the Big Brother house, without a broadcaster to beam you out live. The actual structures that make up the development are simply wonderful to look at. But who built these structures? Who did the R1 billion of the miners' funds pay and enrich to create this breakthrough in modern living-space design?

A quick glance through all the suppliers gives you one company with a black name, Bohlweki Waste Management. This company is a waste removal company, as the name suggests. But no one at the Investec Property Management office that is doing the management for the miners for a fee could tell us if this company was really removing refuse at Melrose Arch or if, indeed, it was black. So of all the architects (over eight architectural firms are involved), of all the engineering firms (also numerous), of all the financial advisors, of all the contractors, there is not a single black firm.

If you asked for the black people involved in developing Melrose Arch, they would most likely refer you to the white people involved in developing Melrose Arch. And the white people involved in developing Melrose Arch would probably tell you that they can't afford to make mistakes, they can't afford to handhold anyone as this is a delicate construction using pension funds and having to show a return of about 20% pretty quickly. They'll probably tell you that they could not find black firms with the credentials to be involved in something of this magnitude. They would say they actually tried and no one of the right calibre came from the black community. You would be hard pressed to argue that they did not try their hardest to find black suppliers.

Okay, so there are reasons for the lack of black suppliers who can participate in the earnings that are generated by using mainly black people's monies in the Sentinel Mining Industry Retirement Fund. Now let's see if black people have businesses in this complex, i.e. are black people participating in the wealth creation that the structures themselves are generating? A quick answer to that question is no. Even the "Zimbabwean restaurant by Zimbabweans" Moyo's in the complex is owned by a Mr Lurie, a white man. This is not surprising as the actual launch of this black-funded white-built Melrose Arch was advertised in the Rosebank/Killarney Gazette (read, we are talking to white people here). What about the posters for upcoming events at this "leafy suburb"-based complex for white peace of mind? Well, let's just say that you won't see them in the Johannesburg CBD and why the hell would anyone want to talk through the *Sowetan*? After all, most miners are illiterate!

So, we have a scenario where white people convinced largely black people to spend black money to build a huge complex for white people to escape from black people in the CBD and enrich white people through a space that is designed to cater for white people. How's that for a scam? Investec did not take a cent from the R103 billion overseas funds in its portfolio to do this. The company did not take a cent from its Corporate Banking division to do this. Investec went to the most insignificant of its portfolios and took largely black money and risked it on Melrose Arch, an untested concept in the South African context. Understand this; if they had built a Sandton City-type mall, the risk of losing the investment would be far lower simply because the Sandton City-type mall concept is well tried and tested, and it works here in South Africa. On the other hand, the risks for something as new and untested in the South African context as Melrose Arch are huge!

As a friend of mine put it, you get the feeling that they asked themselves this question before embarking on this course: "Whose money can we afford to lose? And well, black money came up trumps here. And so Melrose Arch used mainly black money to help white people run away from black people in the Johannesburg CBD. How sick is that?

So we come to the conclusion that Melrose Arch should indeed be called Melrose Ouch! Because the numbers behind that façade hurt, Mandingo! They hurt you and me, big time. We need to wake up. We need to get involved behind the façade where the numbers make or break sense. We need to do this to rise up. Yes, we are not participating yet. In the meantime, though, let's learn to read exactly what's going on.

We hope that this article will help shape your thinking around the analysis of what is presented as the face in the business arena and what is really going on. Learn the language, Mandingo! And rule the world.

BUSINESS TODAY!

I have always said that the real struggle for Africa, the tougher struggle, is the economic struggle. The reason I think it is the tougher struggle is because in Africa, it always starts just after the political liberation struggle ends. At the point of victory, it is tough to convince yourself that the fight actually just began. It is tough because business rules and regulations are easy to shroud in smoke and mirrors to confuse new entrants. It is tough because, often, your economic foes are so paranoid and scared of losing everything that they'll stop at nothing to destroy you

161

before that happens. We have just won our political struggle here in South Africa and, by and large, black South Africans are new entrants in the business arena and you must know how scared, and sometimes paranoid, our South African white counterparts are of losing their comforts.

And so, there it is, the tougher struggle just began for us.

Most African countries won their political wars against their "oppressors" long ago but, sadly, they never even entered the arena of battle when it came to the economic struggle that followed. They lost before the signal for the first round was given and so we had many white South Africans during apartheid saying things like: Look at the rest of Africa! I don't want South Africa to become a banana republic! And: Don't argue because that's what Africans do to well-built economies when they take over politically, they destroy them! And so it was hard for us black South Africans to be heard above the din at South African white dinner parties during apartheid. We had no good examples to counter the arguments. We could only point to who was to blame for the woeful state of the African economy and, generally, we argued that it wasn't us.

Can you and I make South Africa that example of how a people can win politically and be graceful and then go on to win economically and make the whole country prosperous for all the people in it, including "the old enemy"? Can we? I think so. But first we must recognise that the battle for political freedom is only the beginning, and that the economic struggle is the war to win if ever there was a war to win. So this week *O'Mandingo!* explores business. And we start with the very basic question, what is it? What is business and what is our role in it if all South Africans are ever to have a shot at winning against poverty and introducing better business principles to the South African business arena to start off, and then to the world?

So here goes:

You must have heard the phrase "this is my baby" from someone somewhere referring to his or her business. Generally that person means that s/he started this thing, this business, from scratch and nurtured it to the stage where you and I can see it and maybe even go "Wow! What a business!", right? Well, I think a baby is a good way to illustrate what a business is and what we mean by, you know, "business" in general.

Take a young couple, just married, right? They decide they want to have a baby. In today's world they would have to look at their income to see how much this would cost and if they can afford it. If they did not have the money, they would have to save up for this new bundle of joy. Once they have enough money saved, they would engage in coitus with the view to getting the female partner pregnant. In an even greater world, they would both be involved in making sure that the nine months of gestation go very well so that the baby is born healthy. That's stage one.

Stage two. Now the baby is born. In the early days of its life, it really just "takes", right? There's no "hey, could you go fetch my paper kid?" No ma'am/sir! You do not ask it to make you tea. You do everything for it. You do not sleep. You clean it up. You tell it stories. You nurse it through sickness and through health. You worry if it will be okay. Meanwhile the bills to keep it alive and well looked after keep climbing. You educate it and then, if you do a really good job, it looks after you in your old age, if you need it to. This is not unlike building a business.

You are a business! How about that?

Stage three. Now the baby is growing, but the parents must continue to work and generate income, so now they hire a nanny to look after the baby when they are gone. Now the baby is generating income for third parties. You are now a thriving business. Someone invested his or her life and money to make you the productive individual that you have become. First, they paid for your food, clothing and lodging. They took care of your medical expenses, then they got you educated. And now, here you are at your desk or whatever space you work in all day, making money every month. You could be a profitable business.

Let's look at you more closely.

Depending on how well off the family you were born into is, or how bright you were in class, or simply how lucky you are, you got the opportunity to study further than high school and so can command higher salaries than a lot of people. Depending on the moral fibre of that family of yours, you are either well respected and considered upstanding as job offers pile up or well on your way to losing your only job and considered a real pain in the ass! And depending on how good you are at honest introspection, you either become a better human being and fix your flaws or you stagnate and go downhill. And finally, depending on how good you are at managing your cash flow, you are either saving money every month, i.e. profitable, or chasing your own tail every month, i.e. always desperate and penniless in the middle of the month.

As you can see, with babies, the more you put in, the more you get out, and with adults, the more disciplined you are, the more money you can keep. This is not unlike building a business from scratch and maintaining it to the point of keeping it profitable throughout its existence.

Now, who has a baby when they well know they can't afford it? No one except the ignorant, the stupid, the careless and the selfish. Now what makes so many black South Africans believe they can start a business without injecting their own capital?

Now who borrows money to have a baby? The answer is, no one that I know of. Now why don't you save your own money if you want to start a business?

Who claims to own half your child because they introduced you to your spouse? No one that I know of. So why do so many black South Africans believe that introducing two businesses together entitles them to ownership of whatever business entity these two businesses produce plus the profits thereof?

In order to benefit somehow from the birth of a child, you must contribute to its well being, like a nanny does. Now why do so many black South African business players believe that they are entitled to the monthly proceeds of a business they do not actively participate in?

In order to make sure that your baby turns out well, you need to be actively involved in guiding it day in and day out. Now why do so many black businesses behave like it is enough to buy into a business and stand as far away on the sidelines as possible and believe that that business will not turn out sour for them, even as it makes those operating it rich?

I started off saying that the business arena is the next arena of battle and the toughest. Know that as an employee in a company when so many black people in this country are unemployed, you are one of the strongest weapons in our arsenal. Look at it this way: most of us are first introduced to business as employees, directly after our parents have finished investing in making us profitable enough to sell our skills. We start as nannies looking after someone else's baby. This is very good. At best it gives us an opportunity to observe, first hand, how other people raise their babies and learn. At worst we could learn some really bad lessons and develop some really bad habits so we need to stay vigilant. But either way it gives us an opportunity to practise on someone else's baby before we embark on raising our own.

So do this then, learn everything there is to learn about the business you are currently employed in. Go beyond your duties. Learn about the history of that business. Know who the big players in that field are. Find out how that business makes money. Learn about the mechanics of the business and always focus on the big picture, how would I run this business I'm working in and beat the best at it if I were at the helm? Get involved because, as they say, the more involved you are in a baby's upbringing, the more fun you have with it. You see it take its first step. You watch its first toothless grin. And you hear it struggle to call you by name for the first time. Then you attend its wedding and help it raise its own children. This is fun. So get involved. But never slip up on what you get paid to do. The best way to learn then is to try and involve yourself in as many aspects of the business you are in as possible, by offering your help to as varied a number of people in as varied a number of departments as you can. If not, befriend as many people in the different areas of your business as you can, and ask questions. You are in a position to learn, learn, learn and learn in order to be an even more powerful business tool. For yourself, your family, your community and your country. Use that opportunity. You are a rare and special breed remember? Most people in this country are unemployed. Even fewer than the employed people in this country are business owners!

So be an employee with a mission to be an owner so that you can hire more people from your community and build more efficient "business machines" in the future, see? If you are already a business owner, own your business with a mission to grow stronger and larger every day in order to do the same.

And always strive to have fun. Okay?

ACTION!

Affirmative action is a funny thing, isn't it? When you ask black people about it, especially the proud ones, they'll tell you how much they hate it. They'll tell you how much they want to be recognised for their talent and not be given handouts. They'll tell you how much of an insult it is to them, their intelligence and sense of worth! So there, bright blacks don't want affirmative action. Or do they? They certainly seem to be arguing that they do not need it. They seem to be arguing that it takes them too many steps backwards. And you know what? They want to be moving forward. They need to be moving forward. If they move backwards, so does the country, because they are the future!

When you ask the whites, they'll tell you the same thing from a different angle. They'll tell you how the standards drop when affirmative action comes into play. They'll tell you how hard they worked and for how long and how unfair it is that some people, simply because they have a certain skin colour, are being given opportunities. They'll tell you that it's reverse racism. They'll tell you how this is making the country go backwards and they'll point to Sports Minister Ngconde Balfour and give you the recent rugby win/lose statistics to show you what affirmative action can do to ruin a perfectly functioning human machine. Did you not see what the Aussies did to our cricket team recently!

Affirmative action for black people in South Africa seems extremely unfashionable with both blacks and whites.

Those black people who think it is cool do not scream too loudly that this is what they think lest everyone fail to recognise that they too deserve the positions they hold in the workplace. You see, if they said openly that they are for affirmative action they might just be mistaken for freeloaders. And who wants to be known as a person who doesn't quite carry their weight at work? So they rejoice in the dark away from the fashionable crowds who are opposed to this new South African sickness, affirmative action.

Those whites that think it is cool are also hiding. You see they might just be mistaken for condescending, patronising, colonial types who do not think black people can carry themselves. After all, is that not the epitome of racism? Blacks are children you see, they must be looked after. They must be helped along. And one must never forget their limitations. Otherwise one might just force them to bite off a lot more than they can chew. And they cannot chew a lot. They have small mouths. With this sentiment prevailing in this new South Africa, which as we all know, is devoid of any racists, how can any white person worthy of his/her political correctness ever be seen to be so patronising as to say black people need affirmative action?

So there, black people do not want affirmative action. Whites do not want affirmative action. Both camps seem to be arguing that it is a perfect recipe for throwing the country to the dogs. And those who support it are hidden underground but, unlike true guerrillas, they are not fighting a clandestine war to make sure affirmative action for black people specifically goes ahead. Instead, they are, almost by abstention, seemingly saying those who are opposed to affirmative action are correct in their stance. Is it right for these groups to be doing what they are doing? Should we not have affirmative action whatsoever in South Africa today? Would that really move South Africa forward?

Where should we stand on this issue, Mandingo?

When I started in what many black people would argue is the most racist industry in South Africa today, advertising, I was given a desk in a corner with a window overlooking a low building. Some would argue that I was lucky to have a window. In any event, what my physical position inside the building of this company I was working for meant is that I had my back to every supposed colleague I had in that company, including those seated nearest to me. So my sensory perception of what was going on in the company was mainly through my ears. To see or be seen, to even hear properly and be heard, I had to physically turn around! That's a serious disadvantage in the visual department of a visual company, do you follow? In order for me to see, I had to physically impose myself on the building and the people in it. So I was generally seen as a nuisance. I mean, why doesn't this guy sit at his desk! That forced a psychological disadvantage on me, I was an unwelcome guest. As though this was not enough, I was the only African black in this creative department but unlike all other creative personnel in the company, I was made to work alone. People in advertising will tell you that the best work in the creative department of any advertising agency comes from a team comprising a minimum of two creative people – a copywriter and an art director. I had to conceptualise, visualise and write alone. I was not being affirmed. It would be one thing to say I was ignored, but I wasn't. I was being positively downtrodden.

On the other hand there was this Jewish girl who was my age, who started as a writer like me, at the same time as I did, in this very company I was in, and she had the pick of any of the art directors to work with. She was placed in the centre of the creative department. So she was being constantly stimulated visually, aurally and otherwise. The traffic lady always saw her first, if there was a job to be done by a junior, so she got all the good work for juniors. She was being positively affirmed, do you follow? I remember working on a campaign alone and then asking one of her art director mentors to help me visually, since she was off sick. He checked my work, i.e. my concepts, my scripts, etc., as I constantly bounced my ideas off him leading up to the main idea and, when she came back, he gave all the work to her, art directed it and together they presented it to the Creative Director and owner of the advertising agency, a very gifted Jewish man. The only time I discovered what had happened was when the Creative Director called upon the entire agency to show everyone what an example of great creative work looks like and credited this girl and the art director, who took my work, for it! When I went to see the Creative Director about this, he simply said as far as he was concerned, this girl and I were juniors and credit did not count for anything for us. This despite crediting the white junior for my black work!

Those were the old days. Young white people were taken in, looked after through mentor programmes, and guided up the ladder. They were affirmed. The assumption was that they were always going to come through with flying colours. Young blacks like me were given little or no support and actively pushed to think they were never ever going to be good enough and so, where this agency I'm talking about could have produced two great creative people, it concentrated on making sure only one succeeded and spent the rest of its energy making sure the other one failed. That's the joke about apartheid. It was a waste.

I beat the system, Mandingo, because I was never going to take rubbish lying down. After six months in that agency, I did a campaign against woman abuse that I'm still proud of to this day and it was grudgingly judged joint first in the agency. I had beaten teams with a cumulative experience that exceeded twenty years between them. I had conceptualised that campaign, visualised it and written it from my corner of the building with my back to the company's main activities, on my own. I was young. I was enthusiastic. I was never going to be downtrodden. I'm still one of the best admen you'll encounter, but in the end I got tired of all the bullshit that goes with the South African advertising industry and I left the business. This should never happen in a healthy country that wants to take its place amongst giants in the world. It shouldn't. But it does.

The South African workplace is still dominated by white people. By nature they are more comfortable with other white people. And that is no crime. But what it means is that a black kid is always going to have his/her voice drowned out by white people. To advance in life, you must be seen. And you must be heard. The South African black person needs help to be seen and heard in an environment that, despite its best intentions, is geared to be hostile to black people. This is where affirmative action comes in. And this is why I believe every black person, proud and bright or not, should support it.

The Concise Oxford English Dictionary (ninth edition) describes "affirmative action" as "... action favouring those who tend to suffer from discrimination; positive discrimination, especially in recruitment to jobs."

From this perspective, I can see why white South Africans are opposed to affirmative action. In essence, it makes being "previously advantaged" quite unfashionable. On the surface at least, it seems to exclude them. Now that must be hard to deal with, considering Mandela's rainbow sales pitch. I can understand that. How can South Africa be united in strength if it carries policies that exclude some of its people?

Why should white people support affirmative action?

Nobel Peace Prize Laureate Anglican Bishop Desmond Tutu put it best: for as long as your neighbour remains oppressed, you will never be free. White South Africans constitute about 7% of the South African population. But they constitute about 44% of the income-earning group in the country! In essence, this means that a very small minority can afford health care, education, mortgage repayments, holidays, food, etc., while a large majority does not know where or when its next meal will come from. This is a time bomb waiting to explode. And when it does explode, it will blow up white people! This is why white people must support affirmative action too.

Affirmative action is not about making whites poor to make blacks rich. It is about unlocking more wealth, with the view to having more blacks sharing in the wealth of the land. It is the proverbial "grow the cake". Affirmative action is not about firing whites to hire blacks. It is about filling up positions that whites voluntarily leave with black people. Affirmative action is not what I experienced in that advertising agency in reverse. It is about creating two instead of creating one at the expense of the other. Affirmative action is about saving lives. It is about a healthy future. It is about a stable South Africa. It is about avoiding a Zimbabwe-type drive against whites. It needs the support of both black and white people in South Africa, period.

So don't apologise if you are being affirmed. No one walks alone. In any event, every time someone is put in, say, a management position for the first time, s/he is being affirmed because no one really knows if s/he will crack it. We are taking a positive chance on someone. So far, corporate South Africa has been taking a chance on white people and positively forcing black people down. This is totally unproductive and stupid. The future lies in the colourless development of talent. But first we must balance the scales, and this is what affirmative action is here for. When you are affirmed, it is not an insult, it is an affirmation. You are being told that someone somewhere believes in what you can achieve. More and more black people need to hear that message for us to start believing more and more in ourselves.

WHY DO THEY FORGET WHERE THEY CAME FROM?

I was sitting with a friend of mine who likes to razz me about things, just to get me to argue, when he started this conversation:

171

My friend: "You know, Eric, what I don't like about guys like Patrice (Motsepe) and Cyril (Ramaphosa) is that these guys have forgotten where they come from."

Me: "What's so great about where we come from?"

My friend: "What?"

Me: "What's so great about where we come from that we should imprint it in our brains and never forget it?"

My friend: "Come on, Eric, you know what I mean."

Me: "But I don't!"

The truth is that I have heard this argument before and I'm a little sick of it. History is looooong. But I know that those who are proponents of this argument are not thinking beyond three hundred and fifty years. If they were, they would be saying guys like Patrice (Motsepe) remind them of where we come from. You see, beyond three hundred and fifty years, all the way past a thousand years ago, we were the toast of the universe. We were colonisers, not the colonised. Modern Egyptians have inherited the legacy and are now being credited with building the pyramids, but we know that black Nubians like us were the ones who built the pyramids. Beyond three hundred and fifty years ago, we knew the alignment of the stars in the firmament and how this regulated the seasons and our lives. You can trace the origins of Stonehenge to a similar structure in the south of Sudan two thousand years before Stonehenge was built.

Beyond three hundred and fifty years ago, we gave the world its very first institute of higher learning. We gave the world science. We gave it philosophy. We were kings and queens. We ruled. Today archaeologists can scientifically trace cross-ocean trade back to us... African man, African woman. And why would that not be, Mandingo? We are the original people. Geneticists will tell you that. Palaeo-anthropologists will tell you that. Anthropologists will tell you that. Archaeologists will tell you that. We populated the rest of the world and changed to fit the environment. Nations of the world outside of Africa are, in a sense, our children. Beyond three hundred and fifty years ago, we gave birth to the people of the world.

But I know that the "Why do they forget where they come from" brigade is not thinking beyond three hundred and fifty years ago. Three hundred and fifty years ago, Jan van Riebeeck landed in what is called Cape Town today and began what you can safely describe as the massacre and degradation of the original people. Just like other Europeans were doing to the other original people on other parts of Africa, the mother continent. This rape went from being overtly brutal to being so subtle that even those who are doing it today believe they are not doing it, as there seems to be no evidence of it. The education we gave the world was denied us. The opportunities to gain from our own natural resources were rudely yanked away from us. And we were just massacred, man, killed.

The old lion, you see, had grown old and its young had come back to circle it, challenge it and found it wanting. So they took over, brutally. Africa, the mother continent was old, you see, and tired. And maybe she hadn't taught her children manners. Maybe she had only taught them brutality. After all, even though the Moors (us, Africans) were the most benevolent of rulers in the South of Europe and allowed different peoples to practise their different religions under our rule, instead of inflicting ours on them like other colonisers do, for instance, we had taken their kingdoms through brute force and maybe thus taught them what to do to us when some day their turn came to be lords over us. And boy, did they learn the brute force lesson well! Am I saying we had it coming? Maybe.

In South Africa, they exerted their revenge for three hundred and fifty years or more. In that time, we were turned into slave labour, denied even the basic right to family. We were flogged, insulted, flogged again and again, and forced to die working for our captors who grew rich from what was ours. We were pushed into little box houses in horror townships where we were expected to die, killing each other or working for them. What's fantastic to remember about that except that it should never happen again? I am okay with the most successful amongst us forgetting "where we come from" if where we come from means no further than three hundred and fifty years ago. I am actually sure that one of the ingredients for success is to forget about that negative part of our history.

However, if, by "… forget where they come from", my friend means a refusal to contribute to the uplifting of those like them who are still down and it sounds to you like a rational and well-founded argument, I say to you, well, isn't their success a good enough contribution to our collective psyche, that thing at the back of your brain that sometimes says we can be queens and kings again? If Patrice (Motsepe) could run around with a suitcase full of nothing but ideas and have to beg a hospital to bear with him because one of his cheques bounced, and still rise to billionaire status, isn't that good enough as a contribution to our overall total upliftment? Did we fight to be carried or fight for the door to open so we can walk or run ourselves to our chosen destinations?

I will only take issue with "… guys like Patrice…" if they deliberately stand in the way of their fellow man. I will take issue with them if they do what our "children" from the north of where Africa is did when they came back home, to the cradle of mankind, and forced us down, i.e. make it their job to make sure we do not succeed. Other than that, I celebrate every black achievement because it points the way on the journey to where we once were – at the top of the hill, as kings and queens of the universe. Except this time around, we must teach our "children" better lessons, like we did here in South Africa when we said that reconciliation, not retribution, not revenge, is a better way forward, no matter how mean your enemy was to you. Peace.

BOOM GATE POWER

Something wonderful happened the other day. Then it turned complicated. And ugly. Then I thought, what's the point of all this? On sharing this with my friends, I discovered that someone at the SABC had come up with a name for the syndrome that created this chagrin in my life: Boom Gate Power.

The wonderful thing that happened was the near-conclusion of an empowerment process. I met this wonderful woman who told me about the Black Business Support Development Product (BBSDP) at the Department of Trade and Industry (the DTI). In a nutshell, the BBDSP provides grants for black businesses for marketing tools such as market research, corporate identity and computer software. This wonderful woman then helped me fill in the forms and submit them and basically facilitated the whole process all the way through the DTI's inspection process, which ended with me receiving a glorious letter saying I had succeeded in qualifying for the grant. What wonderful news. Of the R81 000 or so that they had approved towards my marketing tools, I only had to come up with 20%, of which 50% would be covered by another DTI-affiliated organisation. In essence, I would end up paying about R8 000 for marketing tools worth just over R80 000. That's if I could jump a few hula-hoops.

Then came the criteria for using the funds and here began the subtle but horrifying nightmare. The first criterion was good. The DTI's BBSDP would not give me the money. They would give it directly to my service providers on proof of delivery of the marketing tools. That was fine. I mean, what if I took the money and bought clothes or went on holiday or paid off unrelated debt or something? I could understand that. Very clever. Then they said I must give them proof that I had paid my 10% share of the total amount before they paid the service provider. That was also okay. Then they said a receipt from my service provider is not enough. What I must do is hand over my bank statement showing that money had gone from my bank account to the service provider's bank account. In addition, I should also hand over the service provider's bank account showing that money had gone into his/her bank account from my bank account. Then and ONLY then, would the DTI's BBSDP pay the service provider the balance.

When we enquired as to what happens if the service provider decided to give the 10% as a discount to somewhat match what the government is doing, we were told no, that is not allowed. My business had to pay the amount. This is okay on the surface until you realise that most people who qualify for the grant actually do not have money. They have businesses that need a boost to generate money, which is why they apply for the grant in the first place. And then we tried another way. What if my uncle paid the 10% directly to the service provider? No, said the DTI's BBSDP. Your sponsor, whether s/he is your uncle or whoever, would have to give you the money for you to pay the service provider! What if my sponsor, like the DTI's BBSDP, did not want to risk giving his/her money directly to me and wanted it to be paid directly to the service provider? No, said the DTI's BBSDP. My sponsor must risk giving the money directly to me even if the DTI's BBSDP thinks this is unwise, as per their payment-to-service-provider policy. Then we thought, okay, one last question, what if I pay my service provider in cash? No, said the DTI's BBSDP, a receipt proving that you have paid your service provider is invalid as pointed out before. You must pay via bank transfer and bring your bank statement to prove this, plus that of your service provider to the DTI's BBSDP. That's the only thing that qualifies! Here it began to sound like your troubles began when you qualified for the funds. It's as though everything is constructed to make sure that only those with money qualify for money aimed at those without money!

Just the other day a friend of mine said we should follow the eastern style of business to make South Africa in particular, and Africa in general, prosper. When he said this, I pointed out that we did not need the high levels of suicide that this model brings, as it does in Japan. Neither do we want the slave labour practices that are apparently prevalent in China because of it. But having noted that, I remembered that one day at Honda, the owner got up and stood on top of a table and said to his staff of less than ten at the time: we are going global. Less than a decade later,

Honda was a global brand that we all know about today. This story made me realise that with all the inherent problems of the eastern model, there's one thing we probably can copy. And that is the enabling environment in which those economies thrive. In Japan, you can say you are going global with very little and end up global in a short space of time. An environment with the same enabling outcome is what made latter-day colossal companies like Microsoft, Oracle and Sun Systems start up, develop, grow and conquer the world from America despite all that country's problems of racism and greed. Australia, forget the plight of the Aborigines a minute here, has done the same thing, from sport through movie and television production to pure business.

In South Africa, Boom Gate Power prevents this from happening. So the DTI's BBSDP is a great idea with loads of benefits for small businesspeople who want to "go global", like myself. But, between the grant that can help this happen and my dream, there sits a Boom Gate guard whose main concern is exercising power and to whom logical steps for enabling me to attain this dream will not even be considered, as he favours rules and regulations above common sense and speed of outcome. Look at this, for instance, say the DTI gives you a grant for research, marketing tools and some software and you could only afford to pay for the 10% of the software. Only, well, sorry, they say to you, you've got to use the whole grant, otherwise you don't get a penny of any of the grant money you qualified for!

Of course, you would think that this is only happening at the DTI and then you hear of a story at the SABC (where the business model has been established to separate certain entities into separate business units and force them to make money almost independently of each other, i.e. archives, which might sell archive material to news, and Henley Studios, which will sell its services to local production, for instance, with finance keeping an eagle eye over all budgets). A finance person returned a budget that allowed for four cameras and four camerapersons, having slashed that down to two cameras and two camerapersons. On being told that this would not work from a production point of view, the same person then returned with a revision of the same budget that catered for three cameras and two camerapersons (as if the third camera could be operated via autopilot!). Now as if that's not the clincher, when the head of the station that needed this budget approved went to talk to this finance person, the finance person turned around and said: Who are you to talk to me, head of SABC X; I do not answer to you. And right there, the boom gate wouldn't go up for the budget to go through. And so an employee at the SABC coined the phrase "Boom Gate Power". I wonder if management on the top floors there even know that this syndrome exists downstairs.

Then you hear that a provincial minister promises a school a library. When the provincial Public Works Department gets the mandate to build the library, they find out that the budget for a proper library can't be under R750 000. The minister's office then comes back and says no, no, no, no. The Minister only promised R300 000 for the library. So let's cut out the preliminaries to bring down the budget. This might seem logical to you, until you discover that in architectural-speak, preliminaries are the basic infrastructural requirements, like telephone lines, office space, security, etc., to deliver the architectural project! Preliminaries are the basic foundation for the management of the project, but the Boom Gate operator does not know that.

I'm sure that this syndrome is way more prevalent than the examples above, and this got me to thinking, why is that? I can only think of one reason. That this country is still stuck in the mentality of appointing trusted political comrades in positions that need skilled leadership and fearless entrepreneurial/ innovative thinking. Younger and more driven South Africans are being left on the sidelines because the country won't take a risk on them to move us toward quicker delivery. The country would sooner have an appointee at a parastatal, especially, who has strong political connections coupled with a strong political background than have a fresh, young, talented, ambitious, I want to change the world for the better, you come along screaming or stay behind kind of leader. And so, places like the SABC, ten years into our democracy, are still full of you found us here, you will leave us here and, by the way, we have seen many like you, who thought they knew it all, come and go and leave us right here type of employees.

And so important change agents like parastatals – the Denels of the world (big losses year on year), the SAAs (farcical Rand/Dollar hedging decisions, big losses), the SABCs (boom gate power-mongering), etc. – are run by people who do not seem to know what the trenches of the businesses they run look like. How, for instance, do you run a company that produces films without having produced or overseen the production of a film in your entire life, taken a crash course in film production, or surrounded yourself with experts in that field? How do you run a team of financial analysts if you've never analysed a single financial document in your life? And you wonder why the level of local television production hasn't improved, and high level people at the SABC are still proud to announce that the reason their local production division is profitable is because they have kept the cost of production the same for ten years, which means, since you and I took over, Mandingo, we have ensured that actors and producers, our cultural guardians, unlike secretaries in corporate South Africa, have earned the same amount even as the Rand went down over a ten-year period! That's a shame because we could be investing more money in better-quality products in order to build a top-class library of television content and reap long-term sustainable profits from it, while we do Africa proud and give her a localised standard to aspire to.

South Africa has been cautious and it was the right strategy for a while. As a country, we had to reward our political cadres. After all, whom could we trust if not those who were besides us in the trenches? We also had the sunset clause to appease nervous beneficiaries of apartheid favouritism in the business arena. But surely the time for this strategy to be dismantled has come and gone now. Surely it's time to move two to three gears up to high-risk, high-reward appointments across the board. Without this shift in thinking, we are bound to lag behind the rest of the world for a little longer than we actually should.

It's time to remove the boom gates, Mandingo, and get rid of Boom Gate Power-mongers and give new, young and hungry cadres a chance to take us forward to quicker and better delivery models of corporate governance. Peace.

THE NEW CASINOS

Some of my friends, learned friends, get paid very high sums of money to spend every working day deciding which companies are going to make how much money for their shareholders in the future. It's a massive business in which companies like Investec are rulers. The professionals in this industry include stockbrokers, asset managers, economic analysts, etc. These are complicated professions, hence the many years of studying as preparation.

Now, let's examine what these professionals do in this business. In essence, these are the guys whose recommendations you would rely on before you invested your money in any company, especially if it were listed in one of the stock exchanges around the world. So, for example, one of these professionals made the call that the miners' pension funds should be invested in the Melrose Arch development in Johannesburg. In twenty years or so, the miners will find out whether or not h/she was right. What these guys do is decide where huge sums of money that do not belong to them should be invested for the highest return on investment. Often, tens of billions of rands rest on the decision of one of these individuals!

As you can see, this can be a highly stressful environment, hence the prevalence of alcohol and substance abuse amongst the elite in this group of professionals. If you think about it, how can this environment not be stressful? It is almost a crystal-ball business, isn't it? No matter how many degrees in economics you have, no matter how bright you are, no matter how experienced, unless you were part of the team that planned the 11 September Twin Tower collapse, you could never have known the sharpness with which the American economy was going to dive around that time, could you? Could you, for instance, have predicted the floods that hit south eastern France recently? Could you have timeously predicted the fall of apartheid and the kind of leader Mandela was to become? Can you tell me what Mugabe is going to do next? All these factors are important in determining whether or not money should go in a certain direction. And these professionals are the best equipped in making these predictions because of their training. But, as you can see, it is a tricky business.

What about you and I, Mandingo? If it is this tricky for professionals, should we be dabbling in the stock exchange to make our money grow?

I will say now that, unfortunately, even the best in this field can only read the history of a company. They will look at the "financials" of a company, i.e. how much money it has made in the past, what assets it has, what liabilities, etc. They will look at all of this along with technical financial elements of this nature to arrive at a judgement call about the company's future. My learned friends are very good at this sort of analysis. That's what they studied hard and train hard to understand. But, just like you and me, they cannot tell if George W. Bush will or will not be caught having sex with an underage girl somewhere; thus, bringing down the entire American economy and causing a second financial crisis in one year because of a renewed lack of confidence in that country's leadership! Like you and me, they cannot tell if, as we speak, the financial director of Sasol is busy siphoning off huge funds from the company coffers with the sanction of that company's CEO.

Coca-Cola is as steady as companies go. But, when the number two guy took over some years back, everything went haywire. People lost money. No one realised that a guy in his twenties was busy making decisions that would bring Barrington's, a century-

181

old, solid bank, down on its knees. If you had your money invested in these companies at the time of the different hiccups, you would have lost it. If you were relying on Barrington's to make a judgement call on where your money should be invested, you would have lost most, if not all, of it!

So what does all this tell us about stock-market investment? First, let's examine this: what are you buying when you buy company stock?

When you invest in a company, you invest in the people running the company and the systems that the company has put in place to make the people in the company function as profitably as possible. So, at the core of it, when I say I am placing X amount of money in Sasol stock, I am proclaiming that, at least until I pull my money out, no one at Sasol is going to do anything that will interrupt the success of Sasol. My money is safe. I am making a judgement call on the future behaviour of certain individuals. If I'm wrong, I lose my money. If I'm right, my money grows. Does this not feel like throwing dice in a casino or pulling some lever and then praying? How can anyone predict the future behaviour of any other individual?

I believe that the world only has so much money circulating at any given time. I believe that businesses simply work to collect as much of that money in their corner of the world as they can. There is a wonderful phrase for it: "Share of wallet". Every business is looking to gain a larger share of your wallet, Mandingo. And one of the easiest ways to do this, i.e. collect other people's money and grow rich, is to "float" your company on the stock exchange. When you do this, you become what Robert Kiyosaki calls "the ultimate investor".

How do you get there?

It's both simple and complicated. Let's take a sweet shop, for example. First, you would buy sweets from the corner café and sell to other kids in school. You would save part of your profits and invest the rest of it back into buying more sweets to sell. If you did this well enough for long enough, you could have enough money saved to open a sweet shop. Now you own a sweet shop. Say it did well enough for you to open more sweet shops. And say these sweet shops do so well and you save enough money to be able to start up or buy a sweet factory to supply them. Say you purchase or open more sweet factories as you open more sweet shops. Now you have Mandingo Sweet Heaven shops all over South Africa and Mandingo Sweet Heaven Factories to supply them and want to expand this business further into Africa. You have a track record. Now you can take a shot at becoming the ultimate investor.

At this point, you prepare the company books to look the best that they can. There are companies that specialise in helping companies do this. You then sell off shares in Mandingo Sweet Heaven Holdings (Pty) Ltd. to the public to supposedly finance your expansion into Africa. In reality, you become this ultra-rich person when the public buys into your company and this dream you have outlined. When they buy into your company, they buy your shares in the company, as you are the founder owner of Mandingo Sweet Heaven Holdings. You are now the "ultimate investor". If each share sells for R7 and you sell five million shares at this price, you will be rich to the tune of R35 million. This is how it is done. And, of course, the idea is to plough much of this money back into the business to fund the expansion into Africa for Mandingo Sweet Heaven Holdings.

Those who buy these shares are banking on the fact that, with your track record, Mandingo Sweet Heaven Holdings shares will go up in price as your expansion plans materialise and they, in turn, will be able to sell their shares to others at a profit. Often, the reverse happens. You buy your shares at R6 a share and when you next look the same share is selling at R4. Some of you might remember that Didata stock went as high as R70 and more. Now the same share is selling at less than R10. What do you think happened to the money that belonged to the person who bought that share when it was R70 and did not sell in time or hung on thinking that the share would improve even as it plummeted?

You, as the investor who buys shares, are not in charge of what happens to the company due to management or other factors, such as war, weather, political policy, etc. You are totally blind and without control. You are playing financial Russian roulette. How does it feel? At best, you will voice your opinion once a year at the annual general meeting for shareholders. Buying shares in any company is a blind bet on the future.

In America, over 1035 companies did this and stole a total of more than US$66 billion from the unsuspecting investor public. US$66 billion! The company that took the most money from people using this system was Qwest Communications (US$2.26 billion). Enron, ninth on the list that *Fortune* magazine (September 02 to 09) compiled, was called "the greedy bunch". Ninth! And you thought they were the really bad guys! AOL Time Warner was third on the list. And most people I know think that this is a good, decent company.

It's not that it is impossible to find good businesses in the stock-market economy. It's just that it is a thorough hit-and-miss job because no one can predict the future. In as much as I can see how you built Mandingo Sweet Heaven Holdings, I can never be sure of how you are going to do in the future. I am at your mercy and at the mercy of the elements and the gods. It's not a very comfortable place to put my money.

So, to go back to our critical question, what does all this tell us about stock-market investment, Mandingo? It says you want to be the ultimate investor. You want to be the person selling off shares. You don't want to be the person trying to guess which share will go in which direction as you search for ways to make wealth. You want to use your money to build your own business. You want to be in charge, Mandingo. It's harder and takes longer as you saw with the Mandingo Sweet Heaven Holdings (Pty) Ltd. example. But at least you are largely in charge of the direction the company takes.

A wonderful Brazilian writer, Paulo Coelho, makes his money by writing bestseller books like his famous *The Alchemist*. His books have been translated into 51 languages and have sold more than 31 million copies worldwide. He is a US dollar millionaire. Asked why he was not putting his money in the stock market to make it grow he asked, what for? With more than US$10 million dollars in the bank, he asked, why would I want more?

Find something you are good at, Mandingo. Work it until it can make you as much money as you need. Don't let greed interfere. And you will be fine and wealthy and happy.

So there it is. Work to be in charge.

SO YOU ARE THE BOSS NOW.
BUT WHAT HAPPENS WHEN YOU LEAVE?

Imagine that you are sitting at an important function with industry leaders of one kind or another in attendance. Imagine that a white person addresses a black one at this function and says: so, you work at such and such a company (meaning one of the parastatals that black South Africans now run), you must know so-and-so (he mentions a black person's name), he's a good friend of mine. Imagine that the black person then answers: Yes. I know him. I fired him. He was asking for more money than I think he is worth. Imagine that someone else asks this very same black person if s/he knows yet another black person in the company s/he works for and s/he answers: Yes. He reports to me.

What do you see here?

I see an idiot who believes that being hired to do something is a platform for power posturing. I see a dimwit who, if, God forbid, you were to make president of any country, would emulate an Adolf Hitler, an Idi Amin or an Ariel Sharon in his/her negative exercise of power because of an inferiority complex of one kind or another. Now stop imagining because this is a true story. What you just read in the first paragraph above actually happened and my guess is that it happens more often than you and I can even begin to imagine.

And that, Mandingo, is one of the most rotten aspects of affirmative action as it is being practised now. We have, in positions of power, candidates who have a lot to learn to fulfill their true potential in the positions they occupy. This is true of anyone who gets a position of whatever magnitude for the first time. But I don't know whether it is because the racial domination of the black race has lasted for so long, especially here in South Africa, that we are now averse to admitting that we don't know lest it re-promulgate the idea that we are inferior. All I know is that not being able to ascertain your true station in life is a long-term disaster because, for instance, instead of acknowledging that things are a bit too fresh around you and working hard to rectify this and becoming familiar and knowledgeable about the fresh surroundings, you spend all your time perfecting the art of "looking" and "sounding" powerful while the other is "doing" things that make him/her truly powerful. And so we get left behind.

A typical result of power posturing is the total disappearance of leadership succession strategies in an organisation. How can a boss who doesn't know enough, won't admit that s/he does not know enough, and is therefore insecure about his/her job tenure, be useful to a subordinate who needs to be taught to grow? If you are all about the big fat office, the big fat salary, if you are all about the big fat title on your big fat business card, it is only normal that what will preoccupy your brain is whether these big fat things will still be around the next day. And so the political game in the office will take precedence over the work that needs to be done for the company to perform at its peak.

The biggest joke, of course, is that the big fat anything in today's corporate world is a big fat relic of a colonial legacy of doing business. US billion-dollar companies are now run in open-plan floors with cubicles for individual offices. Undoubtedly Bill Gates' office is half the size of the office of any of the South African parastatal CEOs. You simply do not need a big fat office or big fat card to run a company well. But you might just need a big fat all-the-above to run it to the ground. Power posturing often leads to corrupt ways of doing business. After all, the classic big–fat–everything story is that of the demise of Enron in the US of A.

A friend of mine once asked me this question: Eric, do you know what's wrong with the SABC? I said I didn't know, what did he mean? He said: the problem with the SABC is that very few members of the British public know or even care to know who the head of the BBC is. I bet you, Eric, he continued, you do not know the MD or CEO or whatever of Radio Highveld or 702 or YFM, for that matter. You might hear the name once in a while when there's a crisis, but generally you don't hear it. Then he said: Eric, the problem with the SABC is that the management is competing with the talent for the spotlight. Where the main man at the BBC, for instance, would understand that the bigger the stars at the BBC the better his job is done, this is not necessarily the case at the SABC. On the contrary, it might be that the bigger the star, the less visible I become as the manager, and so goodbye star, whatever the consequences

I don't know if this is a fair analysis of the SABC. I don't know if it is even accurate. But when I thought more about it, I began to think that even if this were an incorrect analysis of the SABC specifically, it might just be correct in terms of black corporate South Africa in general. And that this could be the main problem with black candidates in corporate positions of power. We are all clamouring for the spotlight, at the expense of each other and the overall health of the organisations we have begun to run. We do not know how to synergise and work together yet. So junior teams have no one to look up to on the rung immediately above them. No one to teach them about good corporate governance, management and teamwork for the good of the bigger picture. All they see are people jockeying for positions, stabbing each other in the back for crumbs, failing to deliver on their job descriptions, abusing each other at every turn, and covering up for each other when disasters, which could have been avoided, happen – lest they lose their jobs. And so the members of the junior teams learn to be those kinds of employees for the future.

It is one of the saddest things.

Yes, a lot of white people do not want us to get anywhere in the corporate world. But, my goodness, we black people are very good at keeping each other and ourselves down. Work to change this, Mandingo. The worst rot within the affirmative action policy as it is being practiced today might just be you and I, and everyone like us who is in a powerful position. Add a lack of understanding of the true demands of that "powerful position" by those in it and there's a disaster. The most horrible part of the affirmative action program as it is being implemented today is that, by and large the first wave of candidates to benefit from it would sooner be surrounded by white secretaries and as many white subordinates as possible than by black ones and, when forced to have black subordinates, they see a threat in them as opposed to seeing the future and working to make it better. That's why we have so many top-position black affirmative action candidates in corporate South Africa and so few black affirmative action candidates in middle management. What is wrong with affirmative action today is that it is not geared to mentor black corporate leaders of the future.

Come, work to change this, Mandingo. Change it!

BACKWARD POWER GAMES

If you are going to change a company or organisation's direction, you must eliminate existing systems and replace them with new ones. And that means replacing the people who call the shots at operational level. If you can't replace them, then make sure the change agents you bring in report directly to you. That adds to your workload, but if you can't do that, forget change. If you can't do one or the other of the two things I just mentioned, you might as well be sending a special force to eliminate a certain enemy and then tipping the enemy off in advance. It's like sending soldiers off to battle and ensuring that they never come back, that they die.

I can't tell you how many times I have been invited by fellow black businesspeople to come and join their companies in order to instigate change, only to be left twisting in the wind with no support as white resistors of change kept pointing to the system and all sorts of other faceless things like "management" as the reasons for no progress.

The first time it happened I had just started my own little advertising agency. It was called Friction and my title was Kaffir in Charge. I had this written on my card. Very sexy. Then came a brother. He ate pap with me and convinced me to close shop and join him in a much bigger operation. On good faith, I went to join the brother. As he had explained to me, his company had just swallowed the bigger white one under which his was incubated up until that point. He needed mine to radically change the creative output of the "new" outfit.

The black operation had swallowed the white one and the two were now swallowing ours to form this amazing creative hothouse. My Friction partner and I joined this bigger, better operation at my behest. Then came delivery time and guess what? None of the power needed to change the agency rested with the brother who invited us. Whenever the brother tried to give us support, the white guys would remind him that he hadn't yet paid off the debt for purchasing this larger stake in the new operation and so had no power. I had changed my whole plan and business life to join a brother who had no power to help me make the changes he envisioned for the agency he had just "acquired". That's where I learned that you can not buy a majority stake from John by borrowing money from John, you see.

A year later I had to leave that outfit.

More recently, I got another call to help change yet another organisation. These black people talk to me about what they envision, about what they want to see happening to shake the organisation they work for. I see their passion, I feel their enthusiasm and I agree to join and help. The first formal meeting I get hauled into has the one black person who talked me into this deal, another black person and a sea of white people. The big black boss then announces that I am never to talk directly to her about anything. As she explained, there were four layers that had to be explored before her office was to be contacted by as lowly positioned a person as me.

In essence, she was saying that whatever I needed to make the changes she wanted to see happening, they would first be checked and approved by all the white people who actually did not want me there in the first place and hated the changes that she supposedly wanted to implement. What is that? I sat there flabbergasted! Yet another black person had taken an opportunity to flex his/her muscles in front of white people at the expense of a black person and totally forgotten to look at the consequences of her muscle flexing. The result was that the whites got more arrogant, more condescending and requests I made took that much longer to be met or I had to scream or kill to get them. The attitude being, who's got your back? The organisation's got ours, weren't you at the meeting when it was laid out?

Then, of course, this MD who created this conundrum for me meets me in the corridors and asks how everything is going! The right answer, of course, is don't put me on the spot here! We are not to talk, you and I, remember? You said it. There are layers of management to go through before we can exchange any knowledge on anything at my level. Why don't you ask the manager who will ask whoever's below him or her who will ask the next lower person and then come to ask me before the process goes back up to your lofty office?

I am here to speed up the changes you want and you lock your door to me and insist I go through the very people who do not want the changes you are introducing simply because this helps you feel powerful, even as you castrate your own soldiers. That is so stupid. And my guess is that it is based on laziness. You want the changes, but you don't want to work for them to happen and, unfortunately, all you have to delegate to are the very white people who do not want your change and you do it because, given a chance between real work and delegating, you'd rather sacrifice real change and have your off days!

Now listen, Mandingo, and listen very carefully. If you are in a powerful position and you need help anywhere on the rung of success in the organisation you are trying to change, first make sure you have the power you need to make the changes. Now make sure you are ready to really work for those changes. Select the soldiers to help you implement the changes. Then make sure they talk directly to you and have your fullest support. Otherwise, please, don't invite any soldiers. Work with whatever you've got in that organisation. And have no change instigated from your office. Be a real house nigger and wear the badge proudly. You'll get my respect.

But I will tell you this, if you have to choose between having power over implementing policy and power over generating policy, you might want to be strong at implementation. And if you choose this, you need the power to empower the people you hire to implement. Do you get me? Don't play power games with your own people because it is still more important to you to show whites how powerful you are at the expense of black people.

PAY! FOR WHAT?!

Every story I have read that talks about financial freedom has had as a core lesson the principle of never holding too tightly to money. You are told that when you clench your fists and hold fast, so that your money does not disappear, you also block your hand from receiving any money. And so, you are told, let the money flow. Allow it to go out so that there's always room for more to come in. I believe that this is one of the strongest reasons why every strong business organisation has a foundation that is dedicated to giving away money. Nedcor, a South African banking institute that netted R3 billion in 2001, has a foundation dedicated to doing just this. So do General Electric, Microsoft, Ford and a host of other big corporations. Moneyed individuals also give money away. Mark Shuttleworth has a Cape Town-based foundation set up for this purpose. Bill Gates has also set up a foundation of his own to do this. So, you are told, let the money flow out. Give it freedom to roam and it will always come back multiplied. The only thing that they seldom talk about when they give this lesson is the answer to the question: in what direction should my money flow?

Who do you give your money to, Mandingo? What is the direction of your money flow?

When I first came to work in Johannesburg, I remember how I used to hustle to get into any place, especially when it was black, you know. I worked as a barman at the Yard of Ale in The Market Theatre precinct in downtown Johannesburg back then. Because of this, Kippie's Jazz Bar experienced much of my hustling prowess. I just never paid to get in. Never. If it took hanging outside until dawn to get in, I would do it. I took this skill to other areas of my financial dealings with black-driven businesses. For some reason, it did not make sense for me to pay to see black musicians play, you know? I mean, after all, they are family right? Why should I pay?

I look back to those days and I feel ashamed, to be honest. I cannot believe that it came naturally for me to believe that if something was produced by white people it had a monetary value and the opposite was true if the same thing were produced by black people. This makes me feel ashamed because deep at the core of this belief system is a black man, me, emulating those people who hate blacks the most for no reason other than that they are black. People who harbour racial bigotry against black people do not put any financial value to anything done by blacks. That's why black people are still earning the lowest salaries in most countries, including South Africa. Sometimes black people's ability to earn more is restricted by other black people who have themselves internalised this belief that there is no monetary value to what blacks produce. And so the cycle of racism and poverty spins harder as those who suffer the most in its wake push it faster and faster.

What is the direction of your monetary flow?

Often I hear black people say to me, you know we young

192

black people start these fantastic clubs and everyone is great. We meet for social events like braais etc. But the funny thing is, they tell me, the minute we start talking some form of monetary contribution to keep this thing alive or grow it, then everyone falls off and the club dies! And so one gets the feeling that black people are more than happy to splash out on white goods and rock up with them at black functions to show them off to their fellow blacks. But when it comes to taking a very tiny portion of the amounts they spend to prop up liquor companies that sell these high-class drinks and car manufacturing companies that sell these top-notch gleaming car machines to help keep an organisation they agree is great, then BOOM! Pay! What for! Are you mad!?!, they scream.

This truth hit me hardest when I went to a function recently organised by ABSIP (the Association for Black Securities and Investment Professionals). At this function I heard, like I did at the previous function of the same organisation, the general secretary Mzila Mthenjane almost go so far as to beg ABSIP members (fondly referred to as Absipers) to pay their R250 annual membership fees. Now here was a room full of professionals, who collectively earn millions of rands per month, and most of them could not see fit to contribute a mere R20 a month to their own association! On the other hand, white people continuously give this very association venues and top-level catering every time the association asks them to do so. Isn't that a shameful irony? For black people to assemble and talk about Africa's need for financial independence, as was the case at this latter ABSIP function, they must be propped up by white money!

And so one gets the feeling that black people want fellow black people to provide freebies while they pay all other communities for everything those communities produce. Now tell me this, isn't that the weirdest thing considering that the one community that needs money more than all other communities, especially here in South Africa, is the black community? Should black people not be more willing to pay for black-produced goods? How are we going to build businesses to liberate ourselves financially if we cannot market those businesses successfully to each other?

It would be interesting to know how many of the people who read *O'Mandingo!* weekly, for instance, have gone to look for and pay to own Sandile Dikeni's collection of poetry, *Telegraph to the Sky* that we recommend here. Forget the reviews by other people, including the people who work on this e-zine. Have you gone to pick it up and review it for yourself at least, and then bought it simply to say, I might not have Shuttleworth's money, but I have taken R80 or so this month and given a brother some royalties?

What is the direction of your money flow? What does your money accomplish, Mandingo?

You do not have to buy rubbish because it is black! You do not have to buy anything simply because it is black. But please, Mandingo, do not refuse to pay for something because it is black. This is the worst form of self-hate. Money is the measure of value these days. You and I cannot get away from this fact. Those who have the most money have the ability to do the most for their communities. Those who do a lot for their communities have the ability to keep their money for as long as possible in their communities before it spins out. To keep this money in their communities, they buy from and sell to each other all the time and only go outside when there is absolutely no one in their community who can provide the product or service that they are looking to pay for. They do not insist on freebies from each other. On the contrary, they attach monetary value to things produced in their communities and then give each other financial support.

And so, when I got to the Bassline Jazz Bar in Melville, Johannesburg, three weekends ago, after the UB40 concert, I was late, but I still paid my fee at the door, and I bought Sandile Dikeni's book. I am proud that I can put a monetary value to things black and take out my money clip and pay for things black with pride. I am over the moon that this is important to me now and that I am growing to internalise it as one of the cardinal principles guiding my life.

And oh, for the record, I am a proud, paid-up member of ABSIP because I believe that it is an excellent organisation that is doing an excellent job in our community specifically, and in the South African economy in general.

A Little Politics Perhaps? Why Not?

FRANKLY INDIAN SOUTH AFRICAN

On the day that the African National Congress (ANC) celebrated its 90th anniversary, Fatima Meer was on television saying that the ANC was to blame for its lack of Indian support! She went on to say something to the effect that the ANC won't even acknowledge that the first resistance movement in South Africa was Indian driven. These comments got me to really thinking about Indian South African support for the ANC specifically, and for this country generally.

I wondered, could it be that Indian South Africans were to blame for the lack of Indian South African support for the ANC?

However, before we examine that question, let's look at Fatima Meer's statement. She says the ANC is to blame for not having Indian South African support. The ANC is a non-racial organisation that garners most of its support from the majority of South Africans, i.e. black African South African people. But if you examine ANC policy, you will be in no doubt that this is essentially a result of the demographic map of South Africa. It is the essential reason why Rajbansi could never be president of South Africa unless he joined the ANC and mended his ways dramatically.

The ANC has always called for support from all communities, including the Indian South African community. It is not a coincidence that some of the most powerful portfolios in government are held by Indian South Africans at the expense of some very able black African South Africans, despite the rumblings of affirmative action for black African South Africans throughout the country. It is not a coincidence that some of the cadres who were involved in such dramatic operations as *"Vula"* are Indian South Africans and that, as a matter of fact, they'd rather be called South African as opposed to Indian or Indian South African. However, this does not change the fact that the ANC has always called for and received support from all South African and international communities and individuals that believe in and want justice, stability, peace and prosperity for all peoples of the world.

Now it is a fact that Indian South African support for the ANC borders on being insignificant to say the least. But I don't think that Fatima Meer is correct when she says that this is the ANC's fault. It could very well be that this is a reflection of the demographic make-up of South Africa, i.e. we have very few Indian South Africans here and so there will always be very few Indian South African supporters for the ruling party. This argument is flawed though because all of us, including Fatima Meer, know that if you sampled any random group of Indian South Africans (except the group that is already in the ANC, of course) you would find that the majority in that group had no time for the ANC at all. In fact, you would find that this very majority actually harboured racist attitudes towards black African people period. Flawed as it might be though, I think that this demographics-driven argument is a far better offering than Fatima Meer's.

You see, the question Fatima Meer is really raising is who is to blame for this Indian South African racism against black African South Africans? And that's the issue I would like to explore here.

Is it the caste system that is embedded in Indian tradition generally that is to blame? We all know that in Indian culture there is such a thing as the caste system whereby the darker the Indian the lower his status in all Indian communities worldwide.

At one point in Indian history, higher-caste Indians would bathe for hours if a lower caste Indian person's shadow fell on their bodies! I am sure that this still prevails in certain parts of India. By extension then you could say that the majority of the people who run and support the ANC are dark and, therefore, in the Indian South African's subconscious, they are a lower level of species and unworthy of Indian support. Now, you can hardly put this at the ANC's door. It is actually an internal Indian problem that must be solved.

Could it be that this Indian South African racism stems from apartheid? Like most clever racist rulers of old, the Nats understood that you needed to create a buffer class between yourself and the most oppressed group in your territory of racist rule. And so the Indian South Africans were allowed more rights, freedoms and better upward mobility in terms of wealth creation than black African South Africans in order to develop into this buffer middle class. Could it be that because of this apartheid policy, Indian South Africans slowly but definitely began to internalise that they were near white and by extension above black? And can you really put this sick mental development at the door of the ANC?

Let's look at this supposedly "ignored" history of the Indian South African struggle that Fatima Meer talks about. And here we will take the most famous of all liberation movement leaders from the Indian South African community, Mahatma Gandhi. Scholars of history will tell you that, when Gandhi was in South Africa, he waged a racist struggle for Indian South African liberation from strife. Yes, he grew into a giant of a man who accomplished seemingly impossible things for his people in the struggle against English colonial rule. But we know, and Fatima Meer must know this too, that in the early part of Mahatma Gandhi's movement to fight for Indian emancipation in South Africa the permeating thought was how can Indians be treated like natives when they are better? This early South African Indian Congress of Gandhi's passed resolutions such as this:

Resolution II*

This mass meeting respectfully protests against the Asiatic Ordinance and humbly requests the Local and Imperial Governments to withdraw the Draft Ordinance for the following reasons:

… (3) … it reduces British Indians to a status lower than that of the Kaffirs and other coloured persons;…

To these kinds of resolutions, Gandhi never objected (it would actually not be far-fetched to assume he drafted this particular racist resolution as he was the legal brain behind the South African Indian Congress of this period). To his credit though, he contributed that if the demands were not met then these "British Indians", not Coolies, should resolve to go to "gaol" instead of getting violent or something like that.

Admirable as this South African Indian struggle is to Fatima Meer, you can hardly call it non-racial. As a matter of fact, when delegates from this very South African Indian Congress were invited to the Non-European Co-operation Conference in 1927, they went under protest, arrived late and then refused to participate in the voting to pass the co-operation resolutions. And can you blame the majority of people in the ANC for not trumpeting this "pioneering" liberation struggle? I will go further and say that it is probably better for the Indian South African community and for Gandhi's legacy to have this black African South African silence on the issue. But I would quickly add that it is extremely unhealthy for the Indian South African community to be silent on the same issue and not to be engaging it honestly and openly.

Look, one of my earliest memories of a shopping experience involves me in a queue in an Indian South African shop. I

*Source: Bhana, Surendra and Pachai, Bridglal (eds.). *A Documentary History of Indian South Africans*. David Philip Publishers, Cape Town: 1984.

remember standing behind this black South African woman who had a R50 note in her hand, presumably from her hard-working husband in the mines. You could tell she did not know the true value of the note. These notes had just been issued. She could not read and was therefore completely at the mercy of the Indian South African merchant who knew this fact. She bought a R3 item and got small change worth less than R10 from this Indian South African trader who then called "NEXT" for me to step up. I watch this happen. But I'm young and I'm tongue-tied by my age. I'm furious but powerless. My whole life spins into a confusion of hatred and disgust and shame and pity and... I stammer out my purchase request and walk out of the shop.

There are many black people with these horror stories of black South African exploitation at the hands of Indian South Africans. None of these Indian South Africans have ever stood up, like the Afrikaner South Africans and the black South Africans at the TRC, and said, "We are sorry. We benefited largely from apartheid; at times we did horrible things to further exploit our fellow South Africans. We are sorry, and as the Jews say, 'Never again'." The Indian South African community has never stood up, spoken in one voice and acknowledged its apartheid sins, asking for forgiveness. And now Fatima Meer has the gall to stand up and blame black people for the lack of Indian South African support for the ANC.

This is disgusting to say the least. What Fatima Meer should do is go back to her community, help it do some serious introspection, and then teach it a non-racist way forward instead of pointing fingers and perpetuating the racism in her community by sticking her head and by extension the heads of members of her community in the sand.

Fatima Meer, I think you've got your wires crossed. You and your people are to blame for the lack of Indian South African support for the ANC. Untangle the wires now and get it right.

WHERE'S THE SEARCH PARTY?

I'm sitting at a restaurant having a political discussion with friends when I sort of disagree with one of them on one of the points he makes. He pushes his point forward. I push mine. He pushes some more. I do the same. He stops and says, Eric, while you were tending flowers in the emperor's garden, I was flying in the army as a kamikaze pilot.

Shut up, Eric. I suffered. I got arrested. I was beaten. Who are you to question any political opinion I hold?

I turned around and said to him that he must never pin his decisions on me. I said that when he chose to do what he did, I wasn't there. I said that I will live with my decisions and he must live with his. At one critical time of the struggle, I said, we needed certain skills and it might be that he provided them and, yes, good for him. I said now the struggle has to continue and guess what? It needs different skills and those might not necessarily be flying as a kamikaze pilot. This man maddened me. I could not believe that he now wanted me to be responsible for what he chose to do and at the same time wanted to denigrate what I did because it did not involve being tortured!

A few months later, I'm sitting at another restaurant with a few friends who turn out to have been in the thick of the 80s movement on the wrong side of the apartheid law. One of them ran a whole defence unit in the East Rand. The other fought to hell and back in the Cape Flats. Both of them battle to sit with their backs to the world at restaurants today. Both of them would sooner die, and would fight to the death before they are taken to jail. The police are on our side now, but the psychological scars these two bare won't let them forget what the policemen represented during apartheid because they encountered them first hand in the most brutal of arenas, the political arena. The one tells you how, at fourteen years of age, tied to a chair, a six-foot policeman knocked him unconscious. Eric, he says, I woke up tied to a broken chair and all I could remember was the approaching fist. I was fourteen years old. I was a child. And this is what they did to me. All I wanted was to go home to my mother, to my family. I was a child.

They both have tears in their eyes.

The other says: "I remember the first person I killed." In that sentence you can tell that he remembers every detail on the man's face, all the emotions it represented before he died. He says: "I did these things. I was a teenager. But if I hadn't taken that man out, he would have killed me. But today I have to live with this image. In all the raids my crew and I were involved in, we never lost one member. But they are all dead now. I'm the only one left and all members of that crew died after 1994 because they could not quite adjust to this hostile new South Africa. The 80s took away my innocence, Eric. That's what I hate the most. I never got a chance to be a child like others did because, for me, it was important to fight – the system had to change. Someone had to fight for that to happen and I did."

Both these friends of mine say they did not fight for any political party. They both say that, for them, it was personal. They could not endure the prejudice they experienced on a day-to-day basis and so felt the deep need to fight. They both say they fought for equality. I fought for equality. I fought because whose business was it to say that because my father was classified one race and my mother another they were lesser beings for falling in love? So I fought. We fought. But now that's all I know, says the one.

I have watched both these friends of mine kick at people who want to get close to them. Women take most of this abuse. I feel as though deep down they, these two friends of mine, feel that since their units were all male, females must be weak. But I'm not a psychologist. So all I'll say is that I've seen these men pushing limits, doing ugly things, alienating people as if to test the people's resolve. It's almost as though they are saying, if you can't take the ugliest side of me, don't come any closer. I've seen these scars and they are from deep gashes in the heart of children turned soldiers now struggling to survive in times of "peace".

And then I hear people say these men belong to the lost generation. And so I ask, where is the search party? We never said they were the "dead" generation! We said they were the "lost" generation. And so I ask again, where is the God damn search party?

One of these friends says he went to see a psychologist. The other one laughs like he knows exactly what the other will say. We wait. I went to see a psychologist, he continues. It began as if I were bothered by something trivial that had happened that day. Then it got deeper and I saw that it came from far back in those street-war days. But then I looked up and realised that my psychologist had this freaked-out expression on her face. So I stopped. If she could not handle it, who could? The other friend laughs again, eyes glassy with tears. He knows what the other friend is talking about. He's been there, he says.

I have problems with aggression, Eric. I'm going to lose my son. I'm driving home and I have to suppress this urge to drive off a bridge. I hate myself so much. I swore at my wife this morning. I called my mother and swore at her. I'm angry, Eric, and I must sit here, in the new South Africa, and still hear people call me names, act racist like my suffering was for nothing! I'm hurting, Eric, and I'm angry. Of course, I'm functioning on the outside. I'm achieving. I've got things in control. But let anyone so much as touch me funny when I did not expect it or talk to me in a strange way when I'm angry about something and I'll rip his head off! I'm angry, I hate myself and I don't know what to do. And now I must pay for a psychologist to fix what this country took away!

The other friend leans over and says, concentrate on your son; it will keep you sane. I think about my daughters and it helps. They link arms. Brothers in pain.

President Mbeki has acknowledged the veterans. June 16 is on our holiday calendar. It would heal so many wounds for President Mbeki, for this country, to look to the 80s, go back and embrace the children we lost there. Tell them we love them whatever they have become. Tell them we are thankful for what they have done. Teach them to see the ghosts of their dead friends, sixteen-year-old fighters who died next to them, as friends coming back to thank them for having carried on and won.

Maybe this question should be addressed to the bureaucrats at the South African Youth Commission, after all, we give them SIXTEEN MILLION rand every year to help the youth but WHERE IS THE SEARCH PARTY?

And when you, Mandingo, see a fellow Mandingo twisting in the wind because of this history, try not to be cocky like I was when I was told that I was a gardener when the heat was on. My good friend wasn't saying I'm useless. He was saying that he is in pain. He was saying he can't even have a political opinion go unchallenged despite all his sacrifices for liberation and peace. He was saying he does not get any slack. He has to fight for his space even in conversation, like everyone else. He was hurting.

Try to look and see the pain, Mandingo. Don't be patronising. Be understanding. Let's heal the wounds.

THE "COLOURED" QUESTION

It is late at night or early in the morning, depending on how your body clock works. Mine says it's late at night. I am standing outside what must be the best cocktail bar in the country at the moment, Six, in Melville, Johannesburg. It's an easy late night early morning by all accounts. There is no aggression on the streets, and 2 a.m. is fast approaching, which means Six will soon be closing.

I'm feeling okay.

Then I hear a man say, "Thabo Mbeki is f*&%*ng up!" I'm a little bored and the prospects are low for a wife at Six on this particular night (I'm looking you know!), so I join the discussion. I ask the question: "What has Thabo Mbeki f'ed up?"

"Take the AIDS issue, for instance," the answer comes, "What kind of man denies the link between HIV and AIDS?"

All this is sounding somewhat intelligent, except I do not

205

remember President Mbeki denying the link between HIV and AIDS. I remember him saying there are more people dying of poverty than there are people dying of AIDS. I remember that this statement was not challenged by anyone at the time. Instead, I remember CNN suddenly showing numerous advertisements urging people to lend a hand, donate money or whatever to help alleviate the plight of the poor around the world. Yes, I do remember him saying that the link between HIV and AIDS has yet to be proven scientifically. But I do not remember him saying the link does not exist.

So now the two complainants, two guys, are left a bit stuck as they can't recall for sure either if President Mbeki did or did not say he believes that there is no link between HIV and AIDS. But there are other problems with this government, I'm told. Me, I'm told, as a coloured man, I feel left behind, the new complaint shoots out at me. Nothing has changed for me as a coloured man. I am caught in between my *broer* and nothing has changed for the coloured man.

I ask if they have heard of a guy called Trevor Manuel, last I checked he was a "coloured" man running the South African Finance Ministry. I ask if the brothers have heard of Patricia de Lille, last I checked she had started her own political party, something that no one except a white person would have contemplated, let alone gone ahead and done, less than fifteen years ago. But these are the exceptions to the rule I am told. How many coloured people do I know that are working in government, I'm asked.

Quite a few, I answer, but okay, say you are right, and there aren't enough coloured people in government. We won't go into how many is enough, but tell me this: what about the newly opened constitutional court in Constitution Hill right here in Johannesburg? Is that not for you too? How about you being able to stand here at night in Melville and speak your mind freely without fear of some racist attacking you like they used to in Hillbrow amongst other places back in the day? Does that not mean your life, as a "coloured" man, has improved?

What about affirmative action, the retort comes. The last time I checked, I answer, affirmative action candidates were women of all races, coloureds, Indians and black Africans. But you know that in practice it does not work like that, Eric. Then, I say, that can't be Thabo Mbeki f*%$*ng up, my *broer*! He does not run the companies for which he has helped write the laws. What it means is that the very same people who were the architects and beneficiaries of apartheid are refusing you a chance to move forward. And in any event, why don't you go to the CCMA and register your complaints? It's free for all, including "coloured" people.

Look, Eric, I'm not a racist, *nê*? I have black family. My grandfather was a proud Sotho man. He stayed here by us. I speak Sotho, Zulu, Tswana you name it. This man, he points at his friend, he spends all his time in Soweto. We are not racists, the friend comes in, we have first cousins who are black. Our blood. We are not racist. But believe me when I say to you that, as a "coloured" man, I feel left behind in this new South Africa. Everyone is benefiting but me.

Maybe it's all in your head, I offer. What! Well, I say, maybe you should not hang on so tightly to being "coloured". No, Eric. I will not do that. I'm coloured. That's me. Why should I deny that? Don't deny it, I say, but remember you are human first. When I sit opposite you and I see a man with the same ideals and goals, I will respond better than I would if all I see is a "coloured" man who just happens to have the same ideals and goals as I do. Being "coloured", being "white", being "black" or "Indian", all these categories come with loads of baggage in this country.

If you say I'm a "coloured man", and you push that line hard on me, a black African, I remember phrases like "you must never go back", the "coloured" saying that meant a "coloured" must NEVER marry a black African. The phrase that meant that marrying white was moving forward. That whites are better

207

and so every "coloured" person must aspire to be as white as possible. That blacks are scum and no "coloured" person should want to be anywhere near them. I remember that you called people like me "*kaffir*" because you thought you were white at times. I remember that, in the apartheid hierarchy, you were higher than me and very proud of it. The tag "coloured" comes with certain stereotypical baggage that will definitely hinder your movement amongst black Africans specifically.

But this does not mean you must deny your mixed heritage. It means that like being black, like being white, it is an accident of nature. You did not earn it. And, if it is a curse because of circumstances at the time, you do not deserve it either. It is an accident of nature. Do not wear it like a badge. Wear your humanity like a badge. I have come to learn that perfection in any endeavour shines beyond superficial things like skin colour. When we remember Isaac Newton, we think of gravity. When we remember Phillip Ameagwali, we think of the Internet. When we remember Nelson Mandela, we think of compassion and reconciliation. These people did not run around saying "I am white therefore I am" or "I'm coloured and so I deserve this and that". They simply pursued their true, life callings. That's how they left legacies for the world to use to advance.

The "coloured" person will forever feel marginalised if h/she continues to believe that being "coloured" is a badge of honour, a sign of being better or more important than being human. Our new democratic systems do not differentiate between the different colours. That's why, at some point, the CCMA was clogged with high-level white people seeking justice in the workplace when it was essentially designed to help lower-level workers like domestic servants.

The new South Africa is not for "coloureds". It's not for "whites". It's not for "Indians". It's not for "blacks". The new South Africa is for all of us. You will not get preferential treatment simply because you are "coloured". So forget it, and get on with the business of being human.

THE 2010 BID

I watched the South African delegation present their bid to the executive committee of the Federation of International Football Associations (FIFA) and cried. I know that you might believe that "tigers don't cry", but I don't. And even if it were true that tigers don't cry, I am not a tiger. I am a man. I am a human being. The last time I checked, both the male and female of the animal species to which I belong, the human race, cry to show certain emotions.

I cried because, man, it was a powerful presentation. It began with video visuals giving a brief history of soccer in South Africa and FIFA's involvement in the demise of apartheid. Then Mandela gave a rendition of the hope soccer represented as a link to the outside world for Robben Island political prisoners like himself. Irvin Khoza took the podium next and gave an African-culture-imbued speech about our elders and their mandate to the young South African Soccer World Cup Bid Committee to bring back the World Cup. Then Danny Jordaan presented the technical readiness of our country to host this big event. And on cue came Abedi Pele to pitch the idea that if South Africa hosts the Soccer World Cup, then Africa will be hosting the Soccer World Cup. Now add the physical presence of South Africa's three living Nobel Peace Prize Laureates (Mandela, Tutu and De Klerk) at the presentation, and top that off with President Thabo Mbeki's presentation about the state of South Africa as a country, and you know that this was moving stuff. In a nutshell, I would say the presentation was inspiring, thought provoking, heartfelt and very powerful.

I said this to my friends as I discreetly wiped off my tears when the 2010 Bid Committee finished its presentation within 28 of the allocated 30 minutes: I don't care if we do not host the 2010 Soccer World Cup, we showed class out there. As far as I was concerned, we had played on one of the biggest stages and showed unbelievable class. Every African who witnessed that presentation would have been absolutely proud and that's a good thing because shackles often begin to break with the banking of beautiful moments of pride. You are freer if you simply have more happy memories of pride. God knows, we Africans need many of those to raise our heads up high and really make this the African century. For the non-African who truly believes that we are good-for-nothing souls waiting for hand outs or whatever racist term s/he chooses to describe the likes of us, the presentation was a beautiful display of the opposite of what this bigot believes and a true eye opener. We were good out there.

Then I caught Danny Jordaan on television talking about how we had pulled this thing off. And he said, well, the president, meaning President Thabo Mbeki, came on board and asked us who was going to be presenting the bid to the FIFA executive committee. On hearing the list, he said, well, you can't not have Madiba, so tell him I'd like for him to go with you. If we are saying South Africa wants to host the Soccer World Cup 2010 for the benefit of all Africans, added the president, then you must also include in your presentation either Roger Mila, Abedi Pele, George Weah or any of the African supporters you have on the team who are not South African. Then, Danny Jordaan continued, the president asked where Archbishop Tutu was. On being told that the Archbishop was in Canada, the president said, tell him to come too, I'm bringing De Klerk. Then the president read everyone's presentation notes and made corrections. Finally, said the president of South Africa, the big man himself, the leading light in world politics today, President Thabo Mbeki, he said, when it's question and answer time, I will answer all the questions. And so it came to pass that we had a winning presentation that brought tears to my eyes.

It did not occur to me then, but it has now as I write, that I don't think that in the entire history of Soccer World Cup Bids for this prestigious event that there has ever been a president of a country who was personally involved with the bid all the way to the actual presentation in order for that country to win the bid.

That makes me sad.

Believe me when I say I think President Mbeki's move to get involved was a masterstroke. I think what he brought to that final stretch was absolute genius, as you can tell from the list above. But I also know that his involvement was a big part of that edge we had over the likes of Morocco, which, by the way, is alleged to have won France's vote on the day. This means that even when it's Africans alone competing, the West (the North to us), custodian of international soccer, will only look at us if our strongest, our best, our busiest are willing to dance to their tune. They still believe that we are small. That's sad and maybe subconsciously some of my tears were for that reason. I would rather believe that some things, like soccer, are beneath my president. But gosh, we need the capital injection more than most. Africa still has to prove to the world its equal status among other continents. And so our best and busiest must find the time to make these points.

And so I am reminded of Patrick Fitzgerald's keynote address at the launch of the book *Voices of the Transition*: How can we have done so much and yet have so much more to do? It's tiring just thinking about this question, but Mandela said it best: at the top of one mountain is a quick view of how many more there are to climb. So, Mandingo, in the words of Ice Cube's character towards the end of the movie *Dangerous Ground*: Don't fall asleep. Stay awake and recognise that we have a long way to go.

Know too, Mandingo, that we will get there. We did not come this far to sit and be passed by or to go backwards. We came this far to go further.

TO VOTE OR NOT TO VOTE – WHAT AN INTERESTING QUESTION

In 1994, when every South African who could was queuing to vote for the first time in a free and democratic South Africa soon to be devoid of apartheid rule, I was shooting a movie called *Nice To Meet You. Please Don't Rape Me*. South African-born,

Dutch-trained, multi-award-winning filmmaker Ian Kerkhof*
was in town. The movie we chose to make as our fellow
countrypersons queued for what seemed like an eternity to get to
that voting heaven, was to depict apartheid South Africa as the
worst form of human rape documented in history. I don't want
to get into a my-horror-is-worse-than-yours territory here, but
this was not a sudden burst of hateful murder that lasted a few
years of brutality. It was a systematic generational genocide of an
innocent people that lasted for decades after previous centuries
of colonial brutality that set it off in the first place. Some of us
South Africans are still walking zombies from the scourge of
this lengthy oppression.

I made the conscious decision not to vote in 1994. Aside from
my seemingly inborn tendency to never go where the crowd
goes, my decision was based on simple logic. I had almost
screamed and jumped high when I heard De Klerk announce
that the ANC had been unbanned. I had heard a lot about the
ANC and its achievements with De Klerk's announcement of its
unbanning as its biggest up to that point. I loved that movement
with all my heart as I do today, even though I have never been
a card-carrying member in its ranks. But deep down I knew, as
I know today, that power changes people in unimaginable ways.
The ANC, I figured, is run by people. When I looked deeper,
I realised I did not know these people. Apartheid had been so
good at keeping me in the dark that I had to work on faith and
take a chance with my first ballot. I never do that. I was not
about to start in 1994 simply because the hype was wonderful
and Madiba, the godfather of peace and reconciliation as we
know him today, had walked free and tall four years earlier.
After all, I quietly reasoned in my soul, freedom also means
freedom not to vote. If the ANC messed things up like many
freedom movements before it on our beloved continent did, I

*Ian Kerkhof has now changed his name to Aryan Kaganof.

would not be complicit; I would reserve my right to criticise. I felt really free.

It's ten years down the line. I have had the unbelievable privilege of sharing a room with Joel Netshitendze (head of the Government Communications and Information Systems, commonly known as GCIS), Gill Marcus (Deputy Governor of the Reserve Bank), Pallo Jordan (Member of Parliament), Smuts Ngonyama (ANC spokesperson) and I recorded our president, Thabo Mbeki, after listening to him change only absolutely vital details in a script for the ANC's election campaign. I feel ashamed for not having had faith in 1994 and going against my natural instinct to wait on the sidelines before diving in. These people taught me in a few sessions how a committee of people can make vital decisions in record time and not make a single mistake. They taught me that the African instinct towards communal decision-making is efficient and alive amongst their ranks. They taught me how to groom leaders as I watched them bring young people into vital meetings and hear them out completely before coming in with much-needed wisdom where necessary or agreeing fully when the youngster was right. Before I had the amazing privilege of watching these leaders of ours in action, I remember asking my uncle, Professor Shepherd Malusi Mayatula, an MP, back in 1995 why the ANC government had turned down US$300 million offered by the Japanese to build hospitals and I was told that, okay, Eric, let's take the money and build the hospitals, where is the money to run them going to come from? What about all the medicinal stock for the patients, how will we pay for that? And how will we pay for staff to man the hospitals? No, Eric, he said, we will concentrate on primary health care to stop people from needing to go to a hospital instead of concentrating on areas that make pharmaceutical companies rich and people weak by intervening too late.

It's 2004 and the tenth year of this beautiful democracy of ours and the question gets asked all the time. What have we gained? People are dying of AIDS! The poor are still poor.

In fact, Economics professors like Sampie Terreblanche argue convincingly, aided by no less a prominent figure than our president's very own brother, Moeletsi Mbeki, that the gap between the rich and poor is at its widest in our history as a country, even as blacks enter the moneyed areas in record numbers today. Trade unions are crying foul because jobs are supposedly being lost in record numbers in certain industries while others, like advertising, remain racist and lily white. What have we gained?

I'm sitting at a coffee shop in Melville and I watch a little van with two white men pull to a stop and accost a black man who is standing with a cloth in his hand on the pavement. It looks very rough, like he will get the beating of his life. They talk to him. I see guns pushing out of their bums. They look like bums themselves. Scruffy. Spoiling for a fight. They get on their cellular phones. Then back in their car marked Crime Stop. The black man walks half a block down the road. The car races towards him again. Threateningly. They fling their doors open. Rush him. The black man doesn't run. He quietly asserts his authority. They circle him. He folds his arms and quietly answers their questions. They get back into their car and drive off. I go up to him and ask what the whole thing was about. In Sotho, he says they want to know what I'm doing on the street. I told them I'm waiting to find cars to wash. They say I must get off. I told them this is public property. They asked for my ID. I told them I don't carry it even though I have one, in any event no policeman has ever asked me for one even though they pass me here all the time. In the end, they said I must not stand in front of that corner shop and he points at it. I look at this brother and smile. Then I tell him he must not worry because we are also watching out for him. He smiles back.

And so I tell you, Mandingo, we have gained the ability to walk and talk with pride. We have gained the amazing feeling that comes from knowing that we too are protected. Even with nothing, we have gained the ability to assert ourselves, quietly, firmly, and win with pride even when hooligans try to bully us off state property. We can be anything we want to be. With this democracy, beyond the sky is our limit.

Come April 14, I am casting my ballot. After all, there is nothing more dangerous than a complacent populace in a democracy. Ask any bright American and he will confirm this.

XENOPHOBIA: A FATHER AND SON CONVERSE

Dumisani says:

You didn't only curb my craving, you outdid yourself. Dad you're quite a piece of work. This week's article was too tight. I'm still trying to "recover", if that's the right word to use. It just blew my mind away. Guess what I'm gonna be doing on April 14 this year! I knew from the beginning that it wasn't a mistake to register, but now you have just removed all available doubt. All praise to democracy and those who fight to maintain it.

Here's one funny thing that I've encountered on my journey of discoveries here at the University of Cape Town (UCT). The majority of the foreign students here that I'm friends with, and their friends, seem to have a serious dislike for South Africa. It seems that South African xenophobia has resulted in reverse hatred for us by the rest of Africa. These guys say that it is the general feeling in their respective countries. There's quite a number of them too: Zimbabweans, Nigerians, Malawians, Zambians, Kenyans and Ghanaians, to name a few. The feeling among these students is that South Africa has set itself aside from the rest of Africa and thinks that it's better than every other African country. Apparently we behave like the America of the continent in the sense that we don't give a hoot about what is going on in the rest of Africa, just the way the US behaves with regards to the rest of the world.

I think this is a worrying factor. It's gone so bad that they are even wishing for South Africa to collapse after a few years.

Back to the main issue, that's why it's so important that we maintain our democracy, not only for our own good, but also to show to the rest of Africa that it is entirely possible. Set the tone, so to speak.

Another thing that I think we as South Africans need to ask ourselves is this: how good is this "wonderful" democracy of ours really if we can't share it with our fellow African brothers and sisters in pure harmony? The same brothers and sisters we relied so much on when we were struggling to get it, the same brothers and sisters who were more than willing to grant a helping hand in our time of need. Do we now just turn our backs on them and say we have achieved our goals, so you guys must all just go fly?

And the father says:

What is worrying, son, is how myopic and ill-informed people who are at a learning institution can be. Today's South Africa is the leading light in African politics. We have been instrumental in helping to resolve internal upheavals in the Democratic Republic of Congo and in Burundi; we helped in the processes that led to Charles Taylor stepping down in Liberia to stop the situation there from becoming intractable; we assisted in resolving the civil war in Ivory Coast, we helped stop a coup in Guinea Bissau recently, even though 60 of the soldiers who were going to get involved are black South Africans. We have never used force except against Lesotho early on in our democracy, and learned that it was wrong to do so. We are in the forefront of the African Union to make sure democracy is respected across the continent. We are pushing hard inside NEPAD to make sure that all of Africa prospers economically. We are not bullies. On the contrary, we have done most of these things through encouraging dialogue as opposed to enforcing our way, like the bully America does. Whenever we negotiate with the West on behalf of our country, we insist that they make the same concessions for the countries around us, like we did with the trade agreement we were fighting for between Europe and ourselves a few years back. Our foreign policy has been underpinned by the thinking that a prosperous South Africa that is surrounded by poor countries with miserable citizens is not sustainable. This is the exact opposite of how America and most Western countries think.

Your friends' criticisms of us with regards to our involvement in Africa are unfounded and based on an inability to assess facts properly. This is utterly worrying because these are people at a university for goodness' sake, where your ability to look at facts and assess them properly is supposed to be at its sharpest!

One can argue that the things I have listed in the first paragraph, which go to how hard South Africa is working to sort out not only our problems but those of the entire continent, as well, are our "thank you" for all the years when we were hosted by other African countries in exile. We haven't turned our back on the continent. We are working together with other continental leaders to make the lives of all Africans better.

The thing about xenophobia is that, as bad as it is, it is not unique to South Africa. If you ask any South African who was in exile in the rest of Africa, they will give you all the derogatory terms used to describe them and emphasise their foreigner status. That does not make it right. But a mature individual who is hosted in a foreign country should expect and accept that this is going to happen, especially on a continent like Africa where people are still fighting to find their space, their food and economic freedom.

Your friends should start by being grateful for what we are doing to help on the continent and for hosting them as we are doing now. Having said that, there is no reason for us South Africans not to realise, accept and be happy with the fact that these are our brothers and sisters. That together we must work to make Africa great. There is no reason for us to be arrogant and insulting and disrespectful. We should never be xenophobic. There is nothing harder than being away from home and I don't know anyone who has done so voluntarily and does not wish to go back at some point.

What your friends must realise, though, is that unfounded and ungrounded criticisms, like the ones they are levelling against us, can easily fuel xenophobia.

Dumisani is Eric Miyeni's son, among other things more important.

THE REAL OPPOSITION STANDS UP WHEN IT MATTERS

I remember sitting at a coffee shop called La Copa in the then hip Johannesburg suburb of Yeoville some years back and listening to this teenager moan. She was a bit upset about the hullabaloo that every older South African black person seems to make about June 16. She kept saying, why are we dwelling in the past? Why can't we just grow up, look to the future and move on? So what if there was a June 16 whenever there was one, she was saying, let's move on okay, now!

I looked at this pretty black girl and mustered as much self-control as I could to stay calm and then I addressed her. I said to her that on June 16 in 1976 when I was ten years old some people got killed and families lost their loved ones, many of whom were at an age as young as hers. I said there were people living today who were stuck in wheelchairs because they got shot on that day. I told her that, for her, what is relevant is that these martyrs, who lost so much on that day, went out on a limb so that today she can be free to say whatever she wants, including saying that June 16 celebrations are a waste of time. And she can say that without fear of negative repercussions. They fought and gave up all that they gave up so that she could be truly free. I said that's why we remember.

Move up to 2002 and I'm sitting at a coffee shop in the now hip white Johannesburg suburb of Melville and listening to a young black man who has taken an important position at the now black-run South African Broadcasting Corporation (SABC). This young black man tells me that he does not care who walks through the door into his important office where he decides which programmes are good enough for the SABC to develop. "If it's s**t, I tell you it's s**t," he tells me. He then tells me that he's not saying this because I'm sitting with him, it's a fact, he says, that the award-winning television series I acted in called *Molo Fish* is s**t!

I ask him what he thinks is good on television. He tells me that the black soap opera *Generations* is s**t. So is *Ezodumo*, he tells me. In fact, he tells me, some black people came to his office and tried to renew this s**t traditional music programme and he told them it was s**t. No offence, he tells me, but s**t is s**t and he is not going to mince his words telling you this whether you are black or white. Basically, he said, there is no colour to this issue, s**t is s**t and *Ezodumo* is s**t. Period! Then he answers my question. He tells me that the only good thing on television is *The Bold and the Beautiful*, the American soap opera.

I found myself back three to four years ago again, mustering my self-control in order to address this young black man as I did that teenage girl. I said, you know, my brother, you are in that important office today, deciding what is s**t or not s**t because people who could not read, people who just knew apartheid had to go, people who came before you, fought and fought hard. Without them, Peter Matlare would not be heading the SABC and you, my brother, would not be deciding what programme is good enough for the SABC and what programme is not. Then I asked him these questions: don't you think you owe it to these ordinary people with no experience, just like you, to spend a little more time explaining politely what was wrong with their presentations so that they can be encouraged to pitch better products to you in the future? Don't you think you owe it to the people who put you in that office to spend more time nurturing potential black talent as opposed to killing it at birth?

He did not agree that he owed anyone anything. He said as far as he is concerned s**t is s**t and that was that. As an example of how much power he has, he told me that he was yanking *Ezodumo* off the air because the black people who came to present to him presented s**t and he was not going to let that programme carry on being aired simply because these people were black. I said I see. And walked away with this bitter taste in my mouth.

And then the weirdest thing happened. About two days later, I heard on the news that the head of SABC 1, Mr Romeo Khumalo, the boss of the young man who does not take s**t, had met with one of the musicians' organisations, was sorry about the *Ezodumo* misunderstanding and that not only would this programme be back on air but it would, in due course, have double the time allocation it had had previously. Then he added that SABC 1 as a whole would cut down on foreign music videos to play more local ones. I thought about that young black man and didn't know whether to laugh out loud, cry like a baby or do both at the same time.

Some claim that South Africa has the strongest minority opposition in Tony Leon and his cronies. I'll give them that because on the surface it seems that way. I'll say *ja*, Tony is vocal and visible because of all that strong Jewish Rand. But he's not the real opposition. He's just trying to halt the country from moving forward in order to keep money in the old hands that apartheid placed it in – the Oppenheimers, the Ellerines and so on and so forth. At least, that's what I believe. So those who think Tony Leon is the opposition are truly mistaken in my opinion. They are missing the point.

The opposition in South Africa has always been the people who laboured under more than three hundred and fifty years of colonial racist rule in this country, the people who faced bullets in Sharpeville those many decades back, the people who took bullets in the chest in 1976. And it will continue to be that for a long time to come. The opposition in this country is what the opposition should be in any strong democracy, the people. President Thabo Mbeki is no one without the backing of the ordinary citizens of this country. This country has no future without the true fulfilment of the ordinary citizens of this country. And when it matters, these ordinary people rise up and rise high to stop the monsters that can eat up our hard-won freedoms. It is such a pity that sometimes the people that these ordinary citizens put up to serve us mistake their positions as platforms of abuse.

And so I say to you, Mandingo, if you believe that you have an important position today, wherever you might be positioned, remember those who put you there. Remember that, when it matters, they will rise up to stop your progress in order to save the progress of the country from being halted. Don't take them for granted. Be humble and let them carry you shoulder high to achieve what they put you there to achieve. And always give back to them with humility whether or not you think what they bring to you is s**t. And, yes, criticise any holiday you want to criticise, including June 16, but remember who made it possible for you to do that freely in this country.

That's it, Mandingo. Reach for the stars but keep your feet firmly on the ground. This is one of the most important principles of *ubuntu*. Live by it.

DECAPITATION

Ahmed Khalfan Ghailani has been caught. This man is under suspicion of being the mastermind behind the massive synchronised bombings of the US embassies in Kenya and Tanzania. Those blasts took 224 lives. Many of those killed were Tanzanian and Kenyan. They had nothing to do with the war between al-Qaeda and the United States of America. At the time of these blasts, I likened this act to someone who comes to visit your house and then starts beating up his wife there. This horrific picture does not come close to defining the kind of mischief this Ahmed Khalfan Ghailani is alleged to have perpetrated in those two African countries. For it to get close on a tiny scale, this man would then have to beat up you and your family in the process of beating up his wife in your house. What this Ghailani character is alleged to have done is the highest form of disrespect, in my opinion.

But it doesn't end there.

I look at what is happening in the Middle East. I look at the form of apartheid that the Israelis continue to impose on their Palestinian fellow countrymen and women. I look at the hatred that is dissolving that part of the world. And I'm sickened to the core. I am sickened by the number of Palestinian deaths orchestrated by the Israelis in the name of security. I am sickened by the number of decrees of hate issued by a succession of Israeli Prime Ministers against their Palestinian cousins because of fear. But the hardest thing for me to say right now is that I am also sickened by the number of children who are blowing themselves up to fight this Israeli terror. It doesn't matter how many times I hear people say Israel has one of the largest stashes of nuclear weapons in the world, that she has the third-biggest army in the world and that the poor Palestinians have no choice since they do not, like Israel, have the backing of an America, a superpower. I am still sickened to the core by the vision of a person seeking to be heard and so blowing themselves up and spreading his or her body little piece of flesh by little piece of bone.

And so I look to Iraq. Saddam Hussein was no good to anyone, least of all his own people. It is agreed that he had to go. Alas, the people behind the war to topple him have no integrity. They falsified intelligence. They lied to their own constituencies and to the rest of the world. They hid their true motives behind some thinly veiled desire for peace and democracy for the people of Iraq. And then they bombed them to smithereens. Talk about an oxymoron – a war for peace. This too sickens me. A world where profit rules over proper values. A world where pushing up the value of any commodity your company is involved in, be it oil, weapons of war, computers or gold, rules above anything else.

And so I am sickened by the whole northern invasion of Iraq. I look at Tony Blair and George W. Bush and all the other key players in that unnecessary war and it takes a great effort to stop myself from throwing up. And so I understand the Iraqi uprising. I empathise with the Iraqi people's need to get rid of these modern-day economic colonisers. But you know what? It is even harder for me to hold down the urge to throw up when I read about the decapitation of American soldiers by Iraqi freedom fighters.

I do not want a part of either side of these conflicts I have described.

And then I look to South Africa and I think you know what? These people could learn from us. First of all, it took decades before our main liberation movement, the African National Congress, moved away from peaceful protest and resorted to violent uprising as a form of protest against the oppressor. And when the resolution was passed, it took more debate to conclude that there would be no soft targets in the armed struggle. It took a lot of discipline, but the direction taken was that we were not fighting individuals, we were fighting a system of oppression. Most important of all, we decided that we were never going to be like or worse than the enemy. The thinking was simple. If you are fighting for good, you will do no evil at all and, if you must do evil, then you will do as little of it as is humanly possible. This very same thinking was responsible for bringing us from the brink of all-out civil strife when Chris Hani, that man of the people, that genius of a leader, was shot dead on the precipice of our takeover from the apartheid oppressor machine. A nation that had been trained earlier could listen and, with discipline, literally let the dark cloud pass when Mandela stood up and said we shall not be derailed from our need for peace, we shall not be taken off the course of good for the betterment of every life on this precious piece of land. The perpetrators would be found and punished, but the country would move forward in preparation for a better tomorrow. And so it came to pass.

I am absolutely certain that the support the struggle against apartheid obtained from around the world came from the simple feeling deep inside every supporter that apartheid was bad but what the ANC would replace it with was good. The prosperity that South Africa is building for her people is supported by the

223

good angels because out here we really do want everyone to have a good life, whatever their background. Countless visitors to these shores have proclaimed that, despite all our problems, they feel an immense sense of goodness here. I want to suggest that it is because we truly do believe in a better world for all who live in it.

When you order your soldiers to literally break the hands of the enemy captives, as one of the Israeli prime ministers did, it creates bad blood and escalates the chances of no end to war. When you send children to blow themselves up as a sign of protest against this evil, you arouse little sympathy from people who might actually believe in your cause. You scare off potential allies. When you bomb a people on the pretext that you want peace, you sicken everyone in the end because people absolutely hate being taken for morons and being lied to. And who amongst us would stand next to a man who just decapitated another for whatever cause and could say, with a smile on his or her face, "This is my brother"?

When you go to a neutral country, kill and maim its innocent citizens in order to get to your enemy with a bomb, well, you are just evil and disrespectful. How can anyone give you support after that?

THE PRICE OF AID

A friend of mine, Jihan El Tahri, made a remarkable documentary film. It's called *The Price of Aid*. The South African Broadcast Corporation (SABC) hemmed and hawed before finally deciding maybe it's not a great idea to screen it! Having seen it, I'm getting more and more convinced that, skewed criticism from the likes of the strangely bitter Max du Preez (creator and editor of that late great newspaper *Vrye Weekblad*) aside, all is not well at the faulty towers, as another friend of mine calls the SABC headquarters. But that's another story. For now, let me give you the lessons denied you by the SABC in *The Price of Aid*.

The Price of Aid is a film that looks, as the title suggests, at what it costs a poor country to accept aid from agencies like USAid. In a nutshell, Jihan follows a bag of donated maize from the donor country all the way to the recipient. The story begins in Zambia where out of nine provinces one is suffering from chronic drought and has no harvests. The country then approaches international donor agencies for help to move food from the north of Zambia where there's plenty to the south where there's a shortage. The country is told that in order for the wheel of aid to be cranked up to help, it must declare a state of emergency. Zambia promptly does this and the wheel is cranked up and tons of maize from America via USAid are placed at the ready to be sent to Zambia. When the Zambians say no, hang on, we do not need foreign maize in the country, we just need transport to move our own maize to the province in need, the powers-that-be say, look, Zambia, we can't move YOUR maize. The only way we can help you is the cheapest way and that is to move maize in from the United States of America. By the way, beggars can't choose how they get helped.

So tons of maize are flown into Zambia. The result is an over-supply of free maize. Local Zambian farmers begin to suffer as their market is almost completely annihilated by this free over-supply. Remember, no matter how low your price, you cannot compete with free. Some farmers even begin to take and sell the free maize. Corruption sets in. By the time the Zambians look up, their entire maize-farming industry is almost totally destroyed. When they look deeper, they discover that the maize that is creating all this havoc and pushing their economy even further down is genetically modified and they were not even told. But like a blessing in disguise, they go to the UN and stop this US-driven aid by telling the world that the true impact of genetically modified food is yet to be known and they do not want Zambians to be guinea pigs.

The Americans are aghast and upset. Now surely you want to ask yourself if someone you are helping turns around and says they do not need your help anymore, you would rejoice as a burden would be lifted off your shoulders, wouldn't you? So why were these Americans upset?

As it turns out, US farmers have, for the longest time, been over-producing maize and other farm produce. Now, can you imagine these farmers burning the surplus food they harvest while so many people in the world starve? Of course not. So they came up with this scam called USAid. What USAid is masquerading as is a food donor vehicle for the world. Oh, my gosh, there are people starving in Zambia, don't worry, call USAid. That sort of thing. What USAid really is is a dumping mechanism for America's surplus produce. Everything that USAid handles must be US produced, US packaged, US transported, US everything. It's a multibillion US$ machine that keeps US people in jobs that probably should have been made redundant by now but haven't. Every year USAid tries to "predict" where the next food crisis is going to be, estimates the cost and lobbies the US government for money to buy all this surplus produce from US farmers in order to dump it in the poor crisis-riddled spot in the world. No crisis, no budget. No budget, no purchasing of surplus American produce. No purchasing of surplus American produce, well, I guess you are back to square one and having to consider burning food! God forbid! Now tell me this, how long before USAid has to create crisis spots around the world to carry out its true mandate of buying all this extra American food to dump on other nations?

And so you come to understand why when Zambia said we need help transporting food to one province only out of nine, the country was told sorry we can only bring loads of maize in. It's the only way. That's why the country was forced to declare an emergency. How else can you provide aid, USAid, if there is no serious crisis? And how can you bring in as much as possible if there is no crisis? The emphasis being, of course, on the words "as much as possible".

Now consider that the US government continues to subsidise its farmers and refuses to let go of this destructive and outdated practice while at the same time insisting that other smaller nations, like South Africa, should not even consider it and you get to see the devil in the mix. You get to see the full stupidity of partisan politics. Logically, considering how much these American farmers over produce, you would think it necessary to stop the subsidies and pull back this over-production, wouldn't you? You would think it prudent to stop creating and sustaining incentive schemes like USAid for these farmers, wouldn't you? But no, says the US. The farming lobby is too strong. You might lose the next election if you do this. The best thing is to create markets abroad, you see. And aid is the perfect entry point just like the bible was in times gone by.

So what is the true price of aid? When they say it's free, are they speaking the truth? Well, as the Zambians quickly found out, the price of aid is very, very high. First of all these bags of USAid maize that they finally blocked through their objection to GM seeds, had no seed. So to plant them, as your own seed would have been killed by the abundance of this new "free" maize that was flooded into your market, you'd have to buy the seed every year from the company that owns the patent to its genetic modification. As one Zambian minister pointed out in the documentary, it might be a matter of time before your debt to the seed-owning company prompted it to come and claim all the land on which you planted its patented crop!

But when you pay too high a price for freebies, whose fault is it? Here I would like to relate two stories. The first one happened in about 1994/95 or thereabouts. I read in the paper that the South African government had turned down US$300 million, yes, US$300 million, from the Japanese who were giving it for the construction of clinics in rural areas. I phoned one of the newly ensconced government officials I knew at the time and asked, what's going on? Can you explain this? I mean everyone knows we need hospitals in rural areas! Very calmly, my uncle, Shepherd Mayatula, a man who has not one, but two Masters degrees in economics, said to me, Eric, say we take this money and build these clinics. Where are the medicines going to come from? Where is the manpower to man these clinics

227

going to come from? And on and on the list continued, what about the cost of maintaining these structures… Then he said, Eric, at this stage we think it best to preach primary health care because if people do not fall unnecessarily sick then we do not need hospitals, do we?

The next story unfolds in 1997/98, or thereabouts. I'm traveling in my car and as usual I am tuned to PM Live on SAfm when the then South African Minister of Health, Nkosazana Zuma, is being grilled for turning down, funnily enough, US$300 million, which was earmarked to help us with the HIV/AIDS epidemic. I remember the minister saying no, we did not turn down the 300 million that was offered. We told the donors that we are first going to look at our own HIV/AIDS programme and if the conditions attached to this "donation" fit well with that programme, then we will accept it. If I'm not mistaken, on the basis of this "first check if it fits" approach, the donation was pulled back and the South African white media went mad for a while.

There are at least two lessons in these stories. One, always look deep into the future to see if what is free today is truly free. Second, always have your own programme, because the programmes that "free" aid come with are not necessarily designed for you. As the Zambians discovered to their dismay, for instance, USAid is designed for US farmers and related industries. It is not designed for Zambians, or any starving nations for that matter.

This is not to say that there are no crisis points that come around in the world from time to time. The point I'm making is that often a crisis is an opening for your destroyer to move in, cloaked as a benefactor. A true sign that you have this kind of devil in the mix is when what appears to be a small hiccup is blown out of all proportion, as in the case of Zambia. Be careful. This is not to say that we should never accept help no matter what. The point, rather, is to say, take your time. It doesn't matter whether you are a country or an individual. It's a hard world out there. Take a good look at the hand that feeds you before you feed. This is not to say that there aren't people and countries out there that really mean well. Rather it is to say, have a test to see if they really do mean well. A good test is what we might want to call the Dlamini-Zuma Test; first come up with a programme to deal with your crisis, identify where you need outside help and if those who offer to help agree that their help must fit your programme, then voilà, as the French might say, you have your well-meaning donor.

FREE AT LAST, FREE AT LAST, WHITE SOUTH AFRICANS ARE FREE AT LAST!

Something extraordinary has happened in South Africa. White South Africans are beginning to dance with rhythm and dress with panache!

There was a time when style was the domain of the dispossessed black South African who, to bolster his/her self image, would go to phenomenal lengths to end up with that R2 000 pair of shoes, R250 pair of pants and that R100 button-down shirt to match. And that's not mentioning the R500 London Fog lumber jacket! I'm talking back when the rand bought US$2! Back when if your South African white male had a safari suit on, long socks to match and a comb in the socks above the *velskoene*, he felt like he was the walking epitome of fashion and the ladies, white ladies, thought, wow, what a man! White man.

Today everywhere I look in Johannesburg, Cape Town, Durban, gee, just about in every South African city, there are white people dressed beautifully. I'm talking real expensive, real stylish. Man! They are styling! Miles away from those floral dresses with the floral hats to match and white shoes with white pantyhose to finish the look. Or those grey suits with grey unpolished shoes to match the grey tie and finish off the white shirt if it wasn't brown. Disgusting. Now, by any fashion Mecca standard, they are styling. From Diesel casual wear to Hugo Boss formal wear. The hippie alternatives amongst them with the uncouth ponytails and dirty, real dirty jeans are like a relic now, a real throwback. Embarrassing. White South Africans are dressing to the hilt to kill. And they are dancing to the beat!

Now, say you had a boss and he said you could wear anything to work that you liked and you looked in your wardrobe and just found one pair of pants and a shirt. You would think your boss was nice, but that's where it would end, isn't it, because regardless of the freedom afforded you, you couldn't exercise it. At times you might even wish he hadn't given you that freedom because all it really did was highlight how little choice you had when it came to clothes. It's almost like a back-handed slap in the face. It's a complete paradox. You are told to fly free and far when you know for a fact that you have no wings.

By this measure and by God, white South Africans are free. They have the know-how, so they can fly anywhere in the world since their black counterparts made the South African passport sexy all over planet Earth. They have the money, so they can buy the best of all fashion since their black counterparts opened our country up to the rest of the world's top fashion houses. Almost all of them are literate, so they understand all the rights enshrined in the constitution that their black counterparts fought and died to put in place for all South Africans. And they exercise those rights with vigour. At one stage the CCMA, which was primarily established to help your lower-level workers such as domestic servants get justice in the workplace, had over 60% of all disputes involving free, white and literate South Africans fighting for their rights in top-level positions! The waiting list was over six months! Presumably, if they had the patience to wait their turn in this long white queue, all domestic workers with a gripe against an employer would eventually get justice.

The bottom line is that white South Africans have the money and black South Africans took the embarrassing apartheid monkey off their backs. So, without guilt, without remorse and with at least as much fear as any black South African with possessions experiences, they are coming out and looking good. Their hips are looser than ever before, so they are finding it easier to rock to a rhythm. They are free at last.

On the other hand, however, black South Africans have exactly the same rights protected by the same courts and constitution as whites. But most of us are illiterate, so we battle to understand our freedoms. We are mostly very poor, so we can't afford to fight for our freedoms when those freedoms are being violated. The HIV/AIDS virus is playing havoc with our potential. We are like that guy who is free to wear anything to work, but only has one outfit. Our circumstances still oppress us. So our freedom deliverance is yet to come. At the moment it's more like "Still in chains, still in chains. Oh my God! Black South Africans are still in chains"!

Where are we going with this? Let's start by describing where we are not going. We do not want white South Africans to be miserable. There is nothing more beautiful to watch than a human being with a swagger in his/her stride. I personally love watching how beautiful white South Africans have become, how sophisticated, the radiance in their midst even though they themselves often don't see how lucky and privileged they are. I absolutely love their newly found dress sense, their love for the gym and overall healthy living, the clean faces, the big smiles. I love that, in every white party I attend, there are more and more white people who can dance to the beat of the song and not ahead of it. It's like a positive energy being unleashed. God knows, this country needs tons of the stuff. So, no, white misery is not where we are going with this.

What we want is to spread this beautiful energising spirit to the rest of our beloved South Africa. Black joy in addition to white joy is where we are going with this. We don't even have to be friends. But together, we want to stop AIDS in its tracks. We want the maximum majority of all South Africans to move above the poverty line and stay there. We want a 90% to 100% literacy rate for the whole country. We want a healthy South Africa that is robust and full of energy because the large majority of people have the money, the know-how and the ability to exercise and protect all the rights they fought together for and died for and then negotiated to avoid a blood bath.

We want all South Africans to sing together and apart: "Free at last, free at last, thank God we're ALL free at last"!

SAVIMBI IS DEAD!

He is dead. And I wish I could simply raise my glass and go "Chin Chin" like most people did when they heard the news. And then stopped. And then did it again when they started to believe he was really dead. And stopped again when doubts set in. And then went "Chin! Chin!" Again. This time with utter certainty, as Savimbi's body was displayed across the world, before he was given a pauper's funeral. But looking at that picture of his body in the paper, on television, on the Internet and everywhere it was splashed across the globe, covered in blood, dead – I could only feel a deep wave of sadness come over me. After all, Savimbi is yet another African black man who died at the hands of other African black men. When will the killing stop?

After thirty years of fighting, you seldom remember what you started the fighting for in the first place. Often, you just carry on because all you remember is that you must win. You lose focus. The people in Sudan will tell you they have religious war for territorial advantage. The people in Somali might tell you that, well, you know, fighting is a way of life now. The people in the Democratic Republic of Congo will tell you something else. You and I might argue that it is an economic thing. Someone might say no, it is colonialism's legacy. But do you really believe that these people really know what the fight is about? I would like to offer that, after some time, the fighting is the only point. And that is the saddest truth about stupid brother-on-brother violence.

But now that Savimbi is gone, will the northerners in Angola show some respect for the southerners? Will the people of Angola who speak Angolan indigenous languages like Umbumdu, Kikongo and Kibumdu speak these languages without being laughed at by the northerners in Luanda where

Dos Santos is from? Are the Portuguese-created problems, such as the Kibumdus' (Dos Santos' language) belief that they are far superior to the Umbumdus (Savimbi's language) and therefore should rule no matter what, fueling the staying power of Savimbi's rebellion, going to be addressed? Will the fighting stop? Or will MPLA continue with what some Angolans regard as the genocide of Umbumdus, like it did after the 1992 elections when even those Umbumdus inside the MPLA were murdered?

For an answer, we can look at other African conflicts. When the Americans took Delta, their most elite fighting squad, into Somalia, they thought all they had to do was kidnap Mohamed Farah Aideed, the then chief warlord in that country. This was going to be a one-week operation. Six weeks later they were still at it when they embarked on what they thought would be a 30-minute operation to end all their operations in that country. They entered Aideed's stronghold. More than 18 hours later they were running back to base on foot. Defeated. They had lost 19 members of their elite squad and 2 of their most advanced and expensive war helicopters. As you might know, just like they failed in Mexico and more recently in Afghanistan, the Americans did not catch Mohamed Farah Aideed. But guess what? Mohamed Farah Aideed is dead now. Somalia took care of this without outside help. But a war rages on in Somalia, and Africa is bearing the brunt of this mindlessness. As a matter of fact, Aideed's son is now one of the chief warlords there. The fighting continues.

Did you not think that, with Mobutu Sese Seko gone, the Democratic Republic of Congo would take its place in the world among other economic giants? Instead, what do we have? The fiasco at Sun City that is rumoured to have cost about R1 million a day with no solution in sight is what we have! Should Tsvangirai even consider the murder of Mugabe to sort out Zimbabwe? Should South Africa strong-arm its neighbours to get its regional stability? I think not. Remember Lesotho. We won the scuffle. But how much good faith do you think a country loses when it tramples upon smaller and less powerful nations to get its way?

Remember America's Vietnam? Can you think for a moment about the animosity in this country between the Afrikaners and the English speaking? Do you know how far back this dates? I believe that the true cost of war is not worth the victories. Do you know how much the French hate the English? What is the true cost of national hate?

Savimbi is dead. Forget that UNITA might break up into smaller groups and create more havoc than it did in Savimbi's time. Forget that and ask yourself this: what will Dos Santos do now that he has the upper hand? We sat our white counterparts down and negotiated a settlement. The miracle in South Africa happened because once we gained the upper hand we let go of the past, showed our "enemy" respect and forged a future that could make ALL South Africans secure. We decided to share with the enemy rather than hog it all for a few blacks that sat at the table. We decided to go for the long haul in order to take our place amongst giants on the international arena. And now, we can say that we were truly inspirational in making the Commonwealth choose our position with regards to Zimbabwe. That position, mind you, says don't pre-empt what will happen. Don't act in haste. And most importantly, don't strong-arm a sovereign state into what you believe is a better way of going about political business. Take your time. Influence. Cajole. Plead. Reason. Be patient and not only will your desired results come, they will last. There are no quick-fix solutions to century-old problems. And very few nations live by that adage more steadfastly than we South Africans. Mandingo, you can be proud.

But what will Dos Santos, the president of Angola, do now that he has the upper hand?

Forget that Savimbi took money and accepted logistical support from the apartheid government of South Africa and the Americans. Forget that, because back then all African countries were simply pawns in the international power game between East and West. It was all about who could control the biggest territory in the world. It had very little, if anything, to do with the people in the countries being supported. So forget where Savimbi got his support back then and ask yourself this: will what made him go to war be fixed so that there is no need for a rebellious UNITA in Angola? Will Dos Santos consider sharing Angola's wealth with more Angolans than his wife? Will this man start thinking of his people first?

This is the main question to answer.

Savimbi is dead. May this signal the death of conflict in Angola. I say this not because I believe Savimbi was the sole cause of conflict in Angola. I say this because there comes a time when you must wonder whether African life has more value or not. If South Africans, black and white, different as day from night, could get together to save all of South Africa for both their disparate interests, why can't the Angolans?

Can they see this? Can the MPLA see this? Can Dos Santos have the humility, the grace and the strength of conviction to put his people first, all his people, including those inside UNITA? Can the remaining leaders of UNITA see this? Can UNITA forget about the diamonds and the wealth that its leaders can't even enjoy except in their fantasies and engage Dos Santos with the view to having prosperity for all Angolans?

Will the ruling party of Angola and the rebel movement come to the table now, shake hands, hug like the brothers and sisters that they are and forge a common and prosperous future for all Angolans? Will they?

Surely they must know that it is time.

Tell them, Mandingo, they must catch a fire, like you and I, and build Africa.

Aaah... Marseilles

WHAT IS THIS PLACE?

Marseilles stinks. Marseilles is beautiful. Marseilles is dirty. Marseilles is rich. Marseilles is poor. Marseilles is hot because it's summer now, over 30 degrees Celsius on some days. Marseilles is cosmopolitan. Marseilles is colourful. Marseilles is hard to define.

Marseilles stinks because people love their dogs here and they walk them everywhere and then let them shit and piss wherever they walk them. It stinks because grown men piss in the city centre in broad daylight while grown women let their children do the same. If squatting weren't more demanding than unzipping one's pants to let the "little big man" out, you get the feeling the women would also piss in the streets because they let their children do what the men do – piss in the street, in broad daylight. However, the women themselves don't, and so I guess Marseilles stinks a little less than it would if they too added to the ranks of the daylight street pissers. But Marseilles stinks nonetheless.

I arrive in Marseilles after being forced to abandon a bag in order to avoid missing my connecting flight in Charles de Gaulle Airport in Paris. I declare my missing bag and am told that it will be delivered to where I'll be staying. No sweat. In the bus on my way to my host's place, I can't but be reminded of Hillbrow in Johannesburg by the big, square, ugly concrete buildings that seem to litter the skyline right down to having clothes billowing away on every balcony. Of course Hillbrow has much prettier buildings than these. They just seem so alike because you can tell that these buildings, like the ones in Hillbrow, are overcrowded with desperate people. Every city has its poor. Marseilles is no exception. What a shame.

237

But then I arrive at St Charles Metro (train station), I step outside and see the Notre Dame monument on a hill in the distance. Now I'm in what seems like old Marseilles and the buildings now beat Hillbrow in the beauty stakes. The streets, however, are truly competing for the "who's the dirtiest of them all" crown. I get the feeling that Johannesburg will get clean quicker and stay clean for longer than Marseilles. This thinking is helped along by the discovery that it is almost a tradition here for garbage collectors to go on strike and leave the city to rot while they fight for their rights. So when the streets are the way they are when I arrive, they are a relief to the natives, seeing as only a few weeks ago, people here were resorting to setting heaps of garbage on fire in order to kill the stench on the streets. The rats were out in full force apparently, having a field day. I wonder where the rich hang out and whether they too experience this stench.

Marseilles' city centre is beautiful though because the buildings look like they were built at the birth of beautiful architecture. It is not a tall city centre. Most of the tallest buildings here are about six storeys high. So it's a short city. But the buildings are old. They are majestic. They are strong and they make the city look stunning. You can tell that a proud and gifted people with style built these buildings. You get this feeling inside some of the cheaper flats too because they have space. But at just under R3000 a month for a bachelor flat, it is not cheap to live here.

I've been here three days now, but to be honest with you, I still can't work out Marseilles' soul. It doesn't seem like a tranquil city you can rest in, but it doesn't seem rough enough for you to fear for your life. Some parts in its outer limits are really ugly, especially the newer buildings. But it is gloriously beautiful in the centre. It's neither fast paced nor slow. It has a port, probably one of the oldest in Europe, but you don't get a sense of heavy maritime commerce on the go here at the moment. It is now more like a tourist attraction destination at the bottom of La Canabiere, one of the main commercial streets here, where the rich anchor their boats.

But it has its Guess stores like Johannesburg. I even saw a Spar grocery store and got a fright. It's an international city. Maybe the best comparison for Marseilles in South Africa is Cape Town. A lot of the streets here are just as narrow as the ones in Cape Town. You get the feeling that you can walk everywhere, things are seemingly so close together. But Marseilles is over two thousand, six hundred years old and if Cape Town is three hundred and sixty years old it is ancient. This probably makes Marseilles more charming. Even the waiters in the places I've stopped at so far to have a bite and something to drink are generally old men.

I can tell you one thing though, Marseilles is more proof that African Americans dominate the world with their music. The forty-something-year-old Frenchman bus driver who takes me from the airport to St Charles Metro has his radio dial on a French radio station that plays mainly hip-hop. One morning, as I sit writing, a car drives by with the music on full blast and all I hear is "We gonna paaaarty like it's your birthday…" It's 50 Cents. He too has taken over Marseilles!

When will black South Africans dominate the world with their export material, I ask myself? I think we are making incredible strides here, in our beloved backyard, in terms of leading the right political and economical evolutions for the betterment of the continent. We had a hand in getting Charles Taylor to leave Liberia, we are helping Burundi foster a fragile peace and, trust me, Zimbabwe will come right. Those are just a few examples. What we need to add to this are tangible products for the world to buy. If only South African money weren't so full of self hate.

The morning after my arrival in Marseilles my bag arrives, fully intact, nothing missing inside. You want to jump up and scream, "Praise the ancestors!" when this happens and you are South African. But it's normal here. I even get a heartfelt apology for the inconvenience. The system works. We can learn a lot from this. Or should I say SAA could learn a lot from this? Next, I must discover where the rich hang out…

WHAT TWADDLE!

I have found where the Marseilles rich hang out. It's in streets like Paradis where they shop. And at cafes and restaurants in and around Vieux Port where they sit, gossip and eat. I wonder if the poor enter their conversations. No. It's not that dogs don't defecate here or that the rich don't spit their chewing gum on the pavement like in the rest of Marseilles. No. That's not it. It just feels that way because it's more like maybe these places get cleaned more frequently. They stink a lot less, if at all. Everything is a lot more sanitised. Serene even. But in Marseillles you are always a block away from stench. But the rich have mastered this cocoon building near the poor to a point where the poor only surface as beggars, if that (and there are tons of them in Marseilles – East Europeans I'm told), otherwise, well, they don't exist. It's almost like Sandton near Alexandra in Johannesburg – the richest suburb, Sandton, near one of the poorest locations in South Africa, Alexandra.

But the rich are sick, hey? And they get the middle class and poor who are trying to be like them to do their dirty work. Like the black foreman in a white farm that drives black slaves. Some things never change. Today, being a day after I came close but was not kicked out of my host's flat and the day I set out to move out anyway, will linger in my mind as one of the most confusing days in my stay here so far. It was infuriating. It was entertaining. It was joyous. When it ended, I hated the French. And the rich showed me this face via their poorer employees.

It started with the hotels. Of all of the hotels I had scouted the day before, I started at New Hotel Vieux Port to look for a room. It was the most expensive on my menu of three hotels but I don't like slumming it so I thought, that's where I'll go. I liked it the most. On this day, however, there's an emaciated poor Frenchman at the counter. I tell him I have been here before and would like to see the room before I make up my mind. He gives me a room on the first floor. I'm like, is that the best room around? He says it's the cheapest. So now I have to explain that

I'm not a cheapskate. I mean this is bad business. On being pressed he gives me an additional key to room 210. Thees eeez ze beste I can dooo, says this pinhead of a Frenchman.

I go up to the second floor. There's no room 210. Some construction workers who are busy renovating the hotel explain that 210 is downstairs, not on the first floor, but one floor down from there. I decide to start by checking room 110 a floor down from where I was, the first room he offered me to look at. It's in the corner. The key gets a bit stuck but the door finally opens. It's a shithole. Now I descend a floor and there's 210. It's also in the corner. It's just been renovated. It's nice except that as I get out I face the scullery or whatever they call those back-of-the-restaurant places. For all I know, I could be the only person with a room on that floor. I go back to this throwback at the desk and I throw the keys at him and storm out. I mean the man had tons of other keys where he pulled these two keys from and he expects me to believe these are the only rooms available at this hotel. What? The rich French don't want to encounter blacks in the corridors?

I wanted to scream: "FUCK YOU AND YOUR SHIT YOU SICKO! SOUTH AFRICA IS RISING AND WE WILL BEAT YOU AT EVERYTHING, THEN MAKE SURE YOU GET THE SHITTIEST ROOMS EVERY TIME YOU VISIT, YOU SWINE!" But I couldn't. First of all it's bad manners. Swearing at the top of your voice at strangers is not cool you know. I did it at an ABSA bank branch back home once and felt terrible thereafter. But second of all, I could not be sure about black South Africa rising. I mean, every time I've done something good in South Africa, like the Eric Miyeni Show on SAfm, white people tried to kill me, trying to kill what I was doing and succeeded in killing it with blacks helping them along or watching passively or waiting for me to fall, then clapping and laughing and screaming *ja*, I won the bet, I knew it wouldn't last anyway. So there, I don't like lying and I wasn't about to scream a lie and be rude in the process. So I dumped the keys on the guy instead and stormed out into the sweltering summer heat of Marseilles.

At the next hotel I say, *Désolé, je parle Francais. Parlez Anglais?* Which means, sorry, I speak French. Do you speak English? Instead of *Desolè, je ne parle pas Francais. Parlez-vous Anglais?* Which means: sorry, I DON'T speak French, do you speak English? She gets me though and says, okay, speak English. I do and explain that every hotel is trying to give me a shitty room. Has she got a decent room I can rent. She says, we have ze roomer, fourth floorer, fifth floorer, sixth floorer, you chooserrr. I ask to see the room and she gives me a set of pictures to look at and says I'm not allowed to inspect the rooms physically. The pictures don't look so good. I don't trust this system. I figure this can't be a good hotel judging by the non-renovated room 110 in New Hotel Vieux Port next door. I leave.

At the third hotel, Hotel Saint Ferreol's, deeper in the city, off a trendy street called Saint Ferreol, they show me a room on the corner right next to the breakfast area. I mean, who wants to wake up and walk into a sea of eating people? I don't. So I ask if they can't get me a different room. *Non*, they say. Eezer ze bester I caner dooo! I couldn't help noting that in this setup as well I would be the only person on that floor, right next to the bar and breakfast area. I say *d'accord* (okay) and leave. Fuck the French. I mean, it's bad to generalise but this is typical of white people, and the French, with their speeches at the UN against the war on Iraq, are no different. Why do these whites hate blacks so much damn it! What did we do to deserve this vermin?

Come to think of it, this ugliness first revealed itself at the French Consulate in Johannesburg before I left to come here. My cellular phone rang and I answered it. Naïve. And this French woman behind the counter just started screaming: "NO PHONER HEEERR. NO PHONER. SWITCH OFF ZE PHONER! GO OUTSIDER IF YOU MUSTER PHONERR!" God! Woman! I thought, don't be so rude, dude. What's up? Then I said sorry, I didn't see the "no cellular phone" signs posted all over the place. I quickly went outside, cut the call short then promptly switched off the phone and went back inside. Now, the French opposed the Americans on the issue of bombing Iraq not so long ago, didn't they? So now why are they sharing this paranoia with the Americans? Chill dude, I thought, I'm not a suicide bomber! And even if I were one, I'd probably choose the American embassy, so what's your problem?

In the next few days of dealing with this French Consulate, I get the feeling that the last thing these people need are tourists! I mean, they wanted my bank balance, they wanted proof that I had bought enough travel cheques to travel, they wanted my passport, they wanted my letter of employment, they wanted my host to get permission from her city council to let me visit, not only that, I had to send her a copy of my passport to do this and it would take ten days for her to get this certificate if she did, then, to top it all, they said I must travel with duplicates of all these papers because I might be asked for them on the way or in France itself! At last they gave me a visa, because I showed them a contract worth more than R100 000 that I had to come back to after my holiday. Phew! I wonder if we ask the same of these people when they want to visit here. I wonder if we are not doing the opposite, bending over backwards to welcome their scum of the earth here.

I'm flippin' depressed now. God! All I wanted was a holiday. I'm in Marseilles to leave money behind, not take a cent out and, trust me, you don't want to live in France. I definitely don't. They have nothing on us these people. It's even likely that our history is richer and older than theirs. Go to Dr Motshega's Kara Institute if you want to double-check this truth. Yes, their modern systems, like public transport, work. But that's if you haven't yet worked out our brilliant minibus taxi system which, I should add, is as efficient as any tram or bus system I've encountered in virtually all the European countries I've visited. Why do you think the German public transport system is better than the French? I'll tell you. It's because the Germans had to re-build theirs after they lost the second European tribal war they started and thus corrected all the defects of their old system. It's the same reason why our three-star hotels are way better than their American counterparts. Ours are newer. Get it? And I'll be damned if there's one nation in the entire first world that beats any African country in terms of potential. And who can bet that our systems won't catch up and surpass those of theirs that might be better today? We must just keep them out while we build our stuff here lest they turn us into a mini-Europe with all its racism and other sicknesses of the mind!

There, I'm done. Sometimes they piss me off these people. Next, I ignore racism and check out the sights...

THINGS TO DO IN MARSEILLES WHEN IT'S HOT

If there's a protest march, join it. People outside South Africa have causes too as you well know. And it's interesting to see how they protest when they do. I joined one protest march here. I was sitting at my chosen hangout where I play chess, Brasserie Les Danaides, when I heard this huge sound and looked up. And there was a swarm of people walking behind a moving van of sorts that was carrying a massive sound system out of which songs were being played. When I asked around I discovered that this was a protest march for all people who work in the Arts. Dancers. Technicians. Actors. Directors. Administrators. You name it in the arts, whoever delivered it was represented.

So I joined in. After all, I have been known to act from time to time even though that's beside the point. It turns out that Jacques Chirac's government and those before it have not bestowed upon people who work in the arts a status like the rest of the workers in France. This means, just like it is back here at home, there are no proper pension schemes for people in the arts, for example. And so there was a movement across France to demonstrate and show that this was not right and should be changed. Marseilles was not left out of this movement.

What was interesting about this march and why I think you should join one if you are travelling and you come across one is this, first of all marches are entertaining when the cops don't interfere and the crowds are well behaved. But second, now that we too are not having violent marches, you could learn some new, interesting tricks of gaining attention for a cause if you ever thought of organising a march to do this.

At my march, for instance, everyone was colour-coded red. Protestors wore at least one red garment to the march – a red T-shirt here, or pair of pants there, or hat, or dress, or combinations of the above, whatever, something on their body was red. As it turned out, I had a red-striped white shirt on, so I fit right in. Serendipity? Next up, maybe because they haven't been taught the toyi-toyi and can't raise as much of a vocal ruckus as we can, they had this massive sound system I mentioned earlier. Wherever we marched, this thing rattled windows, woke people up and forced them to come out and watch and listen and react. Then they had buckets of red paint. Protestors would lie on the street and the ones with the red paint would draw their outlines and write slogans under them. For days after the march, these statements were still on the streets of Marseilles where the march passed. And you could still hear one of Lauryn Hill's protest songs lingering in the air.

Do a march if you can, but also make time to go and visit some of the churches here. And do not forget Notre Dame (Our Lady), of course. Notre Dame is the golden statue of Mother Mary holding baby Jesus that's posted on a Catholic church that's built on one of the highest points in Marseilles. Notre Dame is called the Godmother and was meant to watch over all the ships that docked at and left Marseilles' old harbour all those years ago and I guess still does today except it does so for the rich boaters who boat out for their suntans and maybe catch a fish or two. You watch Notre Dame and you know for a fact that the Statue of Liberty in New York was given to the Americans by the French. You are at the source.

The thing about churches in Europe, and France's Marseilles is no exception, is that they are truly magnificent, both from

245

an architectural perspective and an interior decoration point of view. They are truly beautiful to behold. It doesn't matter if you are not Catholic or Christian; these are magnificent to take in. So do it. Check out the churches and don't leave out the Notre Dame in Marseilles if you are in Marseilles. These churches are a great testament to the true marketing skills of the Christian movement. Besides, they are a good way to spend a few hours. Now this you can probably do when it's cold too and get all that spiritual warmth if you are open to it.

But when it's truly hot, take a boat ride to the Island Freolle. Do it at night if you can and sit at the back of the boat to really see Marseille under the lights. Otherwise, leave in the daytime but come back at night and sit in front when you do. You will see Notre Dame on the hill, lit up, looking out to sea, ensuring your safe return. You will see Marseilles in her physical glory as the wind cools you down when the boat picks up speed and, for a moment, there will be no racism in the world, just beauty, man-made with God's assistance. Physically, Marseilles is undeniably a beautiful city.

Catch any of the summer festivals too. This is a must even if you are old. I was lucky enough to combine my boat ride to Freolle with a festival called Festival Mimi on the island. Go to these things and see the locals go mad to music and join in where you can. There will be magic for you to experience. I'm standing with a clear view of the stage. This man comes and stands right in front of me and almost completely blocks my view. It's been so beautiful up to now. Now what? I wait. And at that very instant the artist on stage says, this next song is about freedom, freedom of the mind, freedom of the soul. We are all freedom fighters here. So let's all unite and fight for freedom. The man shuffles away embarrassed. Need I say he was white? You will experience some magic no doubt, just go with the flow and keep your own rhythm as you play with the locals.

Go to good restaurants that serve local cuisine. This is a must. You can't smell a new place, get your soul touched, let your eyes see, make your ears hear, then allow your skin to tingle and not serve your taste buds with something from the place you are visiting. You will see many McDonalds outlets. They will feel familiar and you will be tempted to go in and gobble up all that horrible junk food that's allegedly depleting the rainforests of the world. Resist this temptation. Eat some local cuisine and have a story for your taste buds to tell.

I went to one restaurant here and had a dish of lamb that literally melted in my mouth and made my eyes glaze over. I have been to many good restaurants in South Africa, including a French one in Pretoria, but I have never tasted lamb done like this. It's a memory for life. I was of course lucky to have an interpreter to help me choose a dish but, hey, you can be brave. If it's a good restaurant, virtually everything on the menu will be good. Try local cuisine, no doubt. I even experimented with bouillabaisse, one of the most expensive dishes I've ever had to fork out money for (R400 and a bit to be exact, for one dish! And I took a friend with!). It is a traditional Marseilles seafood dish that includes eel, scorpion fish, gurnard and three other sea creatures. Le Miramar, the restaurant serving it, is the oldest traditional French restaurant serving it in Marseilles. I hated the dish even as I ate it near a picture of the American actress Sharon Stone who also dined there once as the picture depicts, I'm told. But it's apparently a traditional Marseilles seafood dish and Le Miramar is one of the oldest restaurants that serve it the old traditional way. I don't regret eating it though. It is a memory that gave me taste-bud-knowledge of something new. I don't have to eat it again but at least I know why. And then, to compensate for the taste, came the bonus; the waiter's been to Cape Town, loved it, loved South Africa and can't wait to be back.

And sometimes we think we are not worthy. Sometimes we think our country is not worthy. Sometimes we wait for others to love who we are in order to love ourselves… shame…

Next, I meet the poor of Marseilles.

POOR AND GENEROUS IN MARSEILLES

It is ironic, isn't it? I just finished reading *My Year of Meat* by Ruth L. Ozeki and in it is a scene that describes the generosity of people in the southern states of America, the poor people. You read about this Japanese woman inside an Amtrack train coach being teased to get comfortable by what we call a ticket examiner in South Africa and the scene culminates in song with virtually everyone in the coach offering her a piece of home-fried chicken so she can experience southern hospitality and you see her clap along, delighted and thinking, this would never happen in Japan, such openness, such human interaction, such communal generosity of spirit.

It is ironic because here I am in Marseilles. The first group I interact with is a bunch of chess players, very good chess players, I must add. You can tell by their clothes that they are, well, by Marseilles standards, by the standards at this hangout joint even, poor. It's the clothes. It's their mannerisms. It's the fact that when they are not rolling their own tobacco, they are bumming cigarettes. Day in and day out, when I get to this essentially gay hangout on my way to what I call the Yeoville of Marseilles that is Belle De Mai and my home for the moment, I find these macho, straight guys, a small world in a bigger gay world, playing chess and teasing each other. It's been a week now and I've only won two games because my opponents fell asleep and underestimated me and I took their queens.

I run out of cigarettes. After a futile attempt to direct me to the tobacco shop a little distance away, one of the guys decides he will walk me there. I buy him a pack of Marlboros and, astonished, he exclaims, for me! I say yes. He can't believe it. *Merci, monsier.* He calls me Mr. As we walk back I ask him not to tell anyone. He says, it no matter. Then he quickly corrects himself and says, no problemer and checks if I understand. No problemer, he repeats. It's hard talking when your language is taken away from you. We get back to the other guys and I make out that they are asking if I bought him the pack. How could he hide it? He is always smoking from a pack of ten and here he is all of a sudden with a pack of twenty. *Voila*. They know. I wonder how he manoeuvres around that one. Deep down I feel bad that I made him promise not to tell.

They are an eclectic bunch, this chess-playing lot. There are older, much older men, old French men who join in mainly for the chess. I play one of them and at one point I call myself stupid and he says, Stoopid Buoy and never stops. We laugh a lot about that. He could be my grandfather. He almost wets himself with excitement every time I throw in a French word to show that I'm trying to learn the language. But chess has a universal language anyway. So we are fine.

But there is this poor core group that I'm talking about. There's my cigarette friend, he is the oldest, Rishaaarde. He is dark and you can't quite tell whether he's white or of mixed parentage. Then there's the Marseilles Caucasian native, David. He always looks wasted like he's permanently on drugs or used to be. And then there's the man to beat at chess here, Monem. He tells me he's from Tunisia and reminds me with pride of the South Africa versus Tunisia final at the South African hosted Africa Cup of Nations of 1996. I hear him tell his friends about this and add that Tunisia lost 2-0 without being asked. I love honest men.

On this night, David says to me that they are all going to his place. You canar comer if you wanter. Then he purses his lips and pushes them down on the sides as if to say, no problem. Then he finds the words and says it, no problemer, comer if you wanter. We play, he does that lips thing again, musicer, gamer. *Oui*, you comer. So I go along. How can you refuse such charm. On the way there, Richard insists we stop and get some food. They quibble about what to buy and I suspect who will pay for what and then it's done. When we get to what seems to be Monem and David's flat, Richard cooks spaghetti bolognaise but not before giving us a starter of toasted baguette and some dip that you are supposed to add lemon juice to. It's delicious. When the food arrives, I'm asked to serve myself first. I wasn't even asked to contribute a cent, but here I am being given a taste of southern France hospitality by poor people.

Isn't it ironic? From fiction to reality without missing a beat.

The night continues and I tell Monem that he is very good at chess and he should think about becoming a grand master. He says, I'm good with tactic, you know? But stratejee? *Non.* Not good. I say work at it. He says me? I'm student you know? Student of ze game. Student of chess. Look. He shows me pieces of paper with different moves that he's been working on, *un, deux, trois…* He counts in French and goes way over ten. I'm student, you know? I tell him that the African champion is from Soweto in South Africa. He's surprised. David asks if he is a Grand Master. I say no, he's just over a hundred points short of becoming one. But he did beat the American number one at a chess tournament, I add.

This conversation is all gobbled up in monosyllables and gestures as we try to navigate the language divide. Apartheid, says the Marseilles Caucasian David, he put ze black man down. White man know, he says, if black man play, black man play guder. White man? He does that lips thing again, no guder. I say it's not about colour, anyone with the gift who works hard can be a chess champion. He agrees but says, *non*, apartheid, no guder. I say it's over now. We can all manoeuvre now. He doesn't get it at first. Monem says, I speak English, he points behind his back, searches for the number, fiverr, fiverr years ago, you know? No more. Everybuddy heerrr, is French you know, speaking French and I no speak English, fiverrr years, he also does the lips thing, you speak fast you know, he continues, I no hearrr. I get it. We start again. In the end we get each other. Well, we see, he says. I can just see Monem as a grand master. Man, the guy is good. And fast, very fast.

It's been a beautiful night in Marseilles. And I thank the world for poor people, for their generosity. Imagine if poor people were as selfish and self obsessed as the rich! The ozone layer would be at least as big as the world. The last time I checked it was as big as all of Europe! And what of the soul-touching? We would surely all atrophy and die, wouldn't we? I mean even the rich would die, wouldn't they? I can't remember who said this, but it was poignant. They said the rich travel the world to see and be entertained by the poor. I would add … and thus find meaning in their lives. I mean, how much nicer your down duvets must feel after you saw someone sleeping on a concrete slab covered with plastic to avoid the cold, hey? Those acres of space must feel really comfortable after a poor friend takes you to his or her one-room flat. You feel sad, guilty even, but you feel alive. Slumming it before returning to the fold, they call it – the warm embrace of the trust fund.

It's been a wonderful night in Marseilles. Don't get me wrong. I want everyone to be rich but God, I don't want anyone to lose that common touch the poor seem to naturally carry around. Very little is wasted there. A lot gets recycled there because more can't be afforded. And people share.

My hostess is upset with me. It seems she did not want me to come after all. She has been making sure with every minute and every hour that we share that I feel this intrusion into her life. That I am as uncomfortable as I can be. When we finally talk, she says not even her sister would have dared visit like I did. I ask her why she did not say no? I tell her that I don't have to stay at her place. By many standards, I am quite rich actually, I tell her. I don't say this but inside I'm thinking, I have money, I have property and when I work I get paid very well. So well, in fact, that often I can just sit a whole year or two and do nothing and everything will be fine on the financial front. I'm okay. After those thoughts, I tell her I did not come all the way to Marseilles to have sex with her, you know? I'm adding bits and pieces of the words from my new found non-English speaking friends now, like, you know, at the end of every hard to find English sentence. I don't have to stay here, you know. She doesn't tell me to leave, so I figure I must be here for her to learn some lesson. So I'll stay until she kicks me out. She doesn't. Not yet.

The irony is not wasted on me. People I don't know ask me where I stay and invite me to come over to their crowded flat and live there if I want. This after a few games of chess and someone I think of as a friend, someone I checked with, confirmed with, got a yes from is doing everything in her power to make me feel like a right prick! She's middle class. The middle class love their space. Not as much as the ultra rich, but they love their space too the middle class. I made a mistake. I apologise.

The day before my gourmet meal with my poor friends, I scouted around for hotels and chose one called New Hotel Vieux Port, not to be confused with *"vieux porc"*, which means old pig. It is right by the old harbour at the bottom of Canabier, one of the main streets through Marseilles, decidedly upper class. Tomorrow I move there... if, and only if she plucks up the courage to kick me out. She hasn't done it. Not yet...

AND NOW, ABOUT THE VIRUS...

Just before I left South Africa for Marseilles our leaders were in Maputo in Mozambique. Our President Thabo Mbeki was handing over the leadership of the AU (African Union) to Eduardo Chissano, the Mozambican president, for the next year. But once again Muammar Gaddafi of Libya made headlines with yet another strange comment. He said HIV/AIDS and other diseases like Malaria etc. were good diseases for Africa because they were protecting Africa from the "first world". I guess the logic is that for as long as we have these diseases we will not have an influx of Westerners escaping toxic nuclear waste and the freezing cold and lack of space and high costs of living, etc. to come to Africa for fear of premature, agonising death.

I laughed and nodded when people said Gaddafi was becoming a bit of an embarrassment in his old age and maybe senile like Mugabe up north. But away from all this talk, I began to wonder, have Africa's problems not always involved getting caught off-guard by foreigners bearing gifts of death hidden by smoke and mirrors and covered with sweet talk and fake smiles? I mean, take the Christians for instance, and how they cleared the way for ruthless commerce while we were busy with a crisis of heart concerning leaving our old ways to embrace the new, only to wake up holding the same set of principles – love thy neighbour, thou shalt not kill, don't steal, etc. – as the ones we always had except in a different language and not in a big black book and now, well, we just had the same principles wrapped differently except, this time, we had no land to practise them on. And no money to buy the land back even if this was allowed. And it wasn't.

Africa must rise. To do this, she needs time. To do this, she needs her people to find their way without rough interference from people who are gobbling up the world and always looking for a new source of life to deplete for personal financial gain. Is Gaddafi that senile? Are diseases like HIV/AIDS not buying us this much-needed time? Are the wars on our continent, as much as they must end, not helping in this all-important cause? I wonder.

Take the AIDS virus, for instance. I believe that in tackling it we can learn to stop the greedy part of the West from ruining us because that part ruins nations by employing the same tactics as the AIDS virus does, doesn't it? Or have you not thought about it? Look at it this way: the AIDS virus attaches itself to your body and uses your body to finally kill you, if you let it. What do Westerners do? They don't come out with guns blazing. Not at first. No! They give guns to your brother to kill you and then watch you guys kill each other before stepping in to "help" you sort this out. In the process, you and your brother and sister end up working for them while they steal all your resources.

That is the colonial story of Africa. They tried it here with the train massacres just before the first South African democratic elections in 1994. We know the devastating effect of this tactic from the millions of Hutus and Tutsis, brothers except for the invisible divide created by their colonisers, who massacred each other. And what did the West do? They stood aside. But they did not do this in Eastern Europe! They were in Bosnia and

253

Kosovo to stop it like bats from hell. You know what happened in Cambodia with the Khmer Rouge. Need I add more examples? In normal terms, it is called divide and rule.

So, I say this, in stopping the virus we can learn to stop them. In controlling the virus, we can learn to control them because just like them the virus divides your body to rule. As for Gaddafi, I think he must learn to know what to say at home and what to tell the world. You can't let the enemy see you coming. As a white friend of mine always said, don't send your enemy a telegram telling him what you are going to do to him.

A CONVERSATION IN MARSEILLES

It's a weird feeling being partially deaf and dumb. This is what I am here in Marseilles because my French vocabulary totals a whopping ten words, if that! I really must choose an English- or Shangaan-speaking place for my next holiday. However, on the odd occasion when my host is with me, I get to have a conversation in translation, like my very first serious one.

We were waiting for the bus when this man joined us. He said something to me and I turned to look at my friend. She answered and I gathered he was asking about the bus and she was saying she doesn't know when the last one came by. Then he asked where I was from and I heard my friend say, Afrique du Sud.

"Johannesbooorg?" He asked looking at me. I smiled in amazement. "*Ja, oui,*" I answered. "Gud?" he asked. "*Oui, oui,*" I answered. "No, no, no, no, not gud," he countered. "Marseilles gud." I shrugged. He asked who the president of South Africa was. I said Mbeki. He said no, it isn't. I said Mandela and he said yes that's him and I explained that he wasn't president anymore, Mbeki was.

Then he moved on to the serious stuff to explain what he meant when he said Johannesbooorg "... no... not gud". He said there was racism there. I said, well, there's racism in France too. He said not like in Afrique du Sud and I paused. He said black man not like white man in Afrique du Sud. Apartheid, he said. I said, but that ended in 1994, knowing fully well that we still have our problems.

"Le Zooloo?" he said.

"*Oui*, le Zulu, le Shangaan, le Sotho, le Venda, le… nine," I said raising nine fingers to show the number of indigenous languages in South Africa.

He said, "Le zooloo still not like white man in Afrique du Sud." I shrugged again. In a way he was right. I mean most black people, including the Zulus, are starving in free South Africa while most white South Africans are living way above the poverty line.

He said "White man in South Africa say he is African! This no gud." I asked him why. He said black man, Arab man, pointing at himself, African. Not white man. I said, you know, white South Africans have been in South Africa for over three hundred years. How can they not belong? He said, they are colonial you know? Colonialister, they don't belong. So I asked my friend to ask him where he thinks black Americans belong. He said in Africa. I said where in Africa. He said everywhere. Then he saw the problem with his argument and said "No," waved his finger in the air and continued," … *C'est* different." Then the bus came. We got on and he said "*Au revoir*", and moved deeper into the bus.

Left alone with my host, we continued the discussion. She told me that this happens a lot here in Marseilles, this sort of conversation. She was at a party once and this black man insisted that no white person can ever know more about Africa than a black man, even if that white man spent twenty years in Africa and the black man had never set foot in Africa. Some would argue against this logic, judging by rap artist Ja Rule's behaviour when he was here recently. I mean, the man does not seem to have a drop of white blood in his veins, he looks as black as the best product of the best-preserved slave lineage in America and he thought the township Soweto was a nightclub! I began to ·

wonder which pharmaceutical company he believed gave us the headache pill "Mandela"!

It was the Ethiopian American-based movie-maker Haile Gerima who once said that Africa would lose her identity voluntarily and it would be preserved outside Africa's borders by Africans in exile because memory, remembering their roots, who they are, where they come from, would be more important for their survival. I remember this as my host tells me the story of the black party man who will always know more about Africa than any white person and I think, well, we can't underestimate the power of imagination coupled with story-telling can we?

When your exiled parents relate stories of the village they come from, of the customs there, of uncle Mbhazima's antics, of the village meetings, of the summer sunsets, of the witchcraft, of the stories told around the fires at night, of howling hyenas and roaring lions, of disease and poverty, of the dawn of a new beginning, of their hopes to get back, surely the magic in these stories can give you an insight, even while far away, deeper than that of any outsider with no respectful interest? You will smell the place, dream the place, love the place and embrace the place more with your heart and soul than any outsider could dream to, wouldn't you? And if your parents hated it, you would most likely hate it with the same ferocity fuelled by the same depth of passed down knowledge wouldn't you? Or would you do the opposite still?

Having said that, I know children in Soweto who know more about New York culture than they know about their own. Africa is "… shedding her identity voluntarily". And I know of white American activists who are fighting for the preservation of all that the San people of Southern Africa – also known as the original indigenous occupants of this region (hush, don't say that out loud. What if the Zulus revolt!) – stand for and have made it their life's mission to understand and know these people well and so know more about them than most South Africans, including myself, do. Is culture race bound? Is it bound by geographical location? Or is it a heart-to-heart transmission phenomenon? In the end, my host and I concluded that it is hard to be in exile. We decided that the likelihood is that the black man she was referring to was talking more about self-preservation than knowledge. For him to accept that white people could know more about Africa than he does, and therefore be more African than he was, even if they had been to Africa and he still had to pay the continent his first visit, would be too traumatic a psychological step to take. We concluded that he was actually saying I am an African and, if you are white, you are not. Don't ever claim to be and thus rob me of my identity and place in the world simply because I have yet to set foot there, especially since you never forget to remind me out here in Europe that Europe is not and never will be my home.

This then takes us back to my French friend of Arabic descent who was appalled that, actually, there are white South Africans who call themselves African! I wonder what he would make of the fact that this is a very recent development except amongst Afrikaans-speaking white South Africans who made it a habit those many decades ago to call white English-speaking South Africans "*sout piele*" which, literally translated, means "salty penises". What they meant by this phrase was that the English-speaking South Africans had one foot in Africa and another in England and therefore had their genitals in the sea and thus salty. It was a mockery of the lack of affinity to Africa that most Afrikaners were always proud to have and do to this day for whatever reason and English-speaking South Africans rarely had and still battle to have to this day.

I wonder what he would make of the fact that most English-speaking white South Africans, on setting foot for the first time on English soil, were shocked to discover that their accent was not "English" and so were treated like foreigners in what, while still in South Africa, they thought of as their real home – not black, backward, diseased and appalling Africa. I wonder what he would make of the fact that those very same whites now show their disgust for South Africa in particular by making sure that their money is invested outside the country of their birth because deep down, despite what they say for PR's sake, they hate this country and this continent and actually consider themselves exiles by choice. That a lot of them still carry two passports, one European, another South African just in case, are proud of it and wonder why indigenous South Africans question their intentions whenever they want to partner with them on projects.

Ultimately you want to be free to reside wherever you choose in the world without having to constantly prove your allegiances. Ultimately you want the world to have nations that are not paranoid because they have screwed other nations over and now those screwed-over people want revenge and so are forced to have strict border controls just so they can keep their twin towers and sleep at night. Ultimately it really should not matter where we are from and whom we are except in our hearts and in our human interactions at a one-on-one level.

What is globalisation for if it isn't for a faster sharing of knowledge and resources for the benefit of all mankind? Is this too idealistic? Am I dreaming?

Anyway, that was my first serious Marseilles conversation. It was about politics and race! I think the bus came too quickly, otherwise we would have moved to religion, economics and, with luck, sex. (God! It's hard to make female friends when you are tongue-tied!) These are the conversational subjects that seemingly make the world go round. And Marseilles is no exception.

BLACK PEOPLE ARE POWERFUL

No one is more aware of this power and more fearful of it than racists. And the greatest proof of this fear is embedded in the racism they spew every time they see us. It started centuries ago and novels like Joseph Conrad's racist *The Heart of Darkness* propelled it forward. In these sorts of "classics", black people are portrayed as silent, mysterious, unpredictable, in tune with nature and totally animalistic. And once you are described as an animal, well, you scare "people", don't you?

So they tread carefully around us. They don't know what we are going to do next. They are scared we might just hurt them. We are animals. So when they see us come down the street, they cross over to the other side. When we stop our cars next to theirs, they lock their doors and hope we don't break the windows and snuff out their existence anyway. God, they pray in desperation, let the traffic light turn green. They are scared. We are powerful. They are not. So they will do anything in their limited power to stop us from advancing, because who knows? We might just beat them at their own game, whatever that game might be. And we might kill them while we are at it. After all, this is how they operate. They kill to get ahead. Iraq is a recent case in point. So they reason, why would we not do the same to them?

The only areas where white people have been more successful than we have been are where they've managed to lock us out completely. They created the beautiful game. Football. And the best football player of all time is Pele. Black. When you go to the records of the best students at places like Oxford and Cambridge in England, you will learn that black people are at the top of the pile. Forget that the first-ever university in the history of the world was in Timbuktu, Africa. Forget that their best philosophers, the people who gave them a glimpse of civilisation, like Aristotle, were taught in Africa. Need I remind you that the father of the Internet is Dr Ameagwale. Black. We still don't have a single white person who has run the 100-metre race in under 10 seconds. This does not go down well with racists because they are essentially concerned with enforced white supremacy.

And the cradle of mankind is in Africa, a black continent with spots of mainly hostile and racist whites. The healthiest natural habitats in the world today are in places where people of colour live and have lived forever and longer – South America, the hinterlands of Australia, Africa. And who's busy trying to ruin all that in the name of commercial profit right now if it isn't companies like McDonalds with their insatiable need to keep expanding as they wipe out entire forests to rear cattle for the beef you eat at their junk food outlets spread across the world?

In reality we, black people, should be scared of racists because they do wreak havoc wherever they go. They have murdered millions of people and virtually wiped out entire cultures in places and where they originally come from is made up of systems to control and milk people for financial gain under the guise of civilisation and fake democracies. You are free in and around Europe as long as you do not step out of line. You are free as long as you never question the status quo. You are free as long as you remain scared. Scared of people unlike yourself. Scared of falling sick. Scared of dying. Scared of losing your job. Scared. You are free as long as you are not fearless. So the fearless suffer when they encounter the fear mongers who need them to be fearful in order to continue where their racist ancestors left off. How else do you maintain that castle that has been in your family for generations if people don't fear the power it represents and bow whenever you pass by as they conveniently forget that the blood of slaves built it? And what human being can see what is really going on when their head is bowed in deference?

We are fearless and this scares the living daylights out of racists. But why are they so scared and we are not? I think it's because, deep down, we have nothing to hide and they are guilty. It's scary to have to look inside a cupboard stuffed full of the skeletons of the dead people that you murdered. It's better to act like this does not exist. The problem is that there is no greater reminder of all those corpses than the people who survive the massacres. How can you forget and be secure when the descendants of the people upon whom you visited endless misery are alive? How can you sleep at night? These descendants might rise and call for revenge like they did in Zimbabwe recently when they demanded their farms back. So you remain in bondage inside your big house that was built with the blood of innocents.

Racism is fear based. So, next time you sit at a restaurant and the service takes a little longer than normal as it happens to me sometimes here in Marseilles, remember that. Descendants of racists who are racist themselves don't want to be reminded of the blood they forced out of your ancestors' veins of defiance. They can't possibly sit opposite you, look you straight in the eye and act like everything is normal. It isn't, and their conscience tells them so. After all, deep down, when a hungry black man breaks into a racist white man's house and steals something, the racist white man feels that he deserves it even as his blood boils with anger. He feels that somehow he had it coming. You can't settle down until you have washed your hands clean of the blood of the innocent people you took from. You can't settle down until you have cleared the stench of death from the walls of your crumbling Jericho. But how do you clear your mind of the grim images? How do you stop the nightmares at night? How do you smile during the day and be truly happy?

Christians call it repentance. What they don't tell you is that heaven and hell are on earth. Racists must repent in order to find their heaven. They must acknowledge their wrongdoing to the entire world, apologise from deep inside their souls and seek new, clean, and better ways to collaborate with the people they so abused over the centuries. This is easier said than done, as we know from our truth and reconciliation process here in South Africa. A racist would rather show no remorse, stand chin deep inside his own stinking shit and say that's what was needed then and I did it, so what? No thanks, he adds, I will not take a shower right now if you don't mind. It takes a wise old soul to allow an old foe to embrace her and say, I forgive you. When you ask for forgiveness you pass power to the forgiver young souls figure, and this is not good because I NEED to have power! What children (and that's how I describe racists – children) don't know is that in passing the power to the forgiver you clear space for more, cleaner power for yourself. But alas, children would rather let their pride rule the day. Better that than say,

I'm sorry, mean it and change your ways for the better.

They are not likely to repent, these racists in our midst. This is almost as painful and difficult a process for them as being constantly reminded that they have committed heinous crimes against humanity and they have yet to pay for this. As you can see, these sorts of people are caught between a rock and a hard place.

Now what do we do while they are stuck in this conundrum?

We will resist the seductive charm of their satanic ways. It's okay to be rich, but not at the expense of your fellow human beings and the natural environment that protects us all. We do not have to kill to get ahead. We must take from the great ways of our own sterling past and forge new ways forward. We will see racists for what they are – scared people who need to be taught how to live a life without guilt, a life without fear. We do not need dwarves to be giants. We will not cut them down, but we will stand fearless in their presence at all times. We will keep our new emerging democracies truly democratic. President Mbeki and all the presidents after him will go to the villages every year and ask for guidance and answer for the decisions they make, while we remain free to question everything they do in our name. As for racists, we will engage and question their ways and show them new ones. They have no future without our wisdom. And when they ruin the future, we all pay.

We will remain fearless. After all, when you die, and you have lived a life guided by *ubuntu* (the principle that says you are what you are because of the people around you), as we call it here in South Africa, you make room for yet another great soul.

We will live our lives without fear. Joseph Conrad and his kind were right about one thing, we are animals. And we are proud of it. Animals live a life of dignity. They live truthfully. They take from the environment only that which they need. They listen to the seasons and dance to the rhythm of nature. You will never see a lion hunting down another to feed its young. Animals are fearless and majestic. They are beautiful. They are graceful.

They are proud. They are we and we are they. Together we form the continuum that is Mother Nature. And if being the animals we are scares the living daylights out of people who mistakenly believe that they are not animals, then so be it.

We will live without fear because we hold the power and with this fearlessness, we will shape the future of the human race.

Monuments

IS THERE LOVE AMONGST THE RUINS?

Bob Marley, the man who gave us "Exodus", the best album of the 20th century according to a *Time* magazine poll, said, "... in this great future, you can't forget your past".

It is important to remember.

What can be worrying sometimes is what the world chooses to remember. Recently the mayor of London (England) expressed disappointment and regret at the fact that an application to build a monument to Nelson Mandela in that city was turned down for "aesthetic reasons". The truth of the matter is that if Mandela had been tragically shot and killed in that city there would never have been any aesthetic consideration to building his monument there. It would have been done without question.

This is the same reason the world builds monuments to the holocaust in Germany. It is the same reason why South Africans have the Hector Pieterson Memorial in Soweto. It is the same reason Timothy McVeigh's visitation of horror upon the city of Oklahoma in America is marked by a moving memorial for the beloved 169 dead there. That reason is simple. It is so that the world does not forget in order not to repeat the same mistakes and visit the same horrors upon herself.

But since Germany, there have been holocausts in Bosnia and Rwanda. Since Hector Pieterson's tragic death, more youth were massacred in South Africa in the 80s. To follow the memorial in the Alfred P. Murray Federal Building in Oklahoma, we are going to see another where the Twin Towers fell. The world, it would seem, never learns.

And that's the sad thing about memorials to horrible events. In a sense, they become celebration points for those who succeeded in visiting those horrors upon the innocent victims. In a strange sort of way, they hold those who suffered the losses back by forcing them to keep reliving the pain. Eventually every suffering person yearns after revenge and the collective psyche of the universe yearns to visit upon the perpetrators a similar horror to level the playing field. And so monuments of pain keep multiplying as the centuries pass.

Should we not build monuments to remember the pain we suffer? Should we ban these elaborate grave stones and act like we never walked through the fire? The short answer to these questions is no. We have to remember and so memorials are a must because even as they force us through the fire every time we visit them, they have an incredible capacity to also heal.

So memorials to pain must be built. However, they must not, like they do currently, outweigh and outshadow memorials to towering achievements, to beauty, to joy, to love. South Africa should have as big a monument to Tsietsi Mashinini, the youth leader who led the June 16 student uprising that contributed so much to the fall of apartheid, as it does to Hector Pieterson, the first casualty of that uprising. The world should have as towering a monument to the German Jewish holocaust as it does to the fall of Hitler, the engineer of that holocaust. And of course, America must remember and celebrate the many contributions to world advancement through technology, for instance, as she does the Timothy McVeighs of her world.

And on a personal level, it is as important to remember the many beautiful things that you take for granted on a daily basis as it is to remember the horrible little events that only visit you occasionally. Balance.

MONUMENTS TO SUCCESS
We, the colonised, generally don't like our colonisers. I don't think there's a single group of colonised people in the world that just loves its colonisers. So this is a pretty obvious point. The problem with this dislike of the coloniser by the colonised though

is that often, it blinds the colonised to lessons we would otherwise find easy to glimpse when we look at the same coloniser group. We do not want to be seen to admire "horrible" people, do we?

At the risk of sounding like what African Americans would call an Uncle Tom, I want to argue that we could learn from our colonisers. This does not mean we can't do better, but we could learn too.

A friend of mine, Karam, who is a lawyer and human rights activist, invited me to St John's, a school in Johannesburg, on June 16 last year. He said come through. Eric, I want you to give a little talk about the significance of June 16 to the young people we'll have gathered there for a day of games and teachings about the future and some such motivational stuff for young people. I hadn't planned much to do that day and it sounded like such a beautiful thing to be a part of on June 16, the day the first student casualty, Hector Pieterson, of the 1976 Soweto school uprising, was shot dead, so I agreed.

The children I was to address were black. The school that was hosting this event was St John's, one of the most expensive schools to send your children to in South Africa. I remember the school well because my nephew went there from the very beginning of his school career until he graduated. What I remember most distinctly on meeting him almost directly after he graduated there was what he said to me. He said that he was going to study at Vista college in Soweto and wanted nothing to do with white people for a while. I remember wondering why it was that the longer black people in South Africa spend with white South African people generally, the harder it gets for the black people to like, let alone love, the whites! It's almost like the white people have a built-in mechanism to reject, ridicule, belittle and be disgusted by black people. As a result, black people find themselves being doubly disgusted by and hateful of the very same whites.

You might ask why the opposite is not equally true, i.e. that black people are the ones that make whites hate or dislike them.

267

You might have a point, except that this argument does not take a look at the power dynamics between the coloniser and the colonised, the powerful and the powerless. When you take cognisance of this power dynamic, you quickly realise that the powerless almost always engage the powerful from a position of awe, admiration, envy and respect, if not fear, and so the tone of the relationship between the two is by and large led from the front by the powerful. How it evolves is to a large degree governed by the powerful.

At St John's the black kids are totally outnumbered by the white kids. The majority of the teachers are white. Hell, the school was built for white kids. Black kids are, in a sense, forced upon the school. What would you expect? In this situation I have to argue that the whites at St John's made my nephew want as little to do with whites in general as possible through their interaction with him.

I could never say the same thing for white people who visit black people in South Africa or anywhere in Africa for that matter. Often you hear the visiting whites go on and on about the friendliness of the black hosts and how generous they are despite the little that they have. And their smiles! God! Their smiles in the face of misery are unforgettable and infectious. How they wish they too could lead a life of such blissful happiness even when times are tough! So the colonised, the powerless, have an endearing ability to make the powerful, the colonisers, feel at home and thus like them more (even as they know they do not want to swap positions with them and even as they pity them like lost children) the more time they spend with them. Not so the coloniser, the powerful, the white in the land of apartheid.

This also applies to the liberal whites whose style of inflicting hate is inherent in their need to be in the teacher position, the "I know it all and can help you" position, the "No, thank you, I don't need to know anything about you" attitude, the "Please, shut up and listen because there couldn't possibly be anything of value in your head" position, "Just learn all about me and what I know and you will live a better life", the patronising rubbish that they spew, the "You, black person, are a child" attitude. In the end, this makes us hate them even more. It's a more insidious form of hate-for-whites fermentation inside the souls of black people because it is the most thorough rejection of who we are and what we stand for. The more time black people spend with this type of white, the more hate they feel on disengaging from him. Often I think my nephew encountered this type of white but, hey, I could be wrong. All I remember is that his hatred was palpable and disturbing to witness. Surely he should have been in total love with these people that he spent over twelve of his formative years with! Instead, he wanted "as little to do with them" as possible for the foreseeable future.

But this is an aside. And it definitely isn't what I think we can learn from these people, the descendents of our colonisers, the people Mandela taught us to be friendly to, and we obliged.

What struck me was the majestic quality of the buildings. The imposing portraits of the different headmasters that span over a hundred years of the school's existence. The palpability of the traditions that the school seemed to uphold even in the absence of the teachers and school children, who attended class there. The sheer wealth of it all. I was struck by it because there is nothing like it in my community and I haven't heard of one black South African who is trying to garner support to build a school of half this magnitude for our children.

We have a few billionaires in our midst. Some are buying soccer clubs. Some are looking to enter the movie business. I don't know of one of these rich people in our communities who is seriously pursuing the establishment of an institution that can help our young shape the future for generations forward. It has, and God bless her beautiful soul, taken an African American woman to say: I will build such an institution for little girls in South Africa. That is probably the best gift to this country that Oprah Winfrey can give.

Yes, they colonised us and in the late 1800s when St John's was built, I bet that the money to build and maintain it was pledged by plunderers of our natural resources, men who were loyal to some queen far away in England somewhere who cared nothing for us black indigenous peoples of this land. But you have to give it to them and say, at least with the money they plundered they had the foresight to secure the future with an education institution of such grand proportions as St John's. It took a priest and a few moneyed white men and St John's was made a reality for young white boys, and now we wonder why our young black boys feel aggrieved when they leave that institution!

In any event, there's a lesson from the coloniser. Can you, like him, secure the future in this way?

Requiem

DUMISANI

What does human life weigh? How much is it worth? Should we really care and suffer so much when people we know and love leave this world? Can we, if we want to, find solace in the mantra "God grant me the strength to change the things that I can change, the serenity to accept the things that I can't change and the wisdom to know the difference"?

Dumi gave me a dressing down on Thursday. He was upset with me because he felt that in saying that I should not have to start a scene of which I am the hero by feeding supporting actors lines from behind the camera, that I should be filmed first or at least, as movie-making protocol dictates, be given the option to choose or agree to go last, I was being unreasonable. He did not like that. In his mind, he did not understand what the fuss was about because I would have to read the lines as many times as there were shots in the scene whether or not the camera pointed to me first or last. And so why was I being disrespectful to his director and being unprofessional by writing text messages on my cellular phone when the director was saying he would like me to rehearse the supporting cast before reading my lines for them from behind the camera?

When he stopped dressing me down, I asked him if he was done so I could go back to work. No, he said, why don't I tell him how I feel about this whole thing he just told me. I said, well, Dumi, if you did not get it when I first said it, you won't get it now, so let's just say you've had your say and I've had mine and so we are even, can I go now? When he pushed me more, I said I tried and you just think I'm being a f*&#k and... he interrupted me at that point and said, *ja*, you are. That's when I walked away.

271

· My protest was well founded. Whether he knew it or not doesn't matter. But I understood his anger. Here he was, ready to blow and become the biggest thing on the South African film and television landscape as a producer, the toughest terrain in that field. Here he was with a crew that included, in very high positions, black talent with a 26-year-old at its helm as director. Not only was he, Dumi, producing the most exciting and, in my opinion, beautiful work in South African film and television at the time, he was doing it with what current South African film and television big shots would call "risky" crews, crews that very few if any production houses would touch with a barge pole – young and black. Not only was he telling stories that are relevant to black South Africans without alienating white South Africans, he was doing it on time and on budget. And here I was, Eric Miyeni, complaining about being shot last in a scene. And so when he screamed at me and said: "ERIC, YOU ARE THE KIND OF PERSON THAT IF SOMEONE GOT A SILVER MEDAL, YOU WOULD SCREAM AT THEM BECAUSE THEY DID NOT GET GOLD! *HAAI* MAN, ERIC, YOU ARE EMBARRASSING ME, MAN! AND YOU TALK ABOUT BEING PROFESSIONAL AND YOU ARE BUSY WITH YOUR CELLPHONE WHEN THE DIRECTOR WANTS TO SHOOT A SCENE! HEH EH MAN, ERIC!" He had a point.

In this terrain, this hostile terrain that is the South African film-making terrain, you have to be able to walk with paupers and queens and kings and have them all love you enough to do what you need to be done. Dumi had that talent. But most remarkably, he made them all go with him without sacrificing the original vision of any one of his projects. He was not a *baas* boy. He was passionate and truthful to the vision that we should take over the telling of our stories and do so to the highest standards in the business. So when you get a chance to view *Waiting for Valdez*, the short film that Teddy Mattera wrote, Dumisani Phakathi directed and Dumi brought to life, when you get to view *Mozart*, the film that Micki Dube directed that Dumi also produced and when later you get to see Taye Diggs in *Mr Drum*, the feature length film that Zola Maseko co-wrote and directed that Dumi got made after an eight-year struggle, know that here was a soldier and he was one of us.

I am so happy to say that on the Friday after the Thursday when he dressed me down, Dumi gave me one of those double-fisted fist-to-fist greetings that I believe only black people can come up with and he said, in the most beautiful voice, Erza! Like yeah man, what screaming? When? Where? I love what you are doing on my set, man, let's keep at it, yeah? He just said Erza and I heard all of that because in that one word, in that single tone, in that one smile, he said all of that. And I thought: I love this man. I don't think there was one person in Dumisani's life that did not feel special in his presence. He had a special name for everyone including himself. Dumi was the only person I knew who called himself by a shortened version of his own name. His name was Dumisani, just like my son's, but he called himself Dumi. You'd hear him answer the phone "Hello. Dumi here", like it was the most natural thing.

If he did not have a special nickname for you or a special way of calling you, like he always said Ta Eddie when he called Eddie Mbalo, the bossman at the National Film and Video Foundation, he had something special to share with you alone. A friend of mine Samir tells me how Dumi always whipped out the book he, Samir, had given to him months back and read out something he found amazing in it every time they met! Not only was he special because of this, but I don't think he even remembered the fights he had more than a minute after they happened and so he said his goodbye to me barely twenty-four hours after he had screamed at me with this most gorgeous sounding calling, Erza.

Barely fourteen hours later I heard that he had been shot in the head and killed in the house he was renting. Damn it, man, when I received this news from a mutual friend, Frank, I felt this deep gaping hole in my soul. I just broke down and sobbed.

To this day, a week after the news of the passing away of this stranger really, this beautiful angel, I still get the urge to cry just remembering him and the soul light through his beautiful smile. I cry because in truth, even though I don't know how much life weighs or is worth, something inside me tells me that if anything, life is worth the depth and width of the hole you feel in your soul when the life you are trying to measure is gone. Dumi left a massive hole in my heart and soul and in many others, as testified by his memorial service. To feel less pain, I always try and remind myself of Zola Maseko's beautiful words from his wonderful tribute to the man at the memorial service when he said Dumi had come to teach us what it is to love and be loved, and so his mission was accomplished. Judging by the amount of love in the room on that day when Zola made that moving speech, I can only say, not only was he done doing what he came to do, he also taught us well.

I agree with this and I try to remember it every time the pain stabs, but it's hard because it takes years to produce a Dumi. He had somehow managed to pack over fifty years into his twenty-nine and leapfrogged himself to Godfather status to the point where to me and many others he was ageless. And a swine with a gun walked into his home and snuffed this wonderful life out in as long a time as it takes to squeeze three bullets out of a gun. This is one of our own, Mandingo. And he's gone for what seems a pointless reason when he had so much more to give.

When will it stop!

I leave you to ponder that thought, Mandingo. While you do so, say a little prayer for all the Dumis South Africa is battling to produce, so that they may last longer and move our country, our continent and the world forward to a better plateau.

References

Bodanis, David. *E=mc² – A Biography of the World's Most Famous Equation*. Pan Books, 2001.

Buzan, Tony. *Head First – 10 Ways to Tap into Your Natural Genius*. Thorsons Publishers, 2002.

Coelho, Paolo. *The Alchemist*. HarperSanFrancisco, 1995.

Collins, Jim. *Good to Great*. Random House Business Books, 2001.

Dikeni, Sandile. *Telegraph to the Sky*. University of Natal Press, 2001.

Moore, Michael. *Dude, Where's my Country?* Warner Books, 2003.

Ozeki, Ruth L. *My Year of Meat*. Pan MacMillan, 1999.

Pachai, Bridglal and Bhana, Surendra (eds). *Documentary History of Indian South Africans: Black and white perspectives on South Africa*. David Philip Publishers, 1984.

Acknowledgements

The author and publisher would like to thank the following:
• Robert Jensen for his article published in the *Baltimore Sun*.
• Lemn Sissay for his poem, *Colour Blind*.